MW01679291

FREDERICTON FLASHBACK

Stories and Photographs from the Past

Ted Jones

NIMBUS
PUBLISHING

Copyright © Ted Jones, 2003

All rights reserved. No part of this book may be reproduced, stored in a retrieval system or transmitted in any form or by any means without the prior written permission from the publisher, or, in the case of photocopying or other reprographic copying, permission from Access Copyright, 1 Yonge Street, Suite 1900, Toronto, Ontario M5E 1E5.

Nimbus Publishing Limited
PO Box 9166
Halifax, NS B3K 5M8
(902) 455-4286

Printed and bound in Canada

Design: Kathy Kaulbach, Paragon Design Group

National Library of Canada Cataloguing in Publication

Jones, Ted, 1939-
Fredericton flashback : stories and photographs from the past / Ted Jones.

Fifty articles from the column entitled Fredericton Flashbacks, first published in the Daily gleaner.
ISBN 1-55109-465-7

1. Fredericton (N.B.)—History. I. Title. II. Title: Daily gleaner (Fredericton, N.B.) III. Title: Fredericton flashbacks.

FC2496.4.J65 2003 971.5'515 C2003-905407-1

Canada

The Canada Council for the Arts | Le Conseil des Arts du Canada

We acknowledge the financial support of the Government of Canada through the Book Publishing Industry Development Program (BPIDP) and the Canada Council for our publishing activities.

Table of Contents

Section Four: Natural Disasters and Human Folly

Section Five: Notable Locals

Section Six: Social Life

PREFACE

IN JANUARY 2000, *The Daily Gleaner* invited me to write a regular history column about the capital city of New Brunswick. "Fredericton Flashback" was the result and, on every alternate Saturday since then, it has appeared in the Weekend section of the paper.

By the end of 2003, over one hundred articles will have been published—carefully researched stories of interesting people, historic buildings, and landmark events from Fredericton's past, each enhanced with illustrations (rare photographs and heritage documents). Along the way, many readers have saved these articles for future reference or to send to friends and relatives outside the province. Their boxes of newspaper clippings grew and former students, colleagues, and acquaintances started hoping that the articles might be reprinted in book form. And now the articles/columns have been reviewed, and fifty have been selected and organized thematically for this book. The date of their appearance in *The Daily Gleaner* can be found beside the story titles.

The publication of these articles in book form gives me the opportunity to acknowledge and thank those people who supported me in my research over the last four years. Staff members at the New Brunswick Provincial Archives, the University of New Brunswick Library & Archives, the Fredericton Public Library, and the New Brunswick Legislative Library have been outstanding when I needed assistance, always providing professional and generous service.

Because of their interest and guidance, staff members at *The Daily Gleaner* office have made the "Fredericton Flashback" column enjoyable and gratifying for me. Their expertise in graphics has presented my work in a manner that is visually appealing. To the people of Fredericton, I thank you for your encouragement, your interviews, your photographs, your ideas, and your interest in the wonderful stories of yesteryear. To the patient and co-operative staff at Nimbus Publishing Limited, most of whom I have met only electronically, I express my sincere thanks for your interest in my work and for publishing a wide variety of splendid books that present the rich history of the Atlantic Provinces to the rest of the world. In particular, I offer my appreciation to Dan Soucoup, the genial representative from Nimbus who sat at my kitchen table one winter morning and said, "Your articles could be put into a book quite nicely." Dan's own books and column (in *The Moncton Times & Transcript*) have become a positive literary influence. Finally, my column and this book would not be possible without the sensible advice and proofreading skills of my wife, Anita.

Ted Jones

Section One: Remembering War

SUMMER SHADOWS:
THE STORY OF TWO PARADE SQUARES

AUGUST 18, 2001

Looking northwest across the Officers' Square one hundred years ago. Ladies and gentlemen enjoy lawn tennis while a military band plays in the background. The stone section of the Officers' Quarters is still standing and is now the home of the York-Sunbury Museum; the wooden section at left was demolished in June of 1924, one of the old timbers bearing the inscription "REBUILT 1816."

IN THE BEGINNING, they were separated from the rest of Fredericton by wooden fences that surrounded the military compound when the British regiments were garrisoned in the city from 1784 to 1869.

Barracks Square was located between the Soldiers' Barracks and the St. John River, concealed behind a fourteen-foot-high fence. All that was visible from Queen Street was a large sundial painted on the east gable of the stone barracks. A shadow from a projecting iron rod would be thrown upon the face of the dial, indicating accurate time from 5:00 A.M. until 1:00 P.M.

When retired military captain Patrick Campbell from Scotland visited Fredericton during the summer of 1791, he wrote in his journal that the boards for the fence were "put endways in the ground, so strait and close that a cat cannot get through; and so firmly as to secure every thing within, like a rampart."

Officers' Square was located in front of the Officers' Quarters, between Queen Street and the river, visible behind a low-railing fence. The long second-floor balcony of the stone quarters afforded a splendid view of the parade square, but both the building and the grounds were off limits to civilians without an invitation from the military.

William Cobbett, a young, non-commissioned officer with the first regiment, the 54th, was in charge of the parade squares and was to write later in his autobiography that "many goats belonged to the 54th and, in summer, they picked about wherever they could find grass." Along with the cows and sheep, the goats found excellent grazing in the middle of the Officers' Square.

Because of the fences, the soldiers and officers inside the compound had very little contact with the locals on the outside. As a result, a regular newspaper column entitled "Military Movements" was established in the local press. The Parade Square activities that were recorded were not always witnessed by the public, although the sound of military band music was constantly being heard. People canoeing on the river often drifted by the grounds just to listen.

History was made on both parade squares as early as the summer of 1794 when the first visit of royalty to the capital took place. In June of that year, the Duke of Kent, fourth son of King George III, and father of Queen Victoria, arrived to inspect the troops of the 104th Regiment of Foot.

After Victoria ascended to the throne, her birthday was celebrated each year at Barracks Square with the usual demonstrations of loyalty. The occasion was commemorated by firing a royal salute and a *feu de joie*. His Excellency, the lieutenant-governor, appeared on the grounds; "The British National Anthem" was played in excellent style; and three hearty cheers were given by the troops.

A major historic event shared by both squares took place in the summer of 1842, honouring the thirtieth anniversary of the British victory over the French in Spain at the Battle of Salamanca. A mock battle was staged below Fredericton at a place named for the original site and, after twelve hours of re-enactment, the troops returned to have dinner on the Barracks Square, followed by dancing on the grass of Officers' Square until the wee hours of the morning.

When a general order from the commander-in-chief was issued in 1845, the Officers' Square became the first outdoor smoking area in Fredericton. The use of pipes, cigars, or cheroots had become prevalent among the officers of the Army; as a result, it was requested that all smoking in the mess rooms and adjoining apartments of the Officers' Quarters be discontinued. For those who had acquired the habit, the square was the logical place to congregate.

At the same time, the Barracks Square was becoming the infamous location for the "terrible triangles"—sets of six halberts lashed together, to which early military offenders were tied to undergo floggings with the dreaded cat-o'-nine-tails. Deserters, if caught, were taken to the middle of the square and branded with the letter "D." Fortunately, no civilian spectators were allowed!

The Officers' Square received its first praise and public attention when a detailed description appeared in print in the summer of 1858. Robert Gowan of the New Brunswick Crown Land Office wrote a "Sketch of Fredericton" series for *The Head Quarters* and included the following:

In front of the Officers' Barracks is the Park, usually called Officers' Square, measuring about two hundred by three hundred feet and containing about one and one-quarter acres. The side next the Barker House [hotel on Queen Street] is ornamented with a row of magnificent willow trees, planted in 1802 [by a Scottish soldier in the 104th Regiment] and now forming a thick and continuous mass of foliage. The other sides are planted with trees of divers kinds—elms, balm of Gileads, butternuts, willows. These, though generally but in the early stages of their growth, are gradually adding to the beauty of what is really a very pleasant scene.

As the regiments changed, it was common practise for military families to sell their furniture and other belongings. Thus, the first yard sales in Fredericton were held at Officers' Square. Incoming officers and their wives were ready to purchase.

When the last of the British regiments departed, both squares were left unattended and neglected for a number of years. They became open cow pastures and practising grounds for the popular sport of cricket. They became venues for political soapbox oratory. They also became the most valuable properties in town.

After Confederation, all the military lands in Canada were transferred to the Dominion government by the War Department in England. It was the intention to sell these lands to the highest bidder in order to raise a militia fund for the future maintenance of the force in Canada. In the meantime, the two squares became favourite locations for incendiary and vandalism. Deterioration was rampant.

At Officers' Square, dead branches were left on the old historic willows, the grass was never cut or trimmed, and the walkways were overrun with burdocks. The fence was no longer white but hacked all over from jackknife gougings. Perched on the top railings were "all sorts and conditions of men" who had taken possession of the once beautiful square.

At Barracks Square, the high fence became dilapidated and unsightly, still shutting out a view of the river, always adorned with circus showbills and gaudy entertainment posters. In 1874, Carleton Street was extended through the grounds to the King's Wharf, and

Looking west across the Barracks Square during the World War One years. The Soldiers' Barracks is on the left, the first Provincial Normal School and its annex is on the right.

there were major plans afoot for commercializing the entire drill yard! When a circus company was allowed to rent the space during the summer of that year, a tragic riot was the result.

Before long, local businessmen were travelling to Ottawa, hoping to acquire Barracks Square for the Fredericton Railway Company, and Officers' Square for grand hotel accommodations. There was a definite cause for alarm and, as a result, the public started to protest against private ownership of the squares.

The Militia Department, which still had control, was not as concerned as the local citizens. After a letter-to-the-editor campaign failed to get the mayor to take any action, the citizens approached their member of parliament, who in turn corresponded with the minister of the militia, who announced that the maintenance of the squares was to be placed with Fredericton city council.

The days of summer cow pastures and scuffed cricket fields were ended.

Or were they?

The city fathers agreed to clean up the properties but they voted against any permanent responsibility that would have resulted in long-term improvement and beautification. Except for temporary grass-cutting, gravelled walkways, a few park benches, mended fences, and trimmed trees, the squares would not be receiving perpetual care and protection.

When *The Evening Capital* joined the crusade to preserve the grounds, it was suggested that either a fountain or a bandstand be erected in the centre of Officers' Square. The members of the Fredericton Cricket Club were opposed. They wanted the area left clear for their all-day matches with visiting cricketers from Saint

John. During these tournaments, the balcony of the quarters would be provided with seats for the ladies, and lunch would be served under the stone arches.

Before city council had an opportunity to consider additions to either square, the federal government immediately evacuated everyone from the site and took over the entire compound in 1883 for the establishment of the Infantry School Corps. Fredericton became a military headquarters once again—this time Canadian—until 1914.

During that time, the lawns and grounds of both parade squares were cared for by the military. Flowers beds were planted; old sheds and unsightly barns around the perimeters were demolished; new stables were built. When the low fence around Officers' Square fell down, it was replaced with a decorative cast-iron railing on a granite coping. The high fence around the Barracks Square was built anew and set back from Queen Street to allow for a strip of lawn.

The main attraction at Barracks Square was "Dick," the soldiers' pet bear mascot. From his high pole, he would bow to the Normal School girls next door as he waited for the men to bring him another bottle of beer. He held it between his paws, pulled the cork out with his teeth, and then consumed the contents.

"Guest Nights" or "At Homes" became fashionable during the long summer evenings. Prominent Fredericton families were invited to promenade around the squares before dinner at the officers' mess, with a military band always playing in the background. One hundred years ago, an item in *The Daily Gleaner* carried the headline "Officers' At Home": "There is no more delightful place in the City for a function of this kind than at the beautiful Officers' Square, always a model of neatness, with its spacious level lawn, huge elms and willows, and broad piazzas of the barracks."

Besides croquet and cricket, lawn tennis also became a popular sport at the Officers' Square. There was space for three tennis courts, and the stone quarters was nearby for refreshments. When the Fredericton Tennis Club hosted tournaments, officers of the royal regiment would allow the quarters to be used in the evening, orchestral music being provided for dancing.

At Barracks Square, the favourite sport was baseball, the first game of the Fredericton season always being played just after the troops had finished their drills. Infantrymen and civilians watched the games together on the grounds inside the fence. A number of spectators also cheered the players from the old post office, the first Normal School, and other vantage points.

Following World War One, the military departed once more, again leaving the two parade squares empty, desolate, and "up for grabs." When the properties were turned over to the Department of the Interior for disposal, the citizens of Fredericton demanded that they not fall into the hands of private owners. The people wanted them to become public parks.

In June of 1923, a transfer of the Soldiers' Barracks and Drill Square was made from the federal to the provincial government. It was to become the headquarters for the New Brunswick Liquor Commission and, in the early 1930s, the commission erected a large brick structure in the middle of Barracks Square. Today, that building houses the New Brunswick College of Craft and Design.

The possibility of Officers' Square and Quarters going for commercial use was eliminated in August of 1923 when the federal government passed the property over to the Fredericton branch of the Great War Veterans' Association as trustees with a long lease. This was the result of private citizens and patriotic organizations sending protests and petitions to Ottawa.

By an act of the New Brunswick Legislature, Officers' Square officially became a park in 1956. Since then, there have been several renovations and some interesting additions: two ancient cannons on the border facing the river, a statue of Lord Beaverbrook in the middle facing Queen Street, a memorial to John F. Kennedy in one corner (long since dismantled and moved to UNB).

After two hundred years, both parade squares, now part of a National Historic Site, are still popular spots in Fredericton, especially during the summer months. The sundial on the barracks, no longer hidden by a bank building, is still a constant reminder of the passage of time; the balcony on the quarters, the floor of which was recently replaced, still has one of the best views in the city.

SUMMER SHAM:
SALAMANCA STORY SET STRAIGHT

JULY 20, 2002

Salamanca Cottage had many owners over the years, one of them being the Keeley Institute. This rare advertisement (1895) is courtesy of William Crocket, whose family was the last to occupy the estate.

IT IS THE SEASON for historical re-enactments. From the Changing of the Guard at Officers' Square to the arrival of American Civil War soldiers at King's Landing, tourists and locals are presented with military scenes from the past.

According to *The Royal Gazette*, one of the first military re-enactments to be staged in Fredericton took place in October of 1830. The troops of the garrison, with the Grenadier and Rifle companies of the militia, assembled on what is now the spacious grounds of the cathedral, the line of skirmishes extending from the river bank to the foot of College Hill, "a most imposing and warlike appearance."

In November of the following year, Fredericton was once again "glorified with a Sham Fight," when a gallant stand was made at Mill Creek, below the town, giving the spectators an opportunity to see what the troops would do upon the battlefield against real enemies. Lieutenant-Governor Sir Archibald Campbell and his family were present and were "highly pleased with the day's performance."

Fredericton's most famous re-enactment of all took place on July 22, 1839, when a mock battle was staged to honour the British victory at Salamanca, Spain.

The Salamanca Sham began on the flats below town (where the Morell Park is now located) and moved east toward the hillside now known as Forest Hill. When it was over, the area involved was officially named Salamanca and, as time went on, the place acquired a history of its own:

The Fredericton Railway Company began its line at Salamanca; one of the city's elegant estates was built there; New Brunswick's first Anglican bishop, Canada's oldest-serving senator, and the founder of Fredericton's longest-running newspaper all lived at Salamanca; an alcohol and drug treatment centre was established there (folding in a shadow of mystery); and the only reigning British king to ever visit Canada bid farewell to Fredericton from Salamanca Station.

Over the centuries, historians have presented different versions of the various stories involving Salamanca. Thus, on this anniversary date of the battle in Spain (190 years ago), it is time to set the record straight, starting with the original event of July 22, 1812.

Before 1812, Napoleon Bonaparte had already turned his attention to the Spanish peninsula, insisting that Portugal break off relations with England. However, he had underestimated patriotic spirit: the Spanish and Portuguese were determined to drive the French invaders from the country. When an English army—under the command of the Duke of Wellington—arrived to assist, they successfully drove the French back across the Pyrenees.

At Salamanca, Spain, the British had a major victory, the battle being the most cleverly fought, largest in scale, and most important in results. Ironically, one of the British regiments involved (the 36th Herefordshire) would later be garrisoned in Fredericton from 1839 to 1842.

It was not until the 36th Regiment arrived in Fredericton that the mock battle of Salamanca took place, although Queen Victoria's accession (1837) and her subsequent coronation (1838) have both been stated as the date (but without documentation). When *The Royal Gazette* was printed in Fredericton on Wednesday, July 24, 1839, it carried the headline ANNIVERSARY OF THE BATTLE OF SALAMANCA, "which accordingly took place on Monday last, the 22nd instant."

The Sham Fight began at 8:00 A.M. Major Cairns of the 36th was in command of the opposing force, consisting of one division of the 36th, plus the Royal Artillery, Cavalry, and Rifles of the First Battalion/York County Militia.

Colonel Maxwell of the 36th was in command of the English force, consisting of one detachment of Royal Artillery and five companies of the 36th Regiment.

Cairns marched to the hillside (leading to Forest Hill) and Maxwell to the flats below, both sides halting in order of battle, both waving Salamanca banners. At 10:00 A.M., Lieutenant-Governor Sir John Harvey, accompanied by his family and his attendants, arrived on the scene and joined the hundreds of spectators. A gun was fired as the signal for action, and the manoeuvres began.

Maxwell and the 36th advanced in a colourful line across the field and then charged the hill with fixed bayonets ("glinting in the sun") and blank ammunition. When the barricades ("constructed in the early morning") were demolished, Cairns and the militia spiked and dismounted their guns and fled! William T. Baird of Fredericton was one of the fleeing militiamen at the time, and when he was interviewed by *The Reporter* many years later, he said: "I well remember the appearance of the soldiers as they came up the rise—faces begrimed with powder from biting the cartridges, and white pants soiled and wet with perspiration. The bugle call 'fire and retire' was quickly responded to, and we retreated, continuing the fire in extended order."

Following a "Flag of Truce," the entire 36th Regiment and the York Militia passed by His Excellency in review order and then returned to their quarters.

At two o'clock, the regiment and the militia sat down together at long tables in Barracks Square (behind the Soldiers' Barracks) to a plentiful supply of roast beef and plum pudding, "with an ample quantity of Malt Liquor." On the first sound of the bugle for dinner, local citizens were allowed inside the square to enjoy the several toasts that were given, especially those to the youthful sovereign and the Duke of Wellington, "which were echoed from table to table in continuous cheers."

After dinner, everyone moved to the green grass of Officers' Square and participated in a variety of amusements (sports, dancing, singing), the Salamanca anniversary coming to an end at ten o'clock with a brilliant display of fireworks on the square and on board a scow in the river.

Thus, a glorious achievement of British heroism had been remembered in Fredericton, assisted by one of the corps that had been engaged in the original battle. It is little wonder that the name Salamanca remained a part of local folklore for years to come. And it did!

On the morning of November 6, 1867, carriages and pedestrians from all over Fredericton and York County once again made their way to Salamanca. A battery of cannon was in position to fire twenty rounds; the band of the 22nd Regiment was ready to give a stirring rendition of the National Anthem. The turning of the sod for the first railway ever to be built in Fredericton was about to take place.

At noon, a number of handsome landaus arrived, carrying Lieutenant-Governor Francis Pym Harding, Mayor William Needham and his wife, Mary Ann, the city aldermen, Judge Lemuel Allan Wilmot, clergymen of all denominations, the president and the professors of UNB, members of the Legislative Assembly, and nine directors and seventeen stockholders of the Fredericton Railway Company.

Sheriff Thomas Temple was president of the company, Alexander "Boss" Gibson was one of the directors, and Egerton Ryerson Burpee of Sheffield was the civil engineer. However, it was the lieutenant-governor and Mary Ann Needham who undertook the task of turning the first sod.

The spot selected was at the foot of the hillside, where several meandering brooks emptied into the St. John River near Salamanca Point (site of the Loyalist Cemetery). Mrs. Needham raised the sod with an ornate spade and placed it in a mahogany wheelbarrow. As the crowd cheered, His Excellency wheeled the sod a short distance along the proposed railway line, symbolizing the hours of toil that were to take place before Fredericton would be connected by rail with the outside world.

When the branch line to Hartt's Mills (later Fredericton Junction) was finished, it would connect with the Western Extension railway, which was being built at that time from Saint John to Maine. The northern terminus was the new wooden station on York Street, and the first stop was a small railway shelter with a nearby sign that read SALAMANCA STATION.

The largest private property in the Salamanca area was to become a thirty-three-acre estate on the hillside directly in back of the little railway shelter (between the UNB campus and Forest Hill Cemetery). The original grant of land, dating back to the late 1700s, was smaller and was first owned by Abraham Vanderbeck (proprietor of the historic Golden Ball Inn on Waterloo Row).

When Fredericton barrister Henry Bliss bought the property in 1820, he cleared the land and began to build a pretentious dwelling (high on the hill) that came to be known as Salamanca Cottage. However, after his father (Chief Justice Jonathan Bliss) died in 1822, Henry moved to England and, for the next twenty years, leased Salamanca to a succession of prominent people from Fredericton.

In 1842, Attorney General Charles Jeffrey Peters purchased the place and lived there with his large family (twelve children by his first wife, nine by his second) until his death in 1848. The next occupant was Bishop John Medley, who remained for seventeen years, followed by Captain George Maunsell of the 15th (Yorkshire) Regiment in 1866 and Deputy Surveyor General Andrew Inches in

1867, the last placing the following advertisement in *The Reporter*:

FOR SALE: That desirable residence known as SALAMANCA. This property is pleasantly situated in the vicinity of Fredericton. The dwelling house, in the cottage style, possesses accommodation pertaining to a first-class residence. The grounds are tastefully laid out and planted with ornamental trees. A garden, orchard, and good STABLES are attached. Possession given 15 May 1867.

The Honourable David Wark, age sixty-three and one of the twelve original senators from New Brunswick called by royal proclamation, answered the advertisement and made Salamanca his home for the next twenty-eight years. He acquired adjoining land from his brother-in-law E. R. Burpee, enlarged the main house to three storeys and twenty-one rooms, and added a well house ("over a crystal highland spring") at the top of the hill and a gate house ("for the custodian and his family") at the foot of the driveway.

When Wark turned one hundred in 1904, a special train was sent to Fredericton to convey him to his seat in the Senate. He was living on York Street with his daughter at the time, but he requested that he board at Salamanca Station, and he did. It was his last visit to the national capital before his death the next year and subsequent burial at Forest Hill.

In the meantime, the Wark family had sold the estate for $5,000 to a group of prosperous Fredericton businessmen, all temperance followers, who had purchased a franchise of the Leslie E. Keeley Company of Illinois. For several months in 1895, Salamanca became "the first and only genuine Keeley Institute in the Maritime provinces for the cure of inebriety, the morphine/opium habit, and neurasthenia."

Unfortunately, the venture was plagued with problems from the beginning. Not only did patients escape when the train stopped at Salamanca Station, but the medical doctor in charge suffered from mental depression and suddenly disappeared; his badly decomposed body was found four weeks later in Maine.

Finally, the company was sued for $2,500 by two Fredericton men for claims on bonds. As a result, all furniture belonging to the institute was seized in January of 1896 and sold at public auction, bringing only $400 to help satisfy the judgment. For the next three years, the estate stood empty!

In 1899, Salamanca Cottage became a family home once more when James Harvey Crocket purchased the place and lived there until his death in 1930. He was the son of Dr. William Crocket, former principal of the Normal School and chief superintendent of education, and he had ten brothers and sisters, all of whom had successful careers. James himself was the founder and publisher of *The Gleaner* (a weekly) and then *The Daily Gleaner*, a newspaper he passed on to his two sons—William Wallace and James Alexander.

The estate became known as the Crocket Farm, and son William, with his wife and two sons (Bill and Jim), continued to live there after James H. died. Few changes were made, although a two-car garage with a grease pit was added. It was in the early evening of January 4, 1946, just after William placed his Studebaker in the garage, that he noticed the main house was on fire, the flames spreading with such speed that only the two tall chimneys were left standing after two hours.

The Fredericton Fire Department attempted to pump water up the hill, the hose (resting across the CPR and CNR tracks) holding up two trains in the process. But very little was saved, the loss of the building and its contents being estimated at $20,000. It was never rebuilt, the property being sold to UNB, remaining mostly as woodland with numerous pathways in all directions.

Fourth generation Bill Crocket often visits the site of his childhood home, and, although the apple orchard and the butternut trees are gone, he knows exactly where all the buildings were once located on the vast hillside. There is nothing left of the gate house, the well house, the barns, and the stables, but partial foundations of the main house and the garage remain.

Below the hill, where the train tracks and the little station used to be, Bill remembers an afternoon in June of 1939, when he and his brother went down the hill to place souvenir pennies on the rails, to be flattened later by the train that would carry King George VI and Queen Elizabeth from Salamanca to Saint John.

Because the twelve silver and blue coaches of the royal train were too heavy for the railway line to Fredericton Junction, a smaller train, consisting of five day-coaches, was used for this part of the tour. Over six thousand spectators gathered at Salamanca to bid farewell, the royal couple standing on the observation platform, waving, as the crowds sang "Auld Lang Syne." Her Majesty turned and entered the coach first, followed a few seconds later by the king, after which the train moved slowly away.

Since that memorable moment in history, Fredericton has expanded to include all of Forest Hill and beyond, Salamanca gradually becoming obsolete. The name has appeared recently on the Salamanca Walking Trail and the Salamanca Landing Apartments, both in the vicinity of a busy traffic circle where, once upon a time, a summer sham re-enacted and remembered a famous military battle.

TROPHIES AND MEMORIALS OF WORLD WAR ONE

NOVEMBER 10, 2001

In 1920, one of the six German trophy guns was placed in front of the old Customs House, now the New Brunswick Sports Hall of Fame. In the background is the Queen Street Post Office before its clock tower was removed in 1955.

BEFORE THE NAME WAS CHANGED to Remembrance Day, there was the annual observance of the Armistice which ended the Great War of 1914–1918.

November 11, 1919, was the first anniversary, but technically Canada was still at war because the treaty with Germany had not yet been ratified by all nations engaged in the struggle.

There was no public holiday, but there was a minute of silence at the eleventh hour. There was no memorial ceremony, but there was thankfulness for peace, especially to the people of the British Empire. There was still no buying and selling, but the world was making a slow economic recovery.

In order to return to the prosperity of the years preceding the Great War, a Victory Loan Campaign was underway across the country. In New Brunswick, the capital city was looked upon as the district to over-subscribe with the highest percentage. Fredericton had been a leader in past campaigns but, in 1919, there was an added incentive. A German gun, captured in the war, was to be given to the winning district in each province.

By Armistice Day, the competition in York County had come

down to McAdam Junction with $100,000 and the city of Fredericton with $1,500,000. And both were still going strong! Unfortunately, neither place won, the prize guns going to Albert County instead. It would be another year before Fredericton was able to share in the spoils of the Great War.

In the summer of 1920, the federal government began to distribute across Canada more of the weapons that had been captured by the British and Canadian forces. Fredericton's allotment: four German field guns. Mayor J. A. Reid received the following communication from the director of war trophies in Ottawa: "These trophies, which have been distributed as the property of the people of Canada, have been sent to you with the understanding that the proper care will be taken of them and, in taking over these guns, it is understood that you will agree to this condition."

On June 28, the guns arrived in Fredericton by train and were in the same condition as when they left the battlefields of Europe, the camouflage still being in evidence. At first glance, they were a sorry lot: the breeches were missing, a number of wheel spokes had been shot away, the armour plates were pierced in several places.

For two days, they remained on exhibit in the CNR yards, where they were inspected by returned soldiers and hundreds of citizens. Everyone wanted to learn about the kind of guns that were used against the Canadian boys. Two were 150 mm; two were 77 mm; each had a clearly marked identification number.

Until the city could select a location for the guns, it was decided to store them in the basement of City Hall. But the guns only made it as far as the city dump which, at that time, was located behind city hall. Here they remained and were forgotten during the months of July and August. Not only did they continue to deteriorate, but they were partially dismantled by souvenir collectors.

On September 1, two howitzer guns, also captured from the Germans during the war, arrived in Fredericton, having been allotted to the New Brunswick government to be placed in suitable positions in the provincial capital. Six locations were now needed, and soon.

However, there had been some confusion; the four earlier guns had been intended for the province and not the city. But all six guns, after they were repaired by the provincial government, were to be mounted on concrete foundations and placed on permanent display in various locations in Fredericton. The city's only allotment was to be a German machine gun, arriving later in the fall.

In order that everyone would be satisfied, the provincial minister of public works invited the city to make suggestions for placing the guns and to combine with the province in a formal unveiling and acceptance ceremony. Thanksgiving Day and then Trafalgar Day (both in October) were selected as possible dates, but the war trophies would not be ready by then. Thus, Armistice Day became the earliest date and, according to the minister and the mayor, a most appropriate one.

On Thursday, November 11, 1920, the first big Armistice Day observance took place in Fredericton. It began at noon when the fire alarm sounded a warning to the citizens that the time for a pause of two minutes in all activities had arrived. Work ceased, traffic stopped, pedestrians stood silent.

In the afternoon, the celebration began with a big parade from Phoenix Square (in front of City Hall) to Parliament Square (in front of the legislature). The main attractions were the six German guns, each having been attached to limbers with trained artillerymen in charge. Also taking part were two marching bands, members of the military (Infantry and Artillery), the Boy Scouts, and students from all city schools, the Normal School, and the university.

It was a long parade route, proceeding out York Street to Charlotte, up to Smythe, and then down Queen. Passing the post office, the marchers were reviewed by Lieutenant-Governor William Pugsley, who took the salute on the steps. Arriving at the Legislature, the six guns were placed in position and the program of music and speeches began.

After the guns were presented and accepted, they were taken to various sites in the City, to remain permanently as souvenirs of the great four-year struggle in Europe. One was placed in front of the Customs House (now the Sports Hall of Fame), one at the intersection of King and Brunswick streets in the West End, two at Parliament Square in the East End, and two in front of the Provincial Normal School. (The latter four would eventually be moved to Officers' Square.)

The only other official military trophies in Fredericton at the time were seven old, muzzle-loading, cast-iron cannons located along "the Green." They were leftovers from the imperial regiments of the 1800s and were given to the city by Jabez Bunting Snowball during his term as lieutenant-governor (1902–1907).

The seven colonial cannons and the six German guns were still in their respective places as Armistice Day was quietly observed in 1921. There was no public holiday that year and there was no minute of silence, the city council having neglected to issue a proclamation for the latter.

In 1922, there was a new symbol of remembrance: a bright red Flanders poppy, worn to show a special mark of appreciation for Canada's wartime heroes. The door-to-door distribution was done early in the morning of November 11 by the Red Cross, the Imperial Order Daughters of the Empire (IODE), the Women's Institute (WI), the Great War Veterans Association (GWVA), the Boy Scouts, and various church societies. By noon, every household had been visited, donations had been made, and Fredericton's first poppy campaign was successfully completed.

When the fifth anniversary of the Armistice was observed in Canada in 1923, there was an outstanding event in Fredericton—the unveiling of the Citizens' War Memorial on Sunday afternoon, November 11. It was one of the most impressive in the Dominion and it was erected at an ideal location—the East End triangle, formed by the intersection of Fenety Avenue (lower Queen Street along the Green) and Church and King streets.

Framed by the St. John River on one side and Christ Church Cathedral on the other, the memorial was placed directly in front of the spot where King Edward VII landed when he visited Fredericton as Prince of Wales in 1860.

Never did the people subscribe more readily and more heartily than to the fund for this memorial to their honoured dead. It cost $12,000, of which half was granted by city council, the other half coming from the citizens.

For the construction of the white granite monument, a fourteen-ton shaft was surmounted on a twenty-six-ton die, the latter said to be one of the largest blocks of cut granite in Canada. The total height of twenty-five feet was surmounted with an elegant capstone bearing the coat of arms of the city of Fredericton and that of the Province of New Brunswick.

Located directly in front of the monument was the cenotaph, an empty granite tomb surmounted by a rifle, side arms, and shell helmet, a large granite cross standing at the head.

Behind the cross on the front face of the die was placed a bronze tablet bearing the names of the 109 soldiers from Fredericton who made the supreme sacrifice. The battles in which they died were inscribed on the four sides of the shaft, each side representing one of the four years of the Great War.

Sir John Douglas Hazen, chief justice of New Brunswick and a distinguished former citizen of Fredericton, delivered the dedicatory address. He had been a former mayor of the city, the premier of the province, and minister of naval affairs in the federal cabinet during the war. On November 11, 1923, he spoke as the father of two sons who had served with the forces, one having been killed in action.

Marjorie Osborne, daughter of Lieutenant Colonel W. J. Osborne and sister of Hubert Osborne, whose name was engraved on the bronze tablet, unveiled the memorial. She pulled the cord, allowing a number of Union Jacks to drop from around the shaft, the die, and the cenotaph. The huge crowd burst into applause.

There was silence as the names of the Fredericton men who had laid down their lives were called slowly, one by one. After two minutes were observed as a further mark of respect, three volleys were fired, followed by the sounding of "The Last Post" by bugler Seymour Tyler.

This would be the first of a long line of Armistice Day ceremonies at which Seymour Tyler would flawlessly play the familiar bugle call that orders soldiers to retire for sleep. In later years, he would be joined by bugler John Forrester, who responded with "Reveille," the bugle signal that awakens soldiers in the morning.

Following the unveiling of the Fredericton cenotaph, two churches dedicated special memorials during their evening services: St.Paul's Presbyterian, with a bronze tablet listing twenty-five names; St. Mary's in Devon, with a brass altar cross listing seven names. In the days ahead, other churches followed, each remembering the debt to those who remained overseas but who, at one time, had passed through the Sunday school and had become a member of the congregation.

It was to have been a war to end all wars but, in 1945, there would be 103 more names listed on the Fredericton cenotaph monument, all as the result of World War Two. Not only were these young lives gone but so too were the trophies of World War One. In January of 1942, Mayor Ray Forbes received the following request from the Federal Department of Munitions and Supply:

"We are asking you to donate the trophies from the last war, which you may have stationed in your parks, squares, or other public places of your community, to the Salvage Division of the Treasury Department, so that these pieces can be made over into other implements of war with which to combat the common enemy."

Along with tin cans, toothpaste tubes, tinfoil, and automobile license plates, it was a call for an "all out" war effort, meaning that every available piece of scrap metal had to be salvaged in an effort to keep the war industry at peak production. Fredericton and the province did not hesitate.

At a meeting of city council, the mayor was directed to inform Ottawa that "if these trophy pieces are actually needed for the war effort, the City of Fredericton is perfectly willing to release them."

Ironically, the six German guns from World War One would be incorporated into Canadian munitions and weaponry to fight against another generation of the same enemy.

Marysville and Devon also placed their war trophies at the disposal of the Salvage Committee, Ottawa making all necessary arrangements for the collection. It was soon realized that the souvenirs of the Great War were no longer necessary as a reminder of the great deeds and victories on the battlefields of Europe.

The Fredericton inventory for the salvage also included the seven old nineteenth-century cannons on the Green. The city would not see their like again until 1969, when two old thirty-two-pounder cannons were acquired and mounted on wooden carriages in Officers' Square, where they remain today, pointing towards the St. John River. Originally, they came from the Halifax area in the early 1950s.

On future Remembrance Days, the cannons at Officers' Square will remain silent as they have done for almost two centuries. There will be no presentation of captured guns from world wars. There will be no unveiling of war memorials. There will be no sounds from the bugle of Seymour Tyler, who faithfully took part in all the parades and ceremonies until his death in 1985 at age eighty-eight.

Instead, there will be the remembrance of young men who went to the Fdront, prepared to sacrifice their lives for the Allied cause, striving nobly and successfully to defeat the enemy.

REMEMBRANCE:
THE STORY OF TWO MEMORIAL HALLS

NOVEMBER 9, 2002

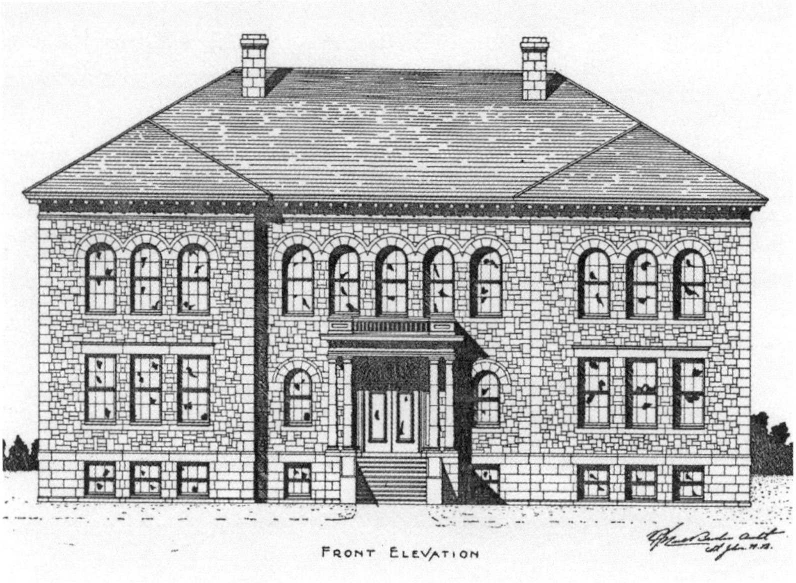

The architect's original sketch for UNB's Memorial Hall. The five windows over the entrance were reduced to three.

EIGHTY YEARS AGO, two of Fredericton's enduring institutions—Christ Church Cathedral and the University of New Brunswick—built memorial halls to honour those who so nobly sacrificed their lives in the Great War of 1914–1918.

Looking back, both of these memorial halls have provided an interesting legacy, from their beginnings in the early 1920s to the present day, especially on November 11 of each year.

Christ Church Cathedral had been without a hall for Sunday school and other church activities since the sale of the old Anglican church hall at the corner of Carleton and Brunswick streets. It had been the first Anglican hall in Fredericton (shared by the parish church and the cathedral). Constructed in 1881 and sold in 1919 to Gaiety Theatre proprietor W. W. O. Fenety for $6,000, it is still standing today after several different occupants over the years.

To provide temporary accommodation for the cathedral Sunday school in 1919, a carriage house adjoining the bishop's residence at 97 Church Street was remodelled and used while the new memorial hall was being built. Fundraising began immediately and, by the winter of 1922, there was enough money.

The architect's original sketch for the Cathedral Memorial Hall. This building was demolished in 1960.

The Very Reverend Scovil Neales, dean of the cathedral, was the chairman of a large building committee consisting of fourteen gentlemen and two ladies (Edith E. Allen and Eliza B. Hunter). The architect was Delancy Robinson of New York, the construction company, Boone and McDonald of Saint John. The contract price: $25,000. The proposed completion date: November 1922.

Cathedral Memorial Hall was built during the summer of 1922 on a vacant lot at 168 Church Street, adjoining the historic deanery on Brunswick Street. The cornerstone was laid in the early evening of July 12 of that year, the impressive ceremony beginning with a choir processional from the cathedral to the proposed site. The gentleman who did the honours of laying the stone was Sir John Douglas Hazen, chief justice of New Brunswick. In delivering his address, he reminisced about his early life in Fredericton: "I am glad that the Memorial Building is to be in King's Ward because it was this ward that first gave me the opportunity of a public position when I was elected to the mayoralty of Fredericton. King's Ward is also the largest ward in the city and the ward with the most beautiful church—the Cathedral."

After the cornerstone was tapped three times with a silver trowel, it was lowered into position, citizens from all over the city observing in silence. Dean Neales said a short prayer and then referred to the contents of the metal box that was to remain inside the stone for all time: "an honour roll with 373 names of the members of the Fredericton Diocese who lost their lives in the War, including the

Deanery and the Parish where each had lived; the Synod journals for 1919, 1920, and 1921; the names of the officers of the various church societies; the names of the sidesmen of the cathedral; a copy of *The Daily Gleaner* for July 12th, 1922."

The hall was to be a one-and-one-half-storey frame construction (with an exterior stucco finish) built on a concrete wall foundation. There were to be two sets of stairs in the main vestibule, one leading up to the auditorium (with stage) on the first floor, the other leading down to the gymnasium (with balcony) in the basement. The first floor was to also have five classrooms and a library. The basement was to house the kitchen and the boiler room, the latter being attached to an outside coal bin. Except for a meeting room over the entrance and a storage room over the stage, the remainder of the second floor was to be left open to the slanted roof above in order to provide ventilation for the auditorium below.

It was not until March of 1923 that the Cathedral Memorial Hall was completed, the final cost reaching $30,000. Although organizations began to use the new facility immediately, the formal opening and dedication did not take place until Tuesday evening, May 15, having been postponed from Easter because the furnishings had not arrived.

The short dedicatory service was conducted by Bishop John Richardson who, in his address, thanked the cathedral women "with all my heart for their courage and optimism—a body of workers unexcelled and unparalled in any diocese as they worked to help finance the hall." They raised $5,000!

When the Diocesan Synod of Fredericton held its fifty-fifth session in the new hall in May of 1924, all the names of the men of the diocese who had given their lives were placed upon the walls. There was also a bronze tablet to the memory of Mr. and Mrs. George Y. Dibblee, benefactors of the hall who, before their deaths, spoke of the need for a hall and then left a financial legacy of $3,300 for the purpose.

In his annual report at the fifty-fifth session, Dean Neales informed the delegates that the hall was an expensive undertaking but that all organizations, clubs, and sports teams had agreed to help pay off the $15,000 debt and to then contribute to the annual upkeep of $1,500. "The hall has already proved to be the greatest value for which it was intended, scarcely a day passing when it is not in use."

When the UNB *Memorial Magazine* appeared in 1919, it included a proposal for a new building that would be a permanent memorial for the 35 UNB students (graduates and undergraduates) who gave their lives during the Great War. As a result, the members of the Memorial Hall Committee met for the first time in January of 1920. All were UNB alumni:

Sir John Douglas Hazen (chairman), Dr. W. W. White, Dr. W. C. Crocket, Dr. H. V. B. Bridges, Dr. A. S. McFarlane, Eliza B. Hunter, Ina (Mersereau) McLeod, and UNB Chancellor C. C. Jones.

It was decided that the purpose of the building as a memorial would be enhanced by providing needed accommodation. Thus, in addition to the convocation hall in the rear (forming the body of a T-shaped plan), there would be a wing on either side of the pillared entrance, containing lecture rooms and laboratories for physics and chemistry. The estimated cost of the proposed building: $75,000.

However, the university had not been particularly fortunate with regard to financial support, especially from the provincial government. By January of 1922, a Memorial Hall Fund Committee was formed to launch a major drive in Fredericton and, subsequently, across the Dominion. Because the estimated cost of the building had doubled, it was absolutely necessary for the province to give $50,000 and the city of Fredericton $25,000. Donations eventually amounted to $40,000, but an additional $30,000 was needed for equipment after construction was done.

By January of 1923, a detailed plan of the new building was prepared by Saint John architect F. Neil Brodie. Nine tenders applied for the contract but it was B. Mooney & Sons, of Saint John, who started construction that summer, working closely with a new building committee chaired by Chancellor Jones and consisting of Murray MacLaren (a future lieutenant-governor), Charles Richards (a future premier), Dr. W. D. Rankine (of Woodstock), and Professor Adam Cameron (of UNB).

Three campus sites were proposed and debated for the location of "Mem Hall" (as it was affectionately called), each in relation to the lower terrace in front of the Old Arts Building: west, centre, and east. The last was chosen so that the university buildings would be prominently positioned for viewing by visitors arriving in the city via the Fredericton Branch Railway, the tracks for which run along the bottom of the hill.

The northeast position was also in the vicinity of the old gate house, near the driveway entrance to the college grounds from University Avenue, thus eliminating considerable excavation for the basement of the new building. The only problem was the inadequate water supply that would be piped from a spring on the college property. A tank for storing rain water would have to be installed.

On a warm Tuesday afternoon, July 23, 1923, Canada's twelfth Governor General laid the cornerstone for Memorial Hall. His name was Lord Byng, the popular commander who had led the Canadians at Vimy Ridge. Thus, his presence in Fredericton on that particular summer day was highly significant. When he replied to addresses from the province, the city, and the veterans, he said: "you have been good enough to refer to the part I played in the War. It was my privilege then to command on the battlefields of Europe the Canadian Corps, that magnificent body of which your men formed an important part. I look forward to meeting the wives and the mothers who so readily gave all they held dear that the world might be free."

After receiving an honorary doctor of laws degree during a special convocation for his visit only, Byng was accompanied by Lieutenant-Governor W. F. Todd and many other guests in attendance to the site of the new building, where a solemn ceremony of laying the cornerstone took place. In the hollow of the stone, a sealed copper receptacle was buried for all time; it contained the following: "The university honour roll, the university calendar for 1923, the *Memorial Magazine*, a copy of the invitation to the cornerstone laying, current Canadian coins and stamps, copies of Fredericton and Saint John daily newspapers, names of the architect and building committee."

In May of 1924, UNB encaenia exercises were held for the first time in the new Memorial Hall. There were forty-four students in the graduating class, two honorary degrees (Charles E. Neill and Harry H. Hagerman) and two masters of arts (G. Alvah Good and Russell S. Sheldrick). The hall would be used for the next twenty-two encaenias, the ceremony moving to the Lady Beaverbrook gymnasium in 1946.

The formal dedication of the new hall would not take place until the encaenia of 1925, at which time Sir George E. Foster was the special guest. A former student and then a professor at UNB, Foster had become one of Canada's leading statesmen. He considered it an honour to dedicate the Memorial Hall and to unveil the bronze tablet (over the entrance to the auditorium), listing the 35 names of the fallen UNB soldiers. He said: "Is this to be a memorial of war? God forbid. It is a memorial to that which underlies all war and which in due time will expel all war—a memorial to duty, a memorial to service, and the will and wish to sacrifice. But to war—no!"

Three individual memorials were also dedicated during the official opening of Mem Hall. A bronze tablet in honour of Charles Fisher (UNB graduate in 1830; Father of Confederation in 1867) was unveiled in the foyer but was later moved to the great hall in the Old Arts Building. His daughter, Frances Fisher, bequeathed $10,000 for the new hall in memory of her father; his nephew, George E. Fisher, was in attendance for the unveiling.

A memorial reading desk in honour of Lieut. John Basil Hipwell (Forestry 1915) and an oak platform table in honour of Capt. Robert Kilgour Shives (Forestry 1913) were donated by their families for use in the new hall. Both young men were killed in action, 1916.

Lady Nancy Astor, the first woman member of the British Parliament, sent a special souvenir for Memorial Hall—a set of four large framed photographs of the private cemetery at Cliveden, the Astor Estate in England. During the War, Viscount Waldorf Astor had turned his estate into a hospital for the care of wounded Canadian soldiers. Lady Astor supervised the work, becoming acquainted with many of the former UNB students. Those who died were buried on the estate, the Astors erecting a war memorial that could be seen in the photographs.

In time, seven stained-glass windows were installed in the auditorium of Memorial Hall, three along each side wall and one over the stage, all with classical or literary themes. One of these windows was given by Frederick R. Taylor, who graduated from UNB in 1896. The others were memorials for the following: the Earl of Ashburnham (who lived in Fredericton for almost two decades); UNB graduate George Fenwick (who died at Passchendaele); Franklin Rankin (who died at Baupaume) and his sister Marjory; UNB classics professor Henry Seabury Bridges; UNB science professor Loring Woart Bailey; and Sir John Douglas Hazen.

By 1960, Fredericton's two memorial halls had experienced many changes. The Christ Church Cathedral hall was demolished in April of that year to make way for a larger and more modern memorial hall at the same location. The University of New Brunswick hall became an arts centre and the home for UNB's resident artists and musicians. The thirty-five names from the Great War are still on the wall.

As Fredericton pauses to remember on November 11, the first Cathedral hall on Church Street and the memorial hall that still stands majestically at the head of University Avenue should be in our thoughts.

DID CIVIL WAR HEROINE ONCE LIVE IN FREDERICTON?

SEPTEMBER 15, 2001

Sarah Emma Edmonds, alias Franklin Thompson.

BUNKER HILL, BULL RUN, Manassas, Fort Sumter, Gettysburg, Charleston, and Harper's Ferry.

Abraham Lincoln, Jefferson Davis, Robert E. Lee, "Stonewall" Jackson, and Ulysses S. Grant.

The places and people of the American Civil War (1861–65) entered Canadian living rooms in the fall of 1990 with a stunning eleven-hour television documentary on PBS. Although the monumental production had several factual errors, there was one grave omission.

In response to a letter from a Fredericton viewer, producer/director Ken Burns said he was not aware of the young York County, New Brunswick woman who disguised herself as a man, changed her name to Franklin Thompson, and joined the First Union Greys, a volunteer militia unit that became Company F of the Second Michigan Infantry Regiment.

Fortunately, physical examinations were not necessary. It was a time in history when clothing, literally, made the man!

Completely fooled by Private Thompson's true identity, commanding officers such as General George McClellan and Colonel Orlando Poe came to admire the soldier with the small hands and feet, whom her fellow comrades innocently called "our little woman" and "the beardless boy."

She was never suspected and she proved her many capabilities when she nursed the wounded in primitive field hospitals, carried the mail long distances on horseback, stood guard for hours by herself, and marched into battle with excitement and enthusiasm.

She became brigade postmaster and aide-de-camp, but her greatest triumph occurred when she volunteered to become one of the Union Army's most elusive spies, infiltrating Confederate lines with eleven successful missions, all without detection, ironically posing as a female on several occasions and one time as a Canadian investigator!

In 1863, she contracted malaria, and rather than submit to a medical examination that might reveal her gender, she deserted and resumed civilian life as a woman, settling down in Oberlin, Ohio.

Frank Thompson was gone forever. Or was he?

It was this second major desertion that was to change her life remarkably. The first occurred at the place where she was born: Magaguadavic Lake in the parish of Prince William, a short distance west of Fredericton.

Her birth name was Sarah Emma Evelyn Edmonson, the last name eventually being changed by the family to *Edmondson* and then by Sarah to *Edmonds*. In 1883, after she confessed her secret life as a soldier, it was discovered that the name *Sarah Emma Edmonds* belonged to one of the most fascinating women in North American history.

But there were no honours during her lifetime.

It was not until 1990 that she was among the first ten women to be appointed to the New Brunswick Women's Hall of Fame; in 1992, she was inducted into the Michigan Women's Hall of Fame.

There have also been dedication ceremonies, historical exhibitions, published biographies, numerous magazine articles, academic studies, and Civil War re-enactments, such as the one that takes place at King's Landing on September 22 (in the parish of Prince William, where it all started).

Now filmmakers want to bring her story to television and the big screen, each one hoping to find the real Sarah and to discover what actually happened to her over the years. Authentic resource material will be their challenge because primary documentation is sparse and scattered, with only small collections of Sarah's letters surviving. Regarding secondary sources, some family descendants differ on certain details; others are unwilling to share information. Along the way, fictional accounts and many errors have embellished the story.

Fortunately, there is Sarah's autobiography: *Nurse and Spy in the Union Army: The Adventures and Experiences of a Woman in Hospitals, Camps, and Battlefields*, published in 1865 in Hartford,

Connecticut, based on her wartime diary (which has yet to be found) and dedicated "To the Sick and Wounded Soldiers of the Army of the Potomoc."

The massive four-hundred-page tome was an impressive accomplishment by a woman in her early twenties with very little formal education. According to the critics, there is skepticism in relation to the book's elaborate organization, elegant literary style, incredible descriptions, and possible fabrication, the last for identity protection on the part of the author.

It sold 175,000 copies and earned its author $100,000 in royalties, all of which she donated to Civil War veterans' associations. Now a collector's item, this rare book is the best starting point for research. In Fredericton, there is a copy at the Legislative Library, the UNB Archives, and the New Brunswick Nurses' Museum.

Another copy made its way into the hands of Jessie (Hamilton) Moffitt of Harvey Station and McAdam who, until her death in 1994 at age ninety-five, read it over and over with keen interest. As Sarah's grandniece, she assisted researchers who came to her door, always defending her great aunt's way of life, always hoping that the printed word would be the truth: "In all the tales my grandmother told me of her sister Sarah, for whom my mother was named, I never heard her speak of her as anything but a girl whose love of adventure and travel made ordinary life seem dull and uninteresting. That she was a possible 'congenital liar,' as well as something worse regarding sexual orientation, was the product of the researcher's imagination."

The grandmother's name was Frances, the first of six children born to Scottish immigrant farmer Isaac Edmondson and his Irish wife, Elizabeth (Leeper). A son Thomas, who was never in good health, was born next, and then four more daughters: Eliza, Rebecca Sarah (who died as a child), Mary Jane, and then Sarah Emma.

There has been a difference of opinion about Sarah's date of birth. Church baptism registers make no reference to her name; parish census records for 1851 are missing. Family legend claims she was born in December of 1841, but when Sarah corresponded with the United States government in December of 1884, she gave her age as forty-five years; that document is now preserved in the National Archives in Washington. Thus, her birthdate might have been 1839, but only if Sarah were telling the truth.

Regardless of the year, she had been born a girl and that was the big disappointment for her father, who wanted only healthy boys to work on his Magaguadvic farm. Although she wore shirts and breeches and succeeded at plowing fields, chopping wood, riding horses, hunting animals, and shooting firearms, the tyrannical Isaac had only one goal for all his daughters—to marry them off as soon as possible!

The choice for Sarah was an older man whom she detested and on whose farm she would be nothing more than a slave. As a result, she planned the first desertion in her life, leaving her family and her childhood home, keeping her future plans and destination a secret.

Years later, *The Capital* newspaper revealed that she came to Fredericton in her late teens and first worked as a seamstress for undertaker Hugh Wiley at his business on Queen Street. She became friends with Wiley's son John, who would later become a Fredericton druggist. During her Civil War years, Sarah sent sums of money to John Wiley, who in turn handed them over to the Edmondson family in Magaguadavic. To protect her disguise, the drafts were always sent in her own name and not that of Franklin Thompson.

After she left the Wiley employment, she took an apartment in the old Fisher homestead on the northwest corner of King and Westmorland Street, where for some time she and her sister Mary Jane carried on a millinery business. Although the Fisher place is no longer standing, it did have historical significance. It was where Peter Fisher wrote *The First History of New Brunswick* and where his son Charles, a future Father of Confederation, was born.

In 1859, Mary Jane returned home and Sarah ventured into the United States, where she donned male attire (for protection) and became a Yankee book agent for the same company that was to later publish her memoirs. In disguise, she returned to Fredericton once more before the Civil War, on her way to Magaguadavic. She stayed all night with the Charles Long family of Long's Creek, just above the city, her true identity never being suspected.

The Capital said that her last visit to Fredericton was after the Civil War was over. Arriving as Sarah Edmonds in female dress, she stayed at the Brayley House on upper Queen Street (now an office complex at #346).

George R. Atherton owned a popular livery stable nearby and it was his son George L. who was hired to drive Sarah to the Magaguadavic area, where she could visit with her family and probably make amends for deserting them, especially the sickly brother whom she loved.

Her young driver was to become a successful druggist on King Street, and when interviewed years later by *The Capital*, he well remembered the drive, "for he was entertained by his lady companion in a very lively and uncommon way, as she gave him the full particulars of her life for the five years that had passed since she had adopted masculine attire."

She was still very much a single person, but with numerous nieces and nephews to provide descendants for years to come. All her sisters had married and now had families of their own: Frances to James Saunders with twelve children; Eliza to John Miller with seven children; Mary Jane to Henry Davidson with two children. Brother Tom was still living at home with his parents.

Returning to Oberlin, Ohio, the place where she had written her book, Sarah would also marry. She met a fellow New Brunswicker from Saint John, a carpenter who had once been a lumber surveyor in Fredericton. In 1867, she became the second Mrs. Linus H. Seelye.

The Seelyes had three children but all of them died in childhood. They then adopted two boys, one of whom married and had five children to carry on the Seelye name and their grandmother's legend. The other son followed in his mother's footsteps, enlisting in the army and going off to the Spanish-American War. He was never heard from again, unlike the missing Franklin Thompson whose story became the highlight of the reunion when the Second Michigan Infantry met in 1884.

Sarah appeared in person and was encouraged by her fellow veterans to apply for a pension and told that they would write the letters of testimony. After hearing her story of faithful service, the United States Congress granted her $12 a month.

She then went one step further and convinced Congress to remove the word "deserter" from Franklin Thompson's record in the muster roll of the Union Army.

Mission accomplished, both in New Brunswick and Washington, she lived her remaining years in Texas, where she became the only female member of the George McClellan Veterans' Post of the Grand Army of the Republic. When she died on September 5, 1898, in her late fifties, she became the only female to be buried in the Civil War plot in Houston's Washington Cemetery—with full military honours!

When Linus returned to Saint John to live in 1913, he told *The Daily Telegraph* that he was working on a book about Sarah which would include her revised memoirs. Before the project was finished, he died while visiting on Grand Manan Island, January 18, 1918, at age eighty-six. There is no marker on his grave at Cedar Hill Cemetery, and the mysterious manuscript, which holds the answers to so many questions about the life of Sarah Edmonds, has never been found.

Today, on a hill overlooking Magaguadavic Lake, in the little burial ground beside All Saints Anglican Church, a weathered tombstone marks the graves of Isaac and Elizabeth Edmondson, and of their son Thomas who died two months before his sister Sarah.

UPHOLDING THE HONOUR OF THE EMPIRE

APRIL 1, 2000

Volunteers from the Fredericton detachment of the RCRI prior to leaving for South Africa and the Boer War. They are in front of the Soldiers' Barracks on Queen Street. Two buglers are on the far right.

WHAT THE PEOPLE OF FREDERICTON saw on All Fools' Day, one hundred years ago, was no practical joke or trick, and they were not unsuspecting victims.

As they passed Edgecombe's Dry Goods Store on Queen Street (later Creaghan's and now the Towne Centre), they stopped to admire a lad standing in the window, dressed in a military uniform, a sword by his side, saluting every person who walked by.

The popular display appealed to the war-spirit sentiment in the city at the time. Young men were intrigued and were ready to volunteer without hesitation. However, only two small Canadian contingents had made the 30-day voyage to South Africa, ready to fight and die for the Motherland.

The Anglo-Boer War, also known as the South African War, started on October 11, 1899, as British imperialism and Afrikaner nationalism met in colonial conflict.

There had been extensive preparation on the part of the Boers (descendants of Dutch colonists) to overthrow British influence in the Transvaal republic and the Orange Free State. Thus, an offer from Canada to equip and send military forces was accepted immediately by England. An outburst of enthusiasm among Canadians followed, notably an intense loyalty in New Brunswick.

For the first contingent, no mounted men were required. Instead, an infantry battalion consisting of eight companies was to be formed with great speed from all parts of the Dominion.

New Brunswick and Prince Edward Island were chosen as the recruiting area for "G" Company and, in New Brunswick, where only 109 men were to be enlisted, depots were opened at Saint John and Fredericton.

At once, there was a deluge of applications, everyone anxious to prove his loyalty to England. Of the thirty-two young men accepted at the Fredericton depot, the following were members of the 71st Battalion of the militia: Herbert Leavitt of Gibson, James Pringle and Fred Walker of Stanley, John Wilson of Burtt's Corner, Samuel Jones of St. Mary's, John McLeod of St. George, and John Perkins, Bruce McFarlane, and John Pickles of Fredericton.

Joining them were militiamen Joseph Mauns Aitken (brother of Lord Beaverbrook) and Pillias Scarth Stevenson, both bank tellers in Fredericton at the time of enlistment. Their employers agreed to pay full salary during the absence and assured the same position upon return.

The remaining twenty-one volunteers, including two buglers, were accepted from the regulars of No. 4 Company, Royal Canadian Regiment Infantry (RCRI), stationed in the city at the time. Harry Fradsham was the only local boy among them, although several gave Fredericton as their home address.

Of the ten volunteers accepted for reinforcements for the Fredericton contingent, five were local boys: John Jones (brother of Samuel), James Robertson, Thomas Wright, James Tennant, and John Wandless, the last an 1896 Provincial Normal School graduate who was leaving his teaching position to join.

A grand public "good-bye" began in the afternoon of October 24, 1899, with a citizens' meeting at city hall. It was an elaborate ceremony with Mayor Harry Beckworth, clergymen, and business people. In the early evening, one thousand were at the CPR station on York Street to hear the battalion band play "The Soldier's Farewell."

Just before the departure for Saint John, there was news that a patriotic fund was being established to pay each soldier fifty cents a day in addition to the Imperial allowance. And city council agreed to insure each Fredericton volunteer for $1,000.

Another farewell took place the next afternoon at the Canada Eastern station on Brunswick Street, when each member of the RCRI detachment was presented with a tin box of choice tobacco and a pipe by the commanding officer. Military wives gave each soldier a parcel containing condensed coffee and concentrated meat.

Chatham Junction was the first stop, where connection was made with the Intercolonial Railway Express, which carried the entire Maritime quota of volunteers to Quebec City. Here, the "gallant thousand" of Canada's first contingent boarded the *S. S. Sardinian* for the journey to South Africa.

By the time the troopship reached Father Point in the St. Lawrence River, the Fredericton boys began to assume the role of unofficial war correspondents. The first letter received by *The Daily Gleaner* was dated October 31 and was published November 2. It was from Bruce McFarlane and reads, in part:

"All our boys got *The Gleaner* at Quebec and it was the only New Brunswick paper we saw after leaving Saint John, but it was enough as it has all the news....When you next hear from me I hope to be pounding the Boers, and then next summer you may hear of me playing ball at Pretoria."

After that, relatives and friends in Fredericton kept watching for the incoming mail and they were not disappointed. Because of the interest throughout the community, many of these letters were released immediately to the local press for all to read.

Corporal Stevenson wrote to his bank manager from the Cape Verde Islands, off the coast of West Africa. He stated that "the men are well and in good spirits, though all are complaining of the poor food. The bayonets are being ground and made sharp. We expect to be hurried to the front as soon as we land at Cape Town."

Those who had failed to go with the first Canadian contingent were determined not to miss the second one, which sailed from Halifax in January of 1900. In Fredericton, the following were selected to join the new force of 1,230 men and 1,240 horses: Fred Everett, William Lynn, George Parker, Carleton Allen (grandson of the chief justice), Frank Hawkins, Miles Boone, Albert Finnamore, George Rutter, and brothers Adrian and James Tibbits (sons of the provincial secretary).

Once he arrived at the front, Gunner Everett of the Royal Canadian Artillery sent his letters directly to *The Fredericton Herald* for publication. From DeAar Junction on April 16, he wrote: "We reached this place last Saturday morning, after a march of over 300 miles, which played havoc with our horses....Here we found two or three weeks' mail that awaited us. Five or six *Heralds* were a welcome addition to mine."

News also reached Fredericton through dispatches from London, England. One of these arrived in mid-May and merely stated "Mafeking has been relieved."

As a result, the whole city turned out to celebrate the victorious event. Church bells and factory whistles joined with the ringing of the fire alarm, as did the whistles on the river steamers. The Union Jack was flying on every building.

From June of 1900 to January of 1901, the Fredericton boys of the two contingents began arriving home to receptions, parades, banquets, and smoking concerts at the soldiers' mess. A wounded Private Fradsham was the first and he was followed by all of the others, with the exception of Private Jacob Scott (RCRI), who was killed in action.

Even after peace was proclaimed, over two thousand more Canadians landed in South Africa. One of the last contingents recruited was the Canadian Mounted Rifles. Among the several Fredericton boys who joined were Arthur Finnamore (brother of Albert) and John James Fraser Winslow (a descendant of one of New Brunswick's original Loyalist families).

By the time of this later enlistment, several volunteers had been attending UNB (William Black, Norman McLeod, Ralph Markham), and others had given up their jobs: Fraser Hazlett was a composer with *The Daily Gleaner*; Archibald McAdam was an employee with Western Union Telegram; Matthew McClenahan was a "printer's devil" with *The Royal Gazette.*

Eventually, all of them returned and became members of the South African Veterans' Association of York County. They met regularly in Fredericton and, on February 27, 1910, a major reunion took place at the York Hotel to celebrate the tenth anniversary of the Battle of Paardeberg, in which Canadian bravery became known to the whole world. Thirty-seven members attended and paid tribute to five departed comrades.

Arthur Finnamore was believed to be one of the last Canadian survivors of the Boer War when he died in 1978 at age ninety-six. He was born in Fredericton and volunteered for South Africa at age eighteen. Two years before his death, he was inducted into the New Brunswick Sports Hall of Fame. He is buried in the Rural Cemetery.

Today, there are no living memories of the Boer War and there appears to be little interest in the war in which Canada sent young men to a foreign country for the first time. Surviving military records and nominal rolls have tended to be inconsistent; souvenirs, uniforms, and flags have faded into obscurity.

Fortunately, a small collection of one soldier's memorabilia is preserved in the provincial archives in Fredericton. The collection includes his pocket maps, one showing the Siege of Ladysmith; his photo album, including one photo of a fallen comrade's gravesite; an amateur publication by the British POWs; and a blueprint of Vereeniging, where the peace treaty was eventually signed, May 31, 1902.

MILITARY LANDMARK DISAPPEARED SIXTY-FIVE YEARS AGO

NOVEMBER 24, 2001

Taken from the highway bridge after the 1903 fire at the Drill Hall, this photo shows the front tower with its damaged roof. The first Provincial Normal School is at far right.

ON NOVEMBER 17, 1936, a demolition crew of twenty men began to tear down the old wooden drill hall, where the Fredericton Armoury stands today.

Four days later it was gone. Only the salvaged lumber and a half-century of historic memories remained.

And gone were the military bands that had played there for some of Fredericton's greatest social events.

The idea for the drill hall was conceived in November 1884, the time of the Riel Rebellion and the same year the Canadian government established four infantry schools, "A" Company being located at Fredericton.

With the departure of the imperial regiments, these schools were to recruit and prepare military instructors who, in turn, would train Canadian militia units during summer and winter camps. After a lapse of fifteen years, Fredericton was to become a garrison town once more.

The old stone buildings of the Military Compound were renovated to accommodate the new Infantry School Corps (ISC) and two militia companies of the 71st "York" Battalion. The drill hall was to be the only new building and it would also be used for arms storage. The little wooden armoury or the Militia Arms Store, which had been built in 1832, was enlarged and converted into a hospital (still standing today, now occupied by Fredericton Tourism).

The commandant for the Fredericton school was to be Lieutenant-Colonel George J. Maunsell, a forty-seven-year-old Englishman from Devonshire. He and his family took up residence in the Officers' Quarters (now the York-Sunbury Museum) and it was here that local contractors could examine Maunsell's plans for the new hall.

The government had selected the upper end of the Soldiers' Barracks for the location, with the front facing Queen Street. Colonel Maunsell suggested a site near the riverbank, with the front facing Carleton Street extension. The commandant won and, as a result, the drill hall would be the first building to be seen driving off the new highway bridge. Construction was to start in the spring of 1885 and Joshua Limerick, who was just finishing Charlotte Street School, was to be the contractor.

It was feared by the locals that an ordinary "shed" would be erected, and that travellers entering the city via the new bridge would not be favourably impressed. However, through Colonel Maunsell's good taste in architecture and his interest in Fredericton, an ornamental as well as a commodious structure was to be built.

The full size measured 138 feet in length and 67 feet in width. The front tower was 18 feet square with a 47-foot height to the deck, on which was surmounted a twenty-seven-foot-high flagpole. Clearly carved at the top was the name DRILL HALL and the date 1885.

There were two storeys at the front of the building and two at the rear, a plain-raftered hall (fifty by ninety-six feet) in the long middle section being completely open from ground to roof with a height of thirty-three feet, ideal for the mammoth Christmas tree that became a tradition for the children of the troops. Along the south side were six armouries, each twelve by fourteen feet; along the north were eight windows, each six by eleven.

There was to be no basement; the floor of the drill area to be unique. According to a military press release at the time, "the floor will be of pebbled stone covered with watered gravel, well-rolled."

Inside the arched entrance, two orderly rooms were on either side of the foyer; one for administration, the other for meetings, such as those for the Soldiers' Temperance Club. Above them, on the second floor, were music rooms that opened onto a balcony that projected into the drill hall. As the ISC or the 71st band played, the troops below would practise their training drills or perform their winter parades.

Although the construction began at the opening of navigation, the project was slowed down because suitable lumber (tongued and grooved dressed board) could not be obtained. However, by midsummer, 1885, "the immense shed," as it came to called, started to fill the northeast corner of Barracks Square at the intersection of Carleton and Campbell streets (the latter now a part of the riverfront drive).

When it was finished that fall, the first person to be given a formal tour was Major-General Sir Frederick Middleton, commander-in-chief of the militia of Canada. He arrived on November 26, fresh from suppressing the Riel Rebellion, and Fredericton treated him like a royal visitor. Hundreds showed up at City Hall, where Mayor George Fenety read an address of welcome.

Outside the new drill hall, while the band played "The Dominion Slow March," Middleton inspected the troops and presented prizes for marksmanship. The pace of the ceremony changed when Lieutenant William Russell of the 71st put the ISC through a series of difficult drills which were performed flawlessly. Officers and spectators were impressed with the young lieutenant.

William Russell had been born, raised and educated in Fredericton. He excelled in sports and drama; he studied law, was admitted to the bar, and was made a junior partner in the prominent firm of Charles Fisher & Son.

In the late 1870s, he attended the old military school which was held on the first floor of the York County Court House (still standing on lower Queen Street). When #7 Company of the 71st Battalion was formed in 1882, he was offered a lieutenancy and accepted. Both Middleton and Maunsell soon realized they had an exceptional officer in their ranks.

On November 29, 1885, Lieutenant Russell and the ISC drilled in the new hall for the first time and the 71st took possession of their bandroom. On November 30, the drill hall was taken off the contractor's hands. The local and military alike began to anticipate a grand opening, but that would not occur until early in the new year.

And what a grand opening it was, Lady Alice Tilley (wife of the lieutenant-governor) being the guest of honour and Colonel Maunsell and his wife being the hosts and patrons. The date: Friday evening, January 22, 1886. The entertainment: a popular musical comedy entitled *The Charcoal Burner*. The performers: the Garrison Drama Club of the ISC and the 71st Battalion.

The Drama Club, of which Lieutenant Russell was a leading member, had gone to great personal expense, working hard and long for several weeks, building a stage and painting the scenery. Handbills were distributed and tickets were sold at local bookstores. The hall's five hundred seats were sold out, mostly to the elite of the city.

All the officers were present, some wearing patrol uniforms, and others, mess jackets and vests. The full band of the corps was also in attendance, directed by Bugle-Major John Hayes, who played a number of solo selections.

The highlight was the play, every part being well performed by the amateur thespians. One actor received more applause than the others and that was Lieutenant Russell. According to the theatre critic of *The Capital*, "Mr. Russell convulsed the house with his humorous representation of the droll character that he played."

The Garrison Theatre was on its way to providing many years of fine drama in the new drill hall. It met the challenge of competing with the professionals who came to town to perform at Lee's Opera House and the City Hall Opera House. One of the early handbills survived and is preserved at the UNB Archives: *Never Too Late to Mend*, under the patronage of Lieutenant-Governor and Lady Tilley, "all proceeds to be devoted to the fund in aid of the proposed Victoria Hospital."

Sir Leonard Tilley was a frequent visitor at the drill hall, his first occasion being on February 25, 1886, following the opening of the provincial parliament. The ISC had provided the Guard of Honour and then accompanied the lieutenant-governor to the hall, where he was to present the highly coveted Kalapore Medal to Lieutenant James D. Perkins of the 71st Battalion.

Perkins had been one of the eight men who comprised the Canadian Wimbledon marksmanship team of 1884, winning the famous Rajah of Kalapore Cup against well-chosen teams from Britain and India. Thus, the medal ceremony, which took place inside the little drill hall by the river and which ended with three cheers for the queen, was long remembered in Fredericton.

Unfortunately, the first year of the drill hall was not all joy and success. In mid-March, Lieutenant Russell decided to further qualify himself and left for Royal Military College in Kingston. Two weeks later he was dead, succumbing to the attack of a savage fever that eventually affected his brain.

It was a tragedy that stunned the city. All military activities were suspended as the officers met at the drill hall to arrange a funeral that was to be like a state event, every detail under the command of Colonel Maunsell.

The streets were lined with sympathetic spectators, and every window was crowded as the largest cortege ever seen in Fredericton proceeded to the Methodist Burial Ground (now the Rural Cemetery). Both military bands were in attendance, muffled drums beating the slow march, church bells tolling in the background. The 71st provided the pall bearers, the ISC the firing party. The order of the procession was strictly observed, and so was the uniform—greatcoat, forage cap, side arms.

When the drill sessions and the drama productions resumed, all officers wore crepe for one month in memory of Lieutenant Russell. However, as the mourning period ended, it was replaced with division: a full year of underlying tension between the ISC and the 71st over equal space within the drill hall.

The harmony was gone. The 71st wanted their own reading and recreation room—at the front of the building, not the "dingy" space allotted at the rear. Because the hall was erected for joint use, the officers on both sides met and agreed to resolve the issue. But it took a special event to bring things back to normal.

That event was a grand military ball on February 9, 1888. Location: the Drill Hall. Hosts: the officers (in full uniform or shell jacket) and their ladies. Guests: the aristocracy of Fredericton (over two hundred invitations delivered).

The rank and file transformed the hall into a magnificent ballroom, all decorations being in harmony with the tradition of the imperial troops of yesteryear. Bayonet stars, crossed swords, and polished rifles adorned the walls, along with evergreen, bunting, flags, and a profusion of military photographs. Hanging from the gallery were the colours of the corps and those of the battalion.

The dancing continued until three in the morning, the program consisting of quadrilles, galops, lancers, polkas, and valses. Above the swirling figures, Chinese lanterns and brilliant chandeliers (suspended from the rafters) threw a blaze of light over the fairy-like atmosphere.

Fifteen years later, a real blaze was to completely destroy the interior, taking with it the elaborate decorations from the coronation of Edward VII. It was one of the most disastrous fires that had occurred in Fredericton for some time.

Shortly after 10:00 p.m., January 11, 1903, in the midst of a blinding snow storm, a resident of Devon was about to walk across the bridge on his way home. When passing the new Arctic Rink (where the public library is now located), he noticed a fire reflection in the drill hall and immediately ran to an alarm box.

It was Sunday; the building was empty, and a stoked coal stove in one of the front offices had got out of control, flames spreading to the second floor, threatening the soldiers' library and the billiard room. There was extensive water damage as firemen attempted to save the tower. The main hall was not as fortunate.

Up to the time of the fire, the drill hall had seen a number of changes. In 1892, the ISC became the Royal Canadian Regiment; in 1896, Fredericton became the regimental headquarters under Colonel Maunsell; in 1898, the colonel retired and returned to England, where he died in 1906 at age sixty-nine.

The unsightly appearance of the burned-out drill hall stood for eighteen months before officials from Ottawa arrived in June of 1904 to inspect the situation. They decided to add a brick facade to the front, an extra storey, and a metallic roof. The interior would be restored to its original appearance.

However, the renovations were not completed until the spring of 1906, at which time the 71st Regimental Band held a three-day bazaar for the grand re-opening. The band paraded through the streets announcing the event, and the crowds were phenomenal. The Marysville train was even held over to meet the demand. With the decorations and the music, it was like old times at the drill hall, and so the bazaar became an annual event for years to come.

By 1934, the facilities at the drill hall were too small and unsatisfactory for the five units of the non-permanent active militia comprising the Fredericton garrison at the time. In order for the city to maintain its position as one of the leading militia centres in the Maritimes, the government decided to build a $46,000, three-storey brick annex at the west end.

But this was still not enough. Two years later, the old wooden hall was demolished to make way for a modern structure of brick, concrete, and steel, to be attached to the new annex. It was ready for occupancy in 1937. Total cost: $36,000.

The new building was to have special features: a basement with a miniature rifle range; a hot-water heating system; a concrete floor covered with tile.

Once again, a drill hall in Fredericton resounded to the marching feet of military troops.

The Second World War was only two years away.

Section Two: Famous Visitors

City Connection with Former Prime Minister

September 29, 2001

Richard Bedford Bennett, Canada's eleventh prime minister (1930 to 1935), had an interesting connection with Fredericton. Later, after he moved to England, he became Viscount Bennett of Mickleham, Calgary, and Hopewell—the only New Brunswick-born member of the British House of Lords.

AS THE WORLD FACES A CRISIS situation against terrorism, Canadians look to their prime minister for strong leadership. Political affiliation aside, it is the most important office in the nation, especially during times of instability and fear.

But how many Canadians can name the twenty people who have become prime minister? How many New Brunswickers know the personal connections that some of the prime ministers have had with the provincial capital?

Sir John A. Macdonald, the first prime minister, made a significant non-political visit to Fredericton in August of 1887. He was accompanied by his second wife, Agnes, whose pleasant memories from a former visit had induced her husband to come and see the city for himself. He had no regrets.

Thousands of spectators from all over the province converged on Fredericton and lined the streets in order to catch a glimpse of the Scottish-born leader, who, at age seventy-three, had already given forty-three years to public life. They were not disappointed.

The heavy schedule of events began with their Monday morning arrival at the York Street Station, where an honour guard and the marching band from the Royal Infantry School were waiting. However, it was the 71st Battalion Band that led the long open-carriage procession through the decorated streets, finishing at Government House. It was here that Sir John and Lady Macdonald were to be the guests of the lieutenant-governor and his wife—Sir Leonard and Lady Tilley.

In the afternoon, the Macdonalds each had a special occasion: she laid the cornerstone of Fredericton's first railway bridge, becoming the custodian of the key to the tin box of memorabilia that she mortared into the stone's cavity; he visited City Hall, greeting hundreds of local citizens, receiving three cheers and a "tiger," responding warmly to a civic address by Mayor George Fenety.

In the evening, the Macdonalds attended a theatrical performance at the opera house, a drama entitled *The Midnight Marriage*, presented under their patronage. Afterwards, the Fredericton Brass Band led a gigantic torchlight parade through the streets, as the Macdonalds were escorted by the fire departments of Fredericton and St. Mary's. All public buildings and many homes were illuminated, wax candles lighting up every pane of glass along the route.

At Government House Road, the horses were taken from the lead carriage and Sir John was triumphantly hauled the rest of the way by a number of cheering admirers. In his farewell speech on the front steps, he said that the torchlight demonstration was the finest he had ever witnessed in Canada.

The next morning, Sir John assumed the role of tourist and, in a lone carriage with Sir Leonard, drove all over the city, visiting the university, the legislature, and the barracks. In the afternoon, the destination was Marysville, where "Boss" Gibson welcomed the prime minister to his elegant mansion, and subsequently gave him a tour of his church, his store, and his famous cotton mill.

It would be thirty-four years before another prime minister would visit and this time it was political. On Monday morning, May 23, 1921, Arthur Meighen, age forty-seven and Canada's ninth national leader, arrived at York Street Station with his wife, Isabel.

Automobiles formed the procession this time and the Fredericton Brass Band led the parade directly to City Hall, where Mayor Jack Reid delivered an address of welcome. Echoing the words of Canada's first prime minister, Meighen was touched by the crowd of several hundred and by the official civic reception.

The Meighens made their headquarters at the Barker House Hotel on Queen Street, where the morning ended with a number of political conferences. Before lunch, there was a quick tour of the city and, in the afternoon, there was an address to the women electors of York and Sunbury counties at the opera house.

However, the main reason for the 1921 visit was to support a York-Sunbury by-election and to address a huge campaign rally at the Arctic Rink on Carleton Street, the building having been converted into an auditorium for several thousand people. It turned out to be the greatest political demonstration by the biggest public gathering ever known in Fredericton.

Meighen was introduced as one of the outstanding figures of the British Empire and was given a tremendous ovation before he began his one-hour speech. He opened with Fredericton, referring to the fact that he was in the capital city of one of the oldest provinces of Confederation, a fact to be appreciated especially on Empire Day.

This eloquent son of a poor Ontario farmer won the hearts of Fredericton but, in the general election that year, his government was defeated and Meighen lost even his own seat. He served as prime minister on one other brief occasion in 1926, earning the ironic description in the history books as one of Canada's most gifted yet most unsuccessful politicians.

The man who defeated Meighen was William Lyon Mackenzie King who, for a total of 7,829 days (almost twenty-two years), was in the top office—longer than any other Commonwealth prime minister. A grandson of the great Upper Canadian rebel leader, William Lyon Mackenzie, he was born in Ontario, remaining an eccentric and a bachelor all his life, believing to the end that it was possible to communicate with the spirit world.

It was Mackenzie King who proposed the grand royal tour of 1939 and then accompanied King George VI and Queen Elizabeth for fifteen thousand miles and fifty-two stops. He was deeply involved in all the preparations and paid meticulous attention to the most minor details. The flowers at receptions and luncheons were to be Liberal red and not Conservative blue!

When the royal procession arrived in Fredericton on June 13, seven limousines carried Their Majesties, the royal attendants, the prime minister, and other dignitaries. As the head of the government in Canada, it was Mackenzie King and not the governor general who was the only privy councillor on the tour.

They drove through a city whose population of 12,000 had swollen to 48,000, a city richly decorated and where Mackenzie King saw to it that correct protocol was followed at all times. The royal standard was to be displayed in two places only: the legislative building at Parliament Square (where the King spoke) and the Lady Beaverbrook Residence at UNB (where a luncheon was served).

Both functions were flawless, the prime minister watching and checking continuously, never more than a few feet away from his royal guests. As a result, the entire tour surpassed all expectations, strengthening national unity and Commonwealth ties and leaving the people of Fredericton with memories that have never diminished.

In the midst of his lengthy tenure, Mackenzie King was defeated by the only person from New Brunswick (so far) who has become prime minister—the realization of the boyhood ambition of Richard Bedford Bennett.

That boyhood was spent at Hopewell Cape, where Bennett was born in 1870. When he was sixteen, he left for Fredericton, where he enrolled in the Provincial Normal School. He boarded with a Aaron and Annie Smith on Brunswick Street, arriving with a small black trunk filled mostly with law books and his Bible.

It was a lonely time with too many "dont's"—no smoking, no drinking, no dancing, no gambling, and no bowling alleys. There appeared to be no studying as well, because he graduated in 1887 with a second-class licence, his first teaching post being at Irishtown (near Moncton) with an annual salary of $160.

In January of 1888, Bennett returned to PNS for another term, this time being awarded a first-class licence and the subsequent position of principal at Douglastown (near Newcastle) with an annual salary of $500. Before moving into national politics, he became a lawyer, practising law in Chatham, befriending the seventeen-year-old office boy whose name was Max Aitken, later Lord Beaverbrook.

After his election defeat in 1935, Bennett, who had remained a bachelor and who had become wealthy from investments and inheritance, retired to an estate in England near that of Beaverbrook. He died in 1947 and chose to be interred in his adopted country, the only deceased prime minister not buried in Canada.

In 1951, it was Beaverbrook who financed a new wing of the UNB library, the entire building being named in honour of R. B. Bennett and Andrew Bonar Law (the only Canadian-born prime minister of England). Beaverbook also made it possible to have the Bennett Papers (600,000 items) deposited in the library. Today, these papers are housed in the Harriet Irving Library on the UNB campus, the former Bonar Law-Bennett Building having become the provincial archives. It is here that Bennett's two PNS report cards are preserved.

There were two other links with UNB: in 1933, Bennett became the first Canadian prime minister to receive an honorary degree, although it was awarded in absentia; in 1944, he established four scholarships with a $60,000 gift.

The first prime minister to arrive in Fredericton to accept an honorary degree from UNB was John George Diefenbaker. He also gave the convocation address on that October 9, 1958. The ceremony was steeped in academic tradition, beginning with the march of the thirty-five graduates and guests from the Old Arts Building to the Lady Beaverbrook Rink. Crowds lined the route to see the legendary "Chief" who was simply known as "Dief."

After Diefenbaker and his wife Olive left the next morning, the man who would replace him in five years arrived in the afternoon. Lester Bowles Pearson and his wife, Maryon, came to Fredericton to attend a provincial leadership convention. Today, "Mike" Pearson is probably best remembered as Canada's first Nobel Peace Prize winner. However, he declined to return to Fredericton, on two occasions, to pick up an honorary degree from UNB.

Pierre Elliott Trudeau, who succeeded Pearson, also declined UNB's offer, but the next two prime ministers accepted: Joseph Clark, the youngest man in the office at age forty, came to Fredericton for encaenia in 1976; John Turner, who held the office for only seventy-nine days, attended convocation in 1968. (It was Sir Charles Tupper, Canada's sixth prime minister, who served the shortest term—sixty-nine days! During his teen years, Sir Charles often visited Fredericton, his father being the minister at Brunswick Street Baptist Church.)

Trudeau did accept an invitation to visit Fredericton on June 1, 1981, to mark the tenth anniversary of the founding of the Council of Maritime Premiers. He arrived in the afternoon and was swarmed with well-wishers wherever he went, his bodyguards struggling with the crowds.

That evening he was to deliver an after-dinner speech at McConnell Hall on the UNB campus. Before he entered the building, he paused to chat with over two hundred schoolteachers who were on hand to quietly demonstrate the current breakdown in salary negotiations with the provincial government.

Did they make an impression? Did the Maritime premiers make an impression? At the end of the evening, a reporter asked Mr. Trudeau for his opinions on the proceedings and received this one reply: "It was an excellent meal of New Brunswick lamb, and the Coquilles St. Jacques was the best I have ever tasted on either side of the Atlantic."

Of all the twenty prime ministers, only one has visited Fredericton High School, the oldest and largest English high school in Canada. On the morning of October 14, 1992, Martin Brian Mulroney arrived at FHS with his bodyguards. Accompanied by his wife, Mila, who, at the time, was using a cane because she was recuperating from a broken ankle, they stopped at the gymnasium door where several teachers were standing. Greetings were exchanged, then Brian and Mila took a few seconds to decide how they would make their grand entrance into the midst of two thousand students.

For over an hour, the students listened to the prime minister defend the Charlottetown Accord before he dropped the hint that they should have the afternoon off from classes in honour of his visit. This gesture was totally unexpected by authorities but it brought forth a thunderous cheer from the crowd. The downside was that many students had to wait for their buses on the usual schedule and that large quantities of cafeteria food already prepared would not be needed.

Mulroney can probably be excused for his little protocol indiscretion, failing to realize that it is the representatives of the Crown who have the privilege of granting public holidays. The prime ministership is a political office and does not symbolize the nation. Yet the office has grown and changed since Confederation, and Canada has become a larger and more complex country. With so many challenging problems facing Canadians, it will be interesting to see if Jean Chrétien, the twentieth prime minister, will lead successfully through the aftermath of the September 11 terrorist attack and into the twenty-first century.

TWO KNIGHTS ON THE TOWN JULY 1881

JULY 21, 2001

THEY WERE FATHERS OF CONFEDERATION, Canadian statesmen, federal cabinet ministers, companions of the Order of the Bath, and knight commanders of the Order of St. Michael and St. George. They were also native-born Maritimers.

Their names: the Honourable Sir Leonard Tilley from Gagetown, Queens County, New Brunswick; the Honourable Sir Charles Tupper from Amherst, Cumberland County, Nova Scotia.

However, 120 years ago, in July of 1881, they were just two knights on the town and that town was Fredericton. What they received from the local citizens was a royal welcome that had never before, or since, been seen in the capital city.

Extensive plans and preparations had been made when the York County Conservative Association met to form the reception committee. The chairman was former Fredericton mayor Edward L. Wetmore, and joining him were a number of prominent gentlemen, including former mayor James S. Beek and the mayor at the time, G. Fred Fisher.

The subscription committee had received generous contributions to cover all expenses for the visit. The transportation committee had engaged thirty carriages for the procession, all to be drawn by white

[FAR LEFT] Sir Charles Tupper

Sir Leonard Tilley

horses, symbolizing the purity of the Conservative Party. It was to be the grandest display in the political history of the city.

The hall committee reported that ample accommodation had been prepared at City Hall for the public meeting, where the two knights were to speak. In addition to the eight hundred seats already there, there would be four hundred additional chairs placed around the hall and in the aisles. The platform had been re-carpeted and then decorated with flags and a coat of arms. Extra furnishings were to be provided by Messrs. Lemont & Sons, flowers by John Bebbington Gardens.

It seemed that every member of the local Conservative Party wanted to get involved and, as a result, a general committee was formed to oversee details of the arrival at the railway depot, the luncheon at the Barker House Hotel, and the dinner at Government House. Well-known people served on this committee.

According to the press of the day, both *The Reporter* and *The Capital*, "It was one of the best organized and most magnificent receptions that has been given to any statesmen within the memory of the people of this City." Not since Confederation had Fredericton seen such elaborate arrangements for properly receiving distinguished visitors.

Thursday, July 26, 1881, was the big day and all Fredericton and York County turned out to catch a glimpse of the two knights. People thronged the sidewalks, filled window casements, and blocked doorways. Enthusiasm and anticipation prevailed.

At 11:00 a.m., the 71st Battalion Band, dressed in military uniforms and helmets, marched from City Hall to the Barker House (across from Officers' Square), reminding everyone that the hour for celebration was approaching. Fifteen minutes later the mammoth cortege of landaus was ready to start.

The parade marshal was Harry Beckwith (a future mayor of Fredericton). He was mounted on a mahogany bay, from where he gave the command to proceed. The band took the lead, striking up "The Flying Dragoons." The barouche which was to carry Tupper and Tilley came next, a four-in-hand with four greys, the two front horses with waving rich plumes, the other two bearing the Union Jack.

Private carriages followed the procession up Queen Street and then out York, all amidst a sea of humanity, colourful bunting, and flags hanging from every store and house. Approaching Union Station, the band began to play "Soldiers at Home"—appropriate music in honour of the two political giants who were about to arrive.

For Sir Leonard, Fredericton was a familiar place. He had been a member of the Legislative Assembly sporadically from 1850 until

1865, during which time he became provincial secretary and then leader of the government. At one point, he and his large family lived in the Odell House that is now the Anglican deanery. His first wife, Julia Anna, who died in 1862, was buried in the Old Burying Ground; his second wife, Alice, who was to be the founder of Victoria Hospital, was the hostess at Old Government House when Tilley was lieutenant-governor from 1873 to 1878.

For Sir Charles, Fredericton had been a place to visit when his father, the Reverend Dr. Charles Tupper, was interim principal of the Baptist Seminary and minister at the nearby Brunswick Street Baptist Church from 1839 to 1843. Young Charles was attending Horton Academy in Wolfville at the time, before studying medicine at Edinburgh University. He eventually became a member of the Nova Scotia Legislature and, like Tilley, subsequently provincial secretary and leader of the government, continuing to visit Fredericton on various occasions.

In July of 1881, they were returning to Fredericton together, travelling on the noon train from Saint John, hoping for as little fanfare as possible. They never realized there would be such tremendous crowds forming a solid phalanx all around the station platform.

When the train reached the curve near the Maryland Road (now Regent Street), the locomotive was switched off and the rumbling passenger coaches slowly rolled into the station and came to a sudden stop. The band played "Onward to Victory," the crowd cheered, and Sir Leonard and Sir Charles appeared on the platform of their private car and raised their hats.

When the carriage procession re-formed and returned to the Barker House, it included the two knights and their entourage (several other members of parliament, personal secretaries, a small press corps). Local citizens and York County residents lined the route, waving their handkerchiefs and using every means in their power to give the guests a great welcome.

Following lunch, Tilley and Tupper hosted a reception in the parlours of the Barker House. In attendance were provincial and municipal dignitaries and York County Conservatives. Outside, in front of the hotel, the Reform Club Band members positioned themselves on Queen Street and provided background music.

The dinner at Government House was hosted by Lieutenant-Governor Robert Duncan Wilmot. It was a quiet affair with just a few other guests, giving the two visitors an opportunity to relax before the main event—the public meeting at City Hall at eight o'clock.

By seven o'clock, people were lined up along Queen Street, waiting for the doors to open, hoping for a good seat. Over one thousand were squeezed into the little auditorium; the rest were turned away. Women had to be accompanied by a man and they had to sit in the gallery.

The seventy-five men who had special seats on the tiny stage were present by invitation only and were the city's leading citizens of the day. Stationed in front of them on the floor was the Fredericton Brass Band. With so little room, it was unfortunate that the acoustic defects of the large Exhibition Building made that venue impossible to use.

When the knights arrived, the applause was unbelievable and it did not subside for several minutes. Sir Charles was the first to speak and he held the attention of the audience for three hours, speaking in a slow and deliberate manner, thoughtfully weighing his words as he proceeded, waiting now and then to be heard above the clapping of hands.

The Reporter and *The Capital* reported that Tupper could not tell exactly why he and Tilley were in Fredericton. Or why they spoke to 10,000 in Saint John the evening before. Or why they were going to Woodstock tomorrow.

It was summer and people were on vacation; there was no general election. Sir John A. Macdonald and the federal Conservative Party had been swept back into power in 1878, ready to achieve their nation-building goals.

Since then, the popular National Policy, with its protective tariff on industry, was established in 1879, and the second and successful Canadian Pacific Railway company, which would complete the transcontinental transport route, was chartered in 1880. As Minister of Railways, Tupper stated that the CPR had been sustained by the largest majority ever received in Parliament and that the transfer of the contract from the government to a syndicate was not fraught with injurious consequences.

Thus, there were definite motives for the visit: to explain, promote, and defend. There was also the competition. Five days before Tupper and Tilley arrived in Fredericton, several members of the Liberal Opposition Party were in the city, giving speeches at Officers' Square, criticizing Macdonald, the Conservatives, and their policies.

When Sir Leonard took the floor, it was eleven o'clock. He said he would speak for only a few minutes, but the crowd wanted more, so he continued until after midnight. As Minister of Finance, he showed a great mastery of details, illustrating clearly how the country was suffering because duties imposed upon foreign goods were not high enough to protect Canadian products. He showed that the National Policy did not bear more heavily on any one province than on another.

In conclusion, both knights gave a seething rebuke to the insinuations that they were jealous rivals for the leadership upon the death of Sir John A. They hoped it would be a long time before the country would lose the services of such an able statesman as the first minister. (And it was, Macdonald continuing in power until 1891.)

Following three cheers for Sir Charles and Sir Leonard and for the Queen who bestowed their titles, everyone moved outside to enjoy a brilliant fireworks display until one in the morning. It was a fitting farewell for these two Maritimers who were at the peak of their political careers, each having taken a leading part in the Confederation movement, being delegates to the Charlottetown, Quebec, and London conferences.

Sir Leonard Tilley would eventually return to New Brunswick to serve a second term as lieutenant-governor (1885–1893). He would die three years later in Saint John at the age of seventy-eight.

Sir Charles Tupper would become prime minister for two months in 1896, resigning after a Conservative defeat at the polls. He would die many years later in England at the age of ninety-four, the last of the Fathers of Confederation to pass away.

Today, the names of Tilley and Tupper are very much recognized in New Brunswick. The birthplace of Sir Leonard in Gagetown is now the a national historic site and museum; the Highland Hill summer estate of Sir Charles in St. Andrews is now preserved as part of the Tara Manor Inn.

For scholars, the Provincial Archives has a unique collection of Tilley's letters penned on Old Government House stationery, and a copy of Tupper's famous 1884 speech on the Pacific Railway resolutions. Holding these aging documents takes one back in history to a time when solid statesmen were in control.

For genealogists who are tracing the Tupper and Tilley lines, descendants of these two great Maritime families continually visit Fredericton. Just recently, Barbara Winn, the great-great-granddaughter of Sir Leonard, and Leigh Tupper, the great-grandnephew of Sir Charles, attended summer openings of the York-Sunbury Historical Society Museum.

For researchers who are still looking for long-lost memorabilia, there is the original thank-you note, signed by the two knights, sent to Fredericton's Conservative Party chairman, July 28, 1881, and printed in the press: "We cannot leave for Ottawa without tendering to your Committee of Reception our hearty thanks for your kindness to us during our brief stay in your City, and for the welcome accorded to us, as well as for the arrangements made by which we were afforded the opportunity of speaking to the Electors of York."

When Queen Victoria Died 100 Years Ago

The Daily Gleaner.

VOL. 11.—No. 19. FREDERICTON, N. B., TUESDAY, JANUARY 22, 1901. PRICE 2 CENTS

THE EMPIRE MOURNS ITS QUEEN.

COWES, Jan. 22.—The Queen passed from life without a struggle. Her end was painless. She expired as one sinks into sleep. At her bedside, when death came, were many whom she loved. Among them were the Prince of Wales, the Princess of Wales, and her son the Duke of York, Princess Louise, Princess Battenburg, Princess Beatrice, the Duke of Connaught, the German Kaiser and Prince Christian.

With them were her physicians, James Reid, A. Douglas Powell, her surgeon, Sir Francis Henry Laking, and the ladies of her Court, her devoted friends and some of her eldest attendants. Among these were her faithful servant from India who helped the Queen in her daily walks about the rooms and who always stood behind her chair while she was dining. So expired, with all that loving care could do to soften the dread ordeal, the most conspicuous character of the Victorian age, the most distinguished British sovereign since William of Orange.

Her Gracious Majesty, Queen Victoria, Passed Away This Afternoon, And the British Nation is Bowed in Grief.

The End Was Peaceful and The Royal Family Was Assembled at the Bedside.

AT DOWNING STREET.

Members of Government and Officals Preparing for Announcement of the Queen's Death.

LONDON, Jan. 22—Lord Salisbury did not go to Osborne, but returned to Hatfield House from London. The Speaker of the House of Commons came to London from Seaford yesterday to confer with the Government regarding the procedure in the event of the Queen's death.

In case she should die Parliament

At York County Court.

The adjourned sitting of York County Court met this morning and the case of Gunn vs. Jones is being tried without a jury. Mr. Jones, of St. John, held a bill of sale upon the furniture etc., of the hotel run a few years ago at Westfield by Mrs. J. G. Gunn. When the furniture was seized a carriage which Percy Gunn claims belonged to him was also taken, and he now brings an action against Mr. Jones to recover the wagon. R. W. McLellan appears for the plaintiff and A. G. Blair, jr., for the defendant.

On a Sunday evening, January 20, 1901, the churches of Fredericton were filled to capacity.

Because of newspaper bulletins and telegraph notices, everyone in the city was aware of the approaching death of Queen Victoria. Thus, there were special prayers and sympathetic references for the longest reigning British monarch in history—sixty-four years!

At Christ Church Cathedral, Dean Francis Partridge, who had come to New Brunswick from England in 1868, closed his sermon by asking the congregation to kneel as they sang "God Save the Queen."

In the nearby cathedral vault were the Letters Patent that Victoria (as head of the Church of England) had signed and sent in 1845, making Fredericton a city for ecclesiastical purposes. Also preserved was the royal Bible she had sent with the Prince of Wales in 1860.

However, the first member of the royal family to visit Fredericton was Victoria's father, the Duke of Kent, fourth son of King George III. He was in command of the British troops in Canada in the 1790s, residing in Halifax for several years, having his own summer residence, the Prince's Lodge, on the shores of Bedford Basin. It was from here, in June of 1794, that he travelled to Saint John and made a two-day trip upriver to Fredericton.

After the duke's daughter became queen, an invitation to visit the colonies was extended to her, in response to her gratitude for the regiment raised and sent to fight for Britain in the Crimean War (1853–56). She declined because of the great distance but promised that the young Prince Albert would visit instead.

When the prince was in Fredericton on August 4 and 5, he stayed at Old Government House and it was there that he received a message from the queen, announcing the birth of his first niece. Immediately, he sent a reply from Fredericton to his mother: "Your telegram reached me in seven days, which is the quickest time ever known."

Forty years after his North American tour, the prince was still waiting to be king. On Tuesday, January 22, 1901, his moment arrived. At 6:30 P.M., his mother passed away at Osborne House on the Isle of Wight, an island in the English Channel and her favourite home.

At age eighty-two, she had been in failing health, a condition precipitated by intense worry over the losses and hardships suffered by British troops in the Boer War. She had remarked frequently that another war would kill her and it did.

As she lay dying, the battles were still raging in South Africa, and side by side with the British troops, there were two large contingents from Canada who had volunteered to "do and die" for their queen.

In return, she held her Canadian subjects in high regard and this was made evident by her last public function—a Majestic review of the Canadian South African troops when they arrived in London. Among the last to see her alive were five young privates from Fredericton who were a part of that parade: John Wandless, James Tennant, T. M. Wright, John Jones and James Robertson.

People back home in the colonies, who never had the opportunity of seeing Queen Victoria, had followed her illustrious reign from the very beginning.

On August 5, 1837, a large crowd of government officials, military officers, and local inhabitants stood in front of Province Hall, the site of the present legislative building, and heard Lieutenant-Governor Sir John Harvey proclaim that "the Princess Alexandrina Victoria is now, by the death of our late Sovereign, King William IV, become our only lawful and rightful Queen of the United Kingdom of Great Britain and Ireland."

The proclamation was then signed by everyone present, including the citizens of Fredericton. Following a royal salute from the royal artillery and the hoisting of colours, the herald at arms (Stephen Miller) proceeded to different parts of the town on horseback, where the proclamation was again read, a military band following and playing "God Save the Queen" in the background.

In honour of the queen's marriage to Prince Albert, February 10, 1840, a grand ball was given at Old Government House in Fredericton. The guests raised their glasses to a long and happy life for the young couple, who were each twenty-one. Unfortunately, the consort was to die twenty years later, leaving the queen a grieving widow for the remaining forty years of her life.

Victoria and Albert had nine children, four sons and five daughters, and it was this next generation who continued to make contact with Fredericton, returning to England with glowing reports about the little garrison town on the St. John River.

After Prince Edward in 1860, Prince Alfred arrived in May of 1861. Like his brother before him, he travelled from Saint John to Fredericton on the steamer *Forest Queen*; however, the recent death of his grandmother, the Duchess of Kent, eliminated all public receptions and parades.

Prince Arthur came next, in September of 1869, also by steamer; he later became Duke of Connaught and Canada's tenth Governor General. In 1879, Princess Louise came by steamer. She was the wife of the then Governor General of Canada, the Marquess of Lorne, and the only child of the queen who married a "subject" and not a "royal."

On June 20, 1887, Fredericton began a week-long celebration of Victoria's Golden Jubilee. The royal salute was given in front of Old Government House, followed by three tumultuous cheers for the queen. Everyone then gathered farther down the road for the laying of the cornerstone of Victoria Hospital, the queen having granted permission to use her name. It would be a small wooden structure with the royal coat of arms over the entrance—the predecessor of the Victoria Public Hospital.

Ten years later, no sovereign was ever before honoured with such loyalty and respect as Fredericton manifested during the Diamond Jubilee. On Sunday, June 20, 1897, there were festive parades to all the city churches, where special commemorative services were held. The elaborately printed programs were kept as souvenirs and many survive today in private collections

Four years later, news of the queen's death plunged the city into deep mourning. Until her funeral on February 2, and long after, black became the predominant colour. It started small with all newspaper columns and all government stationery being edged with black.

But the displays of grief grew to impressive proportions, especially in the business district along Queen Street. The most elaborate belonged to the several large banks. The entire front of their buildings were draped in black and purple, the royal hue prevailing and the stone pillars entwined with black, held in place by purple satin ribbons. Over the porticoes was the familiar portrait of the late queen.

All public buildings of the three levels of government followed suit, hanging heavy black drapings both on the outside and on the interior. Large black letters over the City Hall entrance displayed the motto "Victoria, the Good." Even the United States Consulate (at that time in Fredericton) was heavily draped, the large window being hung with black curtains, caught back with loops of purple. The Stars and Stripes joined the Union Jacks in the city, flying at half mast.

The merchants were kept busy providing the black and purple drapery material that was in demand by hotels, churches, and private homes. But business houses were not to be outdone either. It became almost competitive to excel in the best display possible and this was especially evident with the dry goods establishments, their massive show windows being unmatched in artistic talent.

Jewellery stores placed their silverware upon rich black velvet backgrounds; millinery emporiums created sympathy mottoes in purple flowers upon white floral scrolls; haberdasheries made unique showings of black and purple neckwear, black gloves and hats; shoe stores advertised evening slippers and fine footwear in black patent and leather; photography studios carried a supply of royal family images.

During the ten days of profound mourning, between the death on January 22 and the funeral on February 2, contact was made with Ottawa on several occasions.

Mayor Harry Beckwith and City Council met in special session and passed a resolution of sympathy, on behalf of the citizens of Fredericton, which was telegraphed to the Governor General, the Earl of Minto. The message concluded with a pledge of "continued and hearty loyalty to the Crown of Great Britain."

On January 25, the Royal Standard arrived from Ottawa and was raised at half mast on the flag staff in Officers' Square. The first standard that the military of Fredericton owned, it was flown only once before, during the visit of the Prince of Wales in 1860.

Militia orders accompanied the standard and these were to be observed during the one-month period of military mourning. All musical instruments were to be silent; regimental colours were to be cased with black crepe; medals, badges, and ribbons were to be covered with crepe, as were sword hilts, helmet plates, and bridle straps; black gloves were to be worn, and plumes and feathers were forbidden.

Also from Ottawa came the official orders for a six-month mourning period for the public, followed by six more months of half mourning, during which time there would be an end to all social functions. Because of their passionate devotion towards the great lady of Windsor, the people of Fredericton, at that particular time in history, never questioned this special request.

In the midst of the public mourning, the flags on the legislative building were temporarily raised to the masthead for the provincial proclamation of Edward VII. It was made on January 25 in the assembly chamber. Subsequently, a new oath of allegiance for all those in public office had to be administered on January 29, so that Lieutenant-Governor A. R. McClelan, Chief Justice W. H. Tuck, Premier L. J. Tweedie, and members of the Legislature and justice system could continue in office.

The day of Queen Victoria's military funeral in London—Saturday, February 2—was proclaimed a day of mourning and all businesses in Canada were to be closed. In Fredericton, *The Daily Gleaner* did appear late in the evening, but without any advertisements of any description, making Vol. 11, No. 29 a rare collector's item.

There were two memorial services, both with overflowing congregations: in the morning at St. Paul's, a combined tribute for all churches; in the evening at the cathedral, with a special address by Bishop H. T. Kingdon. All church bells tolled for one hour at noon. For the remainder of the day, the city of Fredericton was silent.

The royal pew at the cathedral (where the Prince of Wales, now King Edward VII, had sat for service in 1860) was suitably draped in black. Adults wore complete mourning clothes; students from the public schools, the Normal School, and the university, attending in groups, wore black armbands; the Daughters of the Empire wore purple ribbons.

On February 4, Victoria was placed beside her Prince Albert in the royal mausoleum at Frogmore House, a mile from Windsor Castle. On the same day in Canada, her statue in Victoria Square, Montreal, was completely surrounded with floral tributes. In Fredericton, the Islington Lodge of the Sons of England wanted a similar monument to be erected in the provincial capital. As a result, the Queen Victoria Statue Fund was born.

Six years later, the proposed statue was still in the news. A committee had corresponded with leading sculptors and a design for a twenty-foot bronze monument had been selected. Because the cost was to be $10,000, two thousand copies of a circular letter of appeal were distributed throughout the city. But the project never seemed to have developed any further and there appear to be no surviving documents to give an explanation.

To perpetuate the queen's memory, Fredericton named streets after Victoria and Albert, and a twelve-acre playground and sports field was called Victoria Park (now Queen's Square). Perhaps the most appreciated memorial at the centenary of her death is the annual observance of her birth on the May 24 holiday.

From England, there have been the continued visits to Fredericton of her children, her grandchildren, and the later descendants. There has also been the lasting influence of the powerful Victorian Era.

"Will My People Ever Forgive Me?"

August 3, 2002

A special committee decorated and illuminated City Hall for a total of $75. Fred B. Edgecombe, a local businessman and one of the volunteer organizers, took this photo just before noon on Coronation Day—August 8, 1902.

One hundred years ago, "Will my people ever forgive me?" were King Edward VII's first words as he awoke from the chloroform, following a life-threatening appendectomy.

Although his question referred to the postponement of the grandest coronation celebration in English history, it might also have suggested the guilty feelings of the sixty-year-old heir apparent in relation to his playboy lifestyle.

Queen Victoria had ruled for sixty-four years. After her passing, in January of 1901, the Prince of Wales, who toured Canada in 1860 as an eighteen-year-old, emerged from the wings as one of the few English monarchs to reach the throne at an advanced age.

Thus, the splendour and magnificence of the coronation for King Edward VII and the subsequent celebration in every Commonwealth town and city would be unparalleled. The date: Thursday, June 26, 1902.

However, with dramatic suddenness, the king became ill on the eve of the big event. He was so close to being crowned, but fate intervened, even though he pleaded with his doctors: "Operation or no operation, I won't disappoint the people. I must go to the Abbey."

If the operation had not been performed without delay at Buckingham Palace, Edward VII would have died. There was no choice but to postpone the coronation. During his convalescence, a new date was set: Saturday, August 9, 1902.

In the meantime, what would happen to the elaborate preparations and travel plans? Could enthusiasm be maintained during the six-week summer interval? Would people return to London and Fredericton and other cities around the world for the postponed celebration?

Throughout Canada, King Edward VII's first coronation date was to be observed as a public holiday. Fredericton began to plan early, hoping to surpass the city's festivities for Queen Victoria's coronation (June 28, 1838). At that time, the entire program was in the hands of the British regiment in garrison, and the results were grand and memorable.

In 1902, City Hall took charge and, from the beginning, Mayor William C. Crocket was wholeheartedly supported by his clerk, C. W. Beckwith, and the ten elected aldermen: Patrick Farrell, John Moore, Asa VanWart, G. W. Clark, Michael Ryan, John Maxwell, David Stockford, George Ross, Darell Jago, and Walter Boyce.

When the first of several public meetings was held on June 5, a number of prominent gentlemen attended and volunteered their services for the various committees. There were also delegates from the Board of Trade, the Tourist Association, the Manufacturers' Union, the Curling Club, the St. Andrew's Society, the fire department, York County Council, and all the fraternal lodges. The only women who were allowed to become involved with the planning were a few representatives from the newly formed IODE.

Two unanimous decisions were reached at these meetings. First, that the towns of Marysville, St. Mary's, and Devon be invited to join with Fredericton in the celebration; second, that the city council be asked to vote a sufficient sum (not to exceed $500) to cover all necessary expenditures.

Older citizens spoke about the day Victoria was crowned, contributing ideas that might be repeated in 1902. James S. Beek, who was the only surviving member from the 1838 planning committee and who was mayor during the Prince of Wales' visit, remembered that the big event for Victoria's celebration was the barbecue where a large ox was roasted whole, the fire having been started the day before: "The ox stood up as in life and his head was on. He was splendidly roasted, and tables were built around him on which were knives and forks, salt and pepper, bread, cheese, cake, and English brew, all in abundance and free to everybody."

Another senior, William H. Anderson (the father of the Countess of Ashburnham) was a young lad of fifteen in 1838 and winner of the big sports event. He never forgot that afternoon: "A fine new football was thrown into the crowd at the flats and was to be the property of any person who could get away with it, the ball to be kicked and not touched with the hands. After a time and much fun, the ball was kicked to the outskirts of the crowd and I got possession of it. Chased by the soldiers and others, I ran, kicking the ball before me, clear to Regent Street, where the chase was abandoned and where I was presented the ball to keep."

In 1902, it was decided that the barbecue would once again be a main feature, $140 being the proposed cost. Mr. Lilly, the local butcher, volunteered to take charge. The roasting of the ox would begin at 8:00 P.M. on June 25 on the Green, so the carcass would be done by noon on Coronation Day. At one'clock, the carving would begin, accompanied by three barrels of lemonade and all the bread that could be eaten by the large crowds expected for the free meal.

The Victorian football game on the flats was to be replaced by Edwardian water sports in front of the Green, and although this would involve canoe races, log rolling, the greased pole, and swimming, it was the tilting match that promised to be the main event. In this match, there would be two occupants in each canoe, one handling the paddle, the other, a twenty-foot padded lance. The object: to knock the opponent out of his canoe and into the water!

It was hoped that the tragedy that accompanied the Victorian fireworks would not happen again. Because of rain in June of 1838, the display had to be postponed until July, at which time the fireworks were set off from a scow moored in front of Old Government House. Lieutenant Keir Inches (age nineteen and of the New Brunswick Artillery) accidentally fell from the scow and was drowned. His body was found the next morning and interred in the Old Burying Ground.

In 1902, a new dimension was added to the mayor's meetings when all city clergymen began to attend and to make their views known. They wanted a union service to be included in the morning schedule and they wanted it to be held in the Methodist Church (now Wilmot United Church). Their request was granted, even though the Church of England had already formed an ecumenical choir at the cathedral and had distributed a program for a special coronation service.

The major undertaking for the planning committee was the organization of five different parades to take place throughout the day, at different times, with different routes, accompanied by three marching bands (each bandsman was to be paid three dollars for the day). Sub-committees were soon reporting on the following: the school parade, to involve one thousand students and two hundred visiting teachers; the trades and polymorphian parade, to have floats depicting local industry, and individual costumes representing ten or more persons; the military parade, to conclude with a drill display at Officers' Square; the torchlight parade, to be led by the City Fire Department (well supplied with coloured fire); the illuminated boat parade, to be composed of canoes, steamers, and naptha launches.

From Ottawa came a proclamation and a suggestion. June 26 was proclaimed a national holiday; 106 Fredericton merchants signed an agreement to close their places of business on that day, thus ensuring a general observance. The oak tree was suggested for every town to plant and to be called King Edward's Tree; Fredericton's IODE adopted this idea, requesting and receiving a place in the day-long program and a site for the tree at Parliament Square.

Thousands of visitors were expected to arrive by railways and steamboats, the transportation companies planning round-trip excursions at reduced rates—"Come to Fredericton and witness the Coronation Day celebration." Both the Canada Eastern and the CPR offered a one-way fare for the round trip. The Star Line steamers, scheduled to travel up from Saint John and down from Woodstock, had the same deal, agreeing to stop at every little place along the river.

As the date approached and Fredericton continued with final preparations, hundreds of thousands of New England residents of British and Canadian birth were already celebrating in Boston. There was a grand military parade of Canadian troops, and a commemorative poem was published by Bliss Carman (Fredericton's native son and Canada's Poet Laureate, who was living in Boston at the time). Entitled "Ode on the Coronation of Edward VII," the twenty-eight six-line stanzas appeared in an elegant hard-covered edition. The opening verse reads:

There are joy-bells over England, there are flags on London town;
There is bunting on the channel, where the fleets go up and down;
There are bonfires alight
In the pageant of the night;
There are bands that blare for splendour, and guns that speak for might;
For another king in England is coming to the crown.

But not on June 26 as planned and not in the style and pomp originally intended. With the news of the king's illness, the royal relatives and the European heads of state returned home. The Canadian military contingent came back and would not go over again. Throughout the Empire, all coronation festivities were immediately abandoned and enthusiasm waned. In Fredericton, the summer holidays continued, many leaving town on vacation. Would it be possible to carry out the celebration at a later date with the same spark of brilliancy?

At the end of July, the committee met and talked about the situation. There was a poor turnout and a lack of interest, but it was decided to start again and prepare for the new coronation date and public holiday of August 9. An attempt worthy of Fredericton would be made in honour of the king who, in his youth, had visited the capital city.

There would be significant changes. The barbecue, the oak tree, and the union church service were cancelled. The merchants would not close until 1:00 p.m., the water sports would be replaced by a baseball game, and Lieutenant-Governor J. B. Snowball would not be able to give an address at Parliament Square because of a previous commitment. The mayor would take his place.

The five parades remained, and although they would not be as elaborate, special features were added: the local boys who had returned from the South African Boer War would march in their khaki uniforms; the members of the St. Mary's fire department would march in new uniforms and bring along an old, hand-operated fire engine and hose cart; each department of the Marysville Cotton Mill would be represented by a special industry float.

The committee members passed a resolution requesting all citizens "to decorate and illuminate residences and places of business, even if it is one Union Jack." They made an appeal to all school children still in the city "to support us in our endeavors to mark the day." And Fredericton's police magistrate issued the following notice: "The setting off of firecrackers will not be allowed on public streets or squares during the big day because it is likely to cause runaway horses."

Following a night of heavy rain, the coronation morning broke in Fredericton with bright sunshine in a cloudless sky, a fresh breeze setting all the flags tangent from their poles. After the Royal Salute of twenty-one guns at 7:00 A.M., there was to be the ringing of church bells and the blowing of steam whistles. But there was only silence!

On the Friday evening before, instructions had arrived from Ottawa stating that permission could not be granted to fire the royal or any other salute because Fredericton was only a flag station and not a signalling depot. As a result, there was disappointment, deeply felt by the military and the citizens. The ammunition and the guns had been ready and the city was waiting for the sounds to be heard simultaneously with those in London during the service at Westminster Abbey.

The other royal symbol had received special permission from the king for this one occasion. Soon after sunrise, the royal standard was hoisted to the top of the tall flagstaff in Officers' Square and there it would flutter until sunset. (The Sovereign's personal flag is traditionally used to indicate the presence of royalty and cannot be displayed at any other time, even upon royal birthdays. Thus, it would be many years before it would once again be raised in Fredericton.)

The day ended with five thousand people standing on the Green, between the two bridges, enjoying a beautiful parade of illuminated boats and canoes along the St. John River. The fireworks followed at ten o'clock and, for the next hour, there was a magnificent display, concluding with the combined bands playing the national anthem as four words flashed across the sky: GOD SAVE THE KING.

A century later, a few souvenirs have survived. A copy of the church service for June 26 and a coronation program for August 9 are preserved in the provincial archives (both had been professionally printed and distributed to all the city hotels at the time). Four copies of Carman's patriotic poem can be found in the UNB Archives, one having been signed by the poet.

The ubiquitous coronation calendar of 1902 is a rare find, but one still exits and continues to grace the wall of an historic Fredericton home. The calendar advertisement promotes Minard's Liniment as a Canadian household remedy; the calendar picture shows King Edward in his ceremonial robes, surrounded by the emblematic shields of all the countries in the Empire.

Regardless of the postponement, it was a glorious time.

TWENTY-FIFTH GOVERNOR GENERAL ONCE LIVED IN FREDERICTON

MARCH 2, 2002

858 Brunswick Street, with Christ Church Cathedral in the background (from an oil painting by the late Ab Knight). Romeo LeBlanc lived in the third-floor apartment.

FIFTY YEARS AGO there was a break in tradition when Vincent Massey became the first Canadian to represent the British Crown in Canada.

Before that time, the seventeen governors general since Confederation had been British aristocrats. Three were closely related to Queen Victoria: the Duke of Connaught was her son, the Marquess of Lorne had married her daughter (Princess Louise), and the Earl of Athlone had married her granddaughter (Princess Alice).

Massey, who had married Alice Parkin of Fredericton, was a widower when he was appointed on January 24, 1952. He assumed office on February 28 and, on March 2, he settled into stately Rideau Hall to begin a successful four-year term. He handled himself with such distinction that his time was extended to 1959.

Since then, all the governors general have been from Canada, but only one has hailed from New Brunswick. Romeo LeBlanc has been the only person from the Atlantic provinces to hold the office (1995–1999), and the first Acadian to do so.

Many years before this achievement was reached, LeBlanc established close connections with Fredericton. In his early career, he was a member of the Teachers' College faculty, during which time he lived at 858 Brunswick Street, a stately residence that still stands across from Christ Church Cathedral.

He came to Fredericton in 1955 at age twenty-eight, his formal education having been completed at a one-room school in Cormier's Cove (Westmorland County), at College Saint Joseph in Memramcook (he was the valedictorian for the class of '48), and at La Sorbonne in Paris (on scholarship).

Returning to New Brunswick, he taught grade school in a little place called Drummond, three miles east of Grand Falls in Victoria County. The province's director of teacher training, Dr. Harrison Chapman, heard about the intelligent young LeBlanc and brought him to Fredericton, where he stayed four years.

In those days, he would have walked "out" to Queen Street in the early morning in order to get to the college, there being a choice of either Church, St. John, or Regent streets. By 8:30 A.M. all four hundred students and the twenty-five staff members had climbed the steps of the Gothic-like entrance, the front doors of which were framed by the same pink granite pillars that survived the fire when the original 1876 Provincial Normal School burned in 1929. It was rebuilt a year later and the centrepiece was a magnificent auditorium, complete with perfect acoustics, a sprawling balcony, and a stage that was the envy of every performer.

Opening exercises were held in the auditorium at the beginning of each day. The thunderous piano chords of music instructor Janis Kalnins escorted each class to its assigned seats, while staff members slowly made their way to the chairs on the stage. The principal, Dr. Dyson Wallace, would stand patiently at the podium, waiting to lead the prayer and a hymn before giving the announcements.

LeBlanc almost always entered from the back of the stage, probably because his office was on the right side of the second-floor hallway that led to the annex or former Model School, a wing that was built in 1912 but left unharmed by the fire. He could travel down a back stairwell that led to a door that opened directly onto the stage. When he did appear, his presence was felt among staff and students.

Urbane and somewhat charismatic, he was the scholar who stood tall, nodding to a few friends, clutching his textbooks in one arm, carrying a clipboard in the other. Once seated, he remained rather aloof, jotting a few notes intermittently.

His colleagues would say later that he was (and still is) a genuine country gentleman, his flawless grooming in well-tailored suits highlighted by black-rimmed glasses, slick black hair, and polished black shoes—a perfect role model for teenage male students in flannel shirts and unpressed slacks who were about to become teachers in classrooms of their own.

But there was more to this man than appearances. A strong character, positive and influential, came through during his years in Fredericton.

Like the students they taught, college staff members were a mix of Anglophones and Francophones; two languages and two cultures came together under the same roof for the one-year program. Ironically, it worked, and Romeo LeBlanc was partially responsible. He understood the young people from rural New Brunswick, and he realized that it was necessary to get the English and French students working together. They did, and the harmony that resulted manifested itself when it came to extracurricular activities.

At Teachers' College in the 1950s there was an abundance of clubs, teams, and special groups, the big one being the yearbook staff and the annual publication of the red-and-blue *Tutoris*. There were seventeen positions for students, and there were four faculty advisors, of whom LeBlanc was the chairman, a position he filled with admirable diplomacy.

It was during this year-long bilingual publication that the yearbook students witnessed another side of him in relation to those qualities that he would display years later as a member of parliament (the longest-serving fisheries minister in Canadian history) and subsequently speaker of the senate. He was firm but fair, organized but relaxed, witty but serious. He was in perfect command of both languages, switching with ease from impeccable English to controlled French.

The four faculty advisors worked well together, providing strong leadership. Thomas Acheson is now deceased but the other two have fond and vivid memories.

Thelma Kierstead: "One could not have found a better colleague. He participated in staff discussions, his opinions always logical and well presented, his point of view always non-confrontational but tactfully and effectively expressed. It is true, his students greatly admired him but, whether they realized he was destined for greater accomplishments, I do not know."

William Biden: "He saw the disadvantages of the Acadians in the education system of the 1950s and he wanted to do something about it; thus, the French students had great respect for his teaching. He did not enjoy math, so he traded with someone else for civics and citizenship, an area more to his liking. He was a hard worker, but he was the *life of the party* at social gatherings."

The faculty social life within the college was limited, although there was the occasional function. The atmosphere of the building tended to be oppressive; having two staff rooms, one for female teachers and another for males, was a contributing factor—either sex seldom entering the other's domain. Even the salaries were different, and with the same qualifications, women were not paid as much as men, married women taking on the status of a part-time employee!

However, noon hours were a different matter. Several of the same staff members stayed for lunch every day and Romeo LeBlanc was among them. The little basement cafeteria adjoined the home economics rooms and here the faculty had a table separate from the students. Eventually, the teachers moved across the hall to the sewing room, where they would have privacy, all of them becoming very good friends.

Shirley Alcoe: "It was during these lively lunchroom discussions that we got to know and respect the real Romeo LeBlanc. The best conversation occurred when he was present. He was keen about everything that was going on in the world and kept the talk flowing, never monopolizing, always being interested in what others had to say as well. He not only *sparkled* during those lunch hours but he *sparked* the discussion."

The late Katherine MacLaggan, the nurse on staff who taught an excellent health course, admired his intelligence so much that she encouraged him to think about furthering his career. And he did!

After classes were through for the day, Romeo LeBlanc would cross Queen Street at the corner of York and enter the James S. Neill building. There on the top floor was the CFNB Radio Station and there he began to record news reports and commentaries for the CBC. World politics always interested him, as did the federal and provincial scenes.

Ed Everett was the studio engineer at the time and never forgot the serious young college professor whose taped messages were fed through land lines to Ottawa and Toronto: "He wanted everything to be technically correct so we did it over and over again."

Thus, the transition into radio journalism had begun. LeBlanc even spent time on his news reports in his little office at the college, his colleagues passing by and noticing that he was concentrating on his tapes, preparing himself for the next stage in a career that would take him to London, Algeria, Cyprus, Berlin, and Washington, as a foreign correspondent for Radio Canada.

Another journalist working for the CBC and living in Fredericton with his wife and family in the 1950s was Rod Chaisson. It was inevitable that he and Romeo Leblanc would become great friends, spending hours together improving their delivery of news reports in English, taping their efforts, listening, and then criticizing the results. According to Thelma Kierstead, "they were tireless in their efforts to be perfect."

On the afternoons he was not recording at CFNB, LeBlanc joined the faculty "lunch group" as they walked over to Keays' Lunch Counter at 72 York Street and continued their earlier discussions over coffee, winding down after the day's classes.

Eventually, the conversation turned to cars and, although LeBlanc did not have one while he was in Fredericton, he was a great help to all the single female teachers who owned cars, telling them what this or that sound meant, taking their cars to the garage and seeing that the right repairs were made.

They also talked about food because LeBlanc was an excellent cook who became known for his splendid spaghetti dinners. Although his third-floor garret apartment was too small for entertaining, he would, from time to time, become the genial host and superb chef at the homes of various colleagues. On the other hand, "He was a charming guest," says Thelma Kierstead, "a real asset to any dinner party, and therefore did not lack for invitations."

The late Franklin Gilmore, who taught science, agreed: "Romeo was affable! He had a sense of humour! He was a full-time student of human nature. He liked to study people and this is why he attended the Saturday night jamborees in the college auditorium. He would sit up in the balcony and watch the audience and their reactions. He did not go for the music or the performers on the stage; it was more fun to observe the people sitting around him, never missing a thing, his mind going all the time. People were his forte!"

Other colleagues, including Helen MacFarlane, Arden Doak, and Beatrice Mahoney, echoed the same sentiments: "Romeo LeBlanc was a people-person who treated everybody the same. He was an independent thinker who loved to join discussions. We thought he was tremendous!"

Eileen Wallace, the librarian, soon realized that LeBlanc would make a great diplomat. "He was thoughtful of others, always making sure that everyone was comfortable. He tended to look after people, no matter who they were, making sure the door was opened for the ladies and that a chair was offered. The little things counted and there was no condescension whatsoever."

Dr. Murray Stewart: "I served on a French and English language curriculum committee with Mr. LeBlanc and found him to be friendly, co-operative, and supportive, but he was an educator who kept a low profile."

Although he sometimes went home to Cormier's Cove, weekends were mostly spent in Fredericton at 858 Brunswick Street, a quiet and picturesque area of the city with the St. John River in full view. The house was built in 1815 on Sunbury Street (now University Avenue) but it was moved around the corner to its present location when "Boss" Gibson had the railroad put through to Marysville, a small CNR station being placed on the east side.

When owner Gilbert Cunningham died in 1949, he left the house to his wife and three daughters. Renovations (on the second floor) followed and the result was three apartments, one of which daughter Pauline shared with fellow teachers Martha Comeau and Jean Marie Carney (a physical education instructor at the college). Whenever the three of them needed a fourth for bridge, it was Romeo LeBlanc who would come down and join the table.

Other times, the tenants on the first and second floors would see that the building was quiet, because they knew the young gentleman scholar on the third floor would be reading, studying, or just enjoying his solitude. His apartment had two large rooms, plus a kitchenette and bath, all with slanted ceilings.

Much has happened in Romeo LeBlanc's life since his four years in the capital of New Brunswick. He went on to other capitals in the world and succeeded beyond expectation. And now he has retired from the world scene and is living back home in Cormier's Cove, having recently been appointed as the sixth chancellor of l'Université de Moncton.

Here in Fredericton, there have been changes too: the Teachers' College has been completely renovated on the inside to become the province's justice building and a major tourist attraction within the military compound; CFNB and Keays' are no longer operating; 858 Brunswick Street now sits in the shadow of a modern apartment complex, the little CNR station having been demolished long ago.

On the eve of his installation as the twenty-fifth governor general of Canada, Romeo LeBlanc remembered his stay in the province's capital. He said the following to a fellow passenger on a flight to Moncton: "I think of all those people during my years at Teachers' College and I treasure their acquaintances and the memories I have of them and my time in Fredericton."

BEAVERBROOK WAS HONOURED FORTY-FIVE YEARS AGO

SEPTEMBER 14, 2002

This 1950 photo of Beaverbrook, taken at a New Brunswick fishing lodge, was attached to each menu at a 1952 dinner in his honour, given by schoolteachers who had been chosen for one of his overseas tours.

AS STUDENTS IN NEW BRUNSWICK begin another year, it is an appropriate time to remember the man who was a great benefactor on their behalf and how he was thanked for his generosity.

The man was William Maxwell Aitken ("Max"), who, after he became the wealthy Lord Beaverbrook, would return to New Brunswick from England every fall for an annual visit. However, the 1957 visit was different from all the others; it was the year that students throughout the province showed their appreciation, and Fredericton was chosen as the site for an enduring symbol of his benevolence.

Although he had been born in Maple, Ontario, and had spent his boyhood in Newcastle, New Brunswick, it was the city of Fredericton that became one of Beaverbrook's favourite homes. (He also had estates in Surrey and Norfolk, three flats in London, three farms in Somerset, houses in the Bahamas and Jamaica, a villa in France, and hotel suites in Montreal, Toronto, and New York.)

Official biographers refer to all these places in detail, but they neglect to mention Beaverbrook's earliest contacts with the capital city of New Brunswick. From the beginning, Fredericton played an important part in his life; in return, he became the city's greatest benefactor.

His first visit was on December 1, 1899. He was nineteen and a struggling insurance agent, his attempts at Dalhousie University, Saint John Law School, and the expanding Canadian West having already failed. When he signed "W. Max Aitken" in the register of the old Queen Hotel on lower Queen Street, little did he realize that in sixty years time he would be purchasing the hotel property for a small Centennial Park, adjacent to his last gift for the city—the Fredericton Playhouse.

In 1899, he might have been in the city on one of his many business deals, but the Anglo-Boer War, commonly known as the South African War, had started that fall, and Max's brother, Joseph Magnus Aitken ("Mauns"), a Fredericton bank teller, was called for duty. Max had also volunteered but had been rejected because of asthma. He travelled to Quebec to say good-bye to Mauns, spending several days celebrating with the troops, probably passing through Fredericton on his way back to Saint John.

During the next twenty years, he hurried in and out of Fredericton on various occasions, but he never stayed overnight. In 1911, his accomplishments in British politics earned him a knighthood in the coronation honours of King George V; by that time, the young Sir Max Aitken was regarded "as one of the most brilliant and successful financiers in the Empire."

Because of poor health in the spring of 1913, he returned to the province of his youth for rest and relaxation. At this time, he began to establish a number of permanent scholarships at UNB, marking the beginning of his many splendid gifts to the university, the city, and the province.

When a new battalion (the New Brunswick Kilties) was organized in 1916, Sir Max was asked to be honorary colonel. He had already been appointed official eyewitness and historian of the Canadian armies in the field, but he took time to send a letter to Fredericton from London. Colonel Percy Guthrie received the following reply: "I am delighted to accept the offer of Honorary Colonel of the 236th." As a result, his picture appeared in *The Daily Gleaner* for the first time in his life.

Sir Max received another honour in 1916—a peerage from King George V. Remembering a little brook next to his home in Newcastle, where he used to feed the beavers, he adopted the name Beaverbrook and used it for the rest of his life. Thus, when his duties as minister of information in Britain's war cabinet were over, he crossed the Atlantic on the liner *Olympic* in June of 1919, returning home to New Brunswick for the first time as a baronet.

He was exhausted and once again in poor health, although he hoped that the Maritime air would restore his energy. A motor trip was planned from Newcastle to Fredericton, with his party arriving in the city on June 18. They had booked a suite of rooms at the same Queen Hotel where he had stayed twenty years earlier. This time he signed his name "Lord Beaverbrook."

It was an all-day trip at that time, Fredericton not being reached until late afternoon. As the car pulled up in front of the hotel, His Lordship rushed forward to shake the hand of a man whom he recognized standing on the street. It was John White of the Canadian Army Medical Corps, a grade-school classmate from the Newcastle days and now an orderly at the Military Hospital on the Woodstock Road. For a moment, in the middle of the sidewalk in downtown Fredericton, the two forty-year-old men with contrasting lifestyles were schoolboys again, smiling, joking, and exchanging stories about the Miramichi.

During an interview with a reporter the next morning, Beaverbrook declined to discuss public matters, but he did express the belief that the Germans would sign the peace treaty. Regarding his personal life, he said, "I have no plans. I'm going to spend my time motoring about New Brunswick until I am in good health again." The visit ended with a flattering editorial and a letter to the editor, the latter from an irate citizen, criticizing the mayor and the city council for not publicly recognizing His Lordship's visit to Fredericton.

Recognition from UNB came two years later when Beaverbrook was given an honorary Doctor of Laws degree and, for the second time, his picture appeared in the local press. The 1921 encaenia was on May 12 and the ceremony took place in the library, which, at that time, was located on the top floor of the Old Arts Building. There were twenty-five degrees conferred, including three honorary ones. However, one was *in absentia* and that was Lord Beaverbrook.

His business interests in England, especially his newspaper empire, made it difficult for him to attend all special events, but his thoughts were continuously with New Brunswick. The scholarships continued to increase, with millions of dollars being invested for young people; the overseas tours for teachers began, with His Lordship being personally involved in the travel details.

After his wife died in 1927, Lord Beaverbrook came to UNB and made plans for the Lady Beaverbrook Residence in her memory. It was opened in 1930 and, to this day, it is still one of the most majestic buildings on campus (with a sixty-foot swimming pool and a squash-racquetball court). The turret clock, with its illuminated dials and chime of bells, was an additional and personal memorial to his late wife.

In 1941, there was the Lady Beaverbrook Gymnasium; ten years later, a new wing for the UNB library (now the provincial archives). To the latter, he gave thousands of valuable books and deposited official collections of personal papers. Even the name, Bonar Law-Bennett Library, was his idea, in honour of his two great friends (Andrew Bonar Law, the only Canadian-born prime minister of England and Richard Bedford Bennett, the only New Brunswick-born prime minister of Canada.)

In time, in Fredericton, there would be the Lady Beaverbrook Rink (1955) on University Avenue, the Somerville House Law School (1959) on Waterloo Row, the Beaverbrook Art Gallery, and the Playhouse. Other parts of the province would receive rinks, parks, libraries, and buildings as well. He placed carillons in churches and even made provision for a bandmaster to conduct the UNB band. And there were the numerous instances of financial help for individuals and associations.

In 1947, at age sixty-eight, Beaverbrook was inducted as chancellor of UNB, the ceremony being a part of the May 16 encaenia. Dalton Camp was the valedictorian that year, Vincent Massey was the recipient of an honorary degree, and His Lordship was the special speaker. He talked about his several positions in Churchill's wartime cabinet, probably the first time that a member of the British House of Lords addressed the university. (The typewritten copy of his speech, with handwritten notations, is preserved today at the provincial archives.)

That evening, Lord Beaverbrook danced at the graduation ball and then hosted a dinner at the Queen Hotel, covers being laid for eighteen guests. They dined in the shadow of a large new hotel, under construction across the street. It would open in 1948 and be named in Beaverbrook's honour (although not financed by him). It would become his residence during his later visits to Fredericton.

Unlike many who have accumulated vast fortunes, Beaverbrook kept returning to his childhood province and kept providing great sums of money so that others could enjoy a fuller life and have the opportunities that were denied to him, especially in the academic field, the sports arena, and the arts and culture areas.

The provincial government would eventually pass legislation, proclaiming his birthday (May 25) as Lord Beaverbrook Day (and a holiday for school children), but the people of New Brunswick wanted to do more to honour their great benefactor. On March 21, 1956, an idea was born when a Fredericton night watchman wrote a letter to the editor, suggesting that every man, woman, and child in New Brunswick give ten cents towards the cost of placing a statue of Beaverbrook in the centre of Officers' Square.

The unique suggestion was made by Donald (Shun) Ryan, who made the first contribution towards the fund—one dollar. "There will be some children who won't be able to donate a dime" he said, "and if I give a dollar that will give them a hand."

Mayor H. S. Wright of Fredericton thought that Ryan's idea was an excellent one and offered to organize the Lord Beaverbrook Testimonial Fund in the capital city and throughout the province. He wrote to the mayors in all other places and to the wardens of the counties, outlining the project. He received a positive response.

Minister of Education Claude Taylor heartily supported the movement for a lasting memorial "to one who has contributed so much to our social and educational welfare, assisting university students with generous grants, providing postgraduate scholarships, and sending five teachers annually for a year's study in England."

Publisher Michael committed *The Daily Gleaner* to do all it could to promote and cover the campaign. An editorial appeared almost every day in the beginning, encouraging people to visit the subscription centre at City Hall: Sign for a Dime, D-Day Is Dime Day, We Can All Spare a Dime. "Shun Ryan's suggestion started it; Mayor Wright's offer kept it alive; now our dimes can make it a success."

The Fredericton Junior Chamber of Commerce joined with other local organizations to promote the plan further. Beaverbrook scholars encouraged the project and sent their donations, although one said that his was a modest contribution, "no measure of my personal debt to Lord Beaverbrook."

Collection boxes were placed in all New Brunswick schools on May 25, 1956—His Lordship's seventy-seventh birthday. Donations were to be voluntary but any child or adult who gave ten cents could write or print his or her name in the books provided. All the names would be permanently sealed in the base of the statue.

On August 1, 1957, a bronze statue of Beaverbrook in his chancellor's robes, nine feet and three inches high, arrived from a famous foundry in Naples, Italy, where it had been cast by well-known Maltese sculptor Vincent Apap. It was placed on a granite base that weighed ten tons, the capstone directly beneath the statue weighing two tons, all three sections of the pedestal rising eleven feet. A plaque on the front gave a brief biography of the Canadian-born peer and publisher.

The unveiling ceremony took place on August 28, 1957, under the chairmanship of Mayor W. T. Walker. A civic and provincial half-holiday was declared so that as many as possible could be present, and the crowds were huge, everyone waiting for a first glimpse of Fredericton's second statue (Robert Burns was the first, Boss Gibson would be the third).

The tribute included a military parade, a band concert, and two special speakers: Premier Hugh John Flemming (who talked about Beaverbrook's many gifts to the province), and FHS student Charles McMillan (who was the 1957 valedictorian and a Beaverbrook Scholarship winner). Shun Ryan himself unveiled the statue.

His Lordship arrived in the city eight days later (September 4) and five hundred people were at the airport to welcome him on his annual fall visit to Fredericton. After viewing the statue the next day and seeing his own image as a testimony of New Brunswick's affection, he placed his response on page one of *The Gleaner*: "To be set up in bronze in Officers' Square by the boys and girls of New Brunswick is an honour I greatly esteem, though I cannot possibly deserve it. Thanks and thanks again."

For the remainder of September and half of October during that particular autumn of forty-five years ago, Beaverbrook continued with a heavy schedule of activities: sponsoring the first annual Lord Beaverbrook Choral Competition, chairing the first meeting of the Board of Governors of the Beaverbrook Art Gallery, addressing the annual conference of the Canadian Education Association and the annual meeting of the Union of New Brunswick Municipalities, attending the annual UNB freshman banquet, visiting the new NBTA headquarters on lower Regent Street, hosting a buffet supper for #333 Squadron/RCAF Cadets, introducing Senator John F. Kennedy as guest speaker at the fall convocation, meeting with Shun Ryan (the result of the last being that Ryan found Beaverbrook to be "just one of the boys").

His final visit to Fredericton was in the autumn of 1962. He presided at convocation for the last time, and he took solitary walks along the St. John River. Two years later, on June 9, 1964, he died in England at age eighty-five. His ashes were brought to Newcastle to be placed in the memorial that stands in the town square.

Will Fredericton ever see or experience his like again? Although he was controversial, unconventional, eccentric and, at times, difficult, the people of New Brunswick should not forget the man who never forgot them. The statue in Officers' Square will help us all to remember his greatness and his generosity.

ANOTHER TIME, ANOTHER ROYAL JUBILEE

MAY 11, 2002

The speakers' platform in front of the main entrance to the legislative building on the afternoon of the Silver Jubilee (May 6, 1935). Lieutenant-Governor Murray MacLaren is delivering his address at the CFNB microphone. In the background, from left to right: Mrs. Laura Tilley, Premier L. P. D. Tilley, Mrs. Olivia MacLaren, Mrs. Dora Richardson, Archbishop John Richardson (top of head only), Major W. Gordon Jones (ADC), Mayor W. G. Clark, Mrs. Harriet Clark, Mrs. Blanch Dysart, Miss Mary Dysart, the Hon. A. A. Dysart, leader of the opposition.

IN THIS GOLDEN JUBILEE year of Queen Elizabeth II, 2002, there will be people around the world who will remember the great Silver Jubilee celebrated for her grandfather—King George V.

The date was May 6, 1935, and, in New Brunswick, all roads led to the capital city, where day-long festivities honoured the monarch who had been on the throne since 1910.

George V had been no stranger to Canada, having made two visits before he became king. The first was a brief stop in Ontario in 1891 during his career in the Royal Navy.

He was twenty-six at the time and wandered off on his own to inspect a harvest exhibition at a local town hall. A large peach caught his eye but, when he innocently reached out to pick it up, a young police officer, unaware of the sailor's identity, rushed forward and gave the prince a sharp crack across his fingers with a baton. Startled but maintaining his composure, the sailor-prince dropped the peach and passed on. The incident was not forgotten.

During a major cross-country royal tour ten years later, the prince and his wife (Princess May of Teck) came to Canada as the Duke and Duchess of Cornwall and York. Stopping at one of the many Ontario train-station platforms, the prince immediately recognized the young officer from ten years before, who was now chief of police. As the earlier incident was recalled, they both burst into laughter.

During the 1901 tour, the duke and duchess arrived in New Brunswick on October 17, their one official stop in the province being Saint John and not Fredericton. This caused negative feelings between the two cities because Fredericton had been negotiating for months to have the Royals amend their itinerary and visit the capital.

However, the Canadian visit was part of a larger Commonwealth tour lasting several months. Owing to the pressure of time and the cost of transportation, only twenty-four hours were allotted for New Brunswick. Because Fredericton was located off the trunk lines of train travel, the capital city was not to have the honour and pleasure of extending a greeting to the heir apparent.

But the city kept trying and, as the time drew near, the Dominion government began to consider Fredericton's request for the duke and duchess to take a boat trip up the St. John River to the capital—similar to one the Duke's father (King Edward VII) had made forty years earlier when he was the Prince of Wales. Was financial support available for such a venture again?

Four special trains had already been provided for the tour, two of them just for the conveyance of grooms, horses, and carriages. Another was for the governor general, the prime minister, their colleagues, and friends. The last was for the duke and duchess and their entourage—ten elegant coaches with luxuriously decorated staterooms and the first instance of telephone service throughout an entire train.

This left one area for the government to cut back upon—military displays. They were kept to a minimum, saving enormous sums of money by not mobilizing thousands of soldiers to impress a prince. According to one official:

"Canada is not, nor never was, a military power. It is useless to endeavour to impress the Prince with the idea that she is one. He will be much more impressed by the evidence of her progress, by her stately buildings, her well-dressed, well-educated people, and her advancement in art and science."

In Fredericton, the Honourable Archibald FitzRandolph offered his beautiful Frogmore residence (still standing on Beaverbrook Street) for the accommodation and entertaining of Their Royal Highnesses should they visit. The offer was declined but Fredericton loyalty to the throne was not diminished.

Instead, the citizens of the capital city went to Saint John, a special passenger train with thirteen coaches carrying hundreds to the port city. The railway also transported the 71st York Regiment from Fredericton, along with its brass band, and 155 "upper class" citizens who had received invitations to be presented to the prince and princess at an evening reception. In addition, a great crush of people travelled by the river steamers.

At Barrack Square in Saint John, two special delegations from Fredericton had the opportunity of meeting the prince. The first was from City Hall—Mayor William Crocket, city clerk Charles Beckwith, and two aldermen. They presented the city of Fredericton address—words of welcome exquisitely written in purple ink upon fine parchment. Bound in red morocco and surmounted by the Fredericton crest, the scroll had been previously on display in McMurray's Book Store window.

The second group comprised twenty-five Boer War heroes from Fredericton, who joined 105 others from New Brunswick to receive (individually) the South African War medal from the prince. One of these veterans, Captain J. Caverhill Jones, was also presented with the Sword of Honour.

At the end of the Saint John ceremony, His Royal Highness concluded his public reply with these words: "Had time permitted, it would have given me great pleasure to have visited Fredericton, as my father had done forty years ago."

Unfortunately, history was not to repeat itself in this instance, no matter how close. And ten years later, Fredericton would be celebrating the coronation of the young prince, his father having died the year before on May 6, 1910.

Coronation Day for Their Majesties King George V and Queen Mary was June 22, 1911. Among the forty Canadian cavalrymen who rode Guard of Honour in the London parade, there was a young man from New Brunswick by the name of William Henry McFarlane. When he returned home, he brought a tiny wedge of the King's coronation cake, a treat given to each guard. (Today, this sweet souvenir is in the possession of his son Howard, who lives in Fredericton.)

The coronation was celebrated royally in Fredericton and, to make the event even more special, Mayor Charles Thomas and city council extended the Freedom of the City to all school children for the day. That meant that none of them could be arrested, no matter how much noise they made!

Amidst brilliant decorations, over one thousand school children and the High School Cadet Corps paraded to Parliament Square in the morning, where Lieutenant-Governor L. J. Tweedie presented each one with a coronation medal and a Union Jack. When the Fredericton Brass Band began to play "Rule Britannia," everyone marched to Scully's Grove for an afternoon of baseball games.

In twenty-five years' time, these same children would be young men and women getting ready to celebrate the Silver Jubilee.

Because Fredericton was chosen as the city to host New Brunswick's official jubilee celebration, plans and preparations began months in advance. As a result, it was an event quite unlike any other in the capital's history, and the credit belonged to a general citizens' committee under the chairmanship of C. Hedley Forbes.

The elaborate decorations came first; a proclamation from Mayor W. G. Clark requested that citizens and merchants trim their homes and businesses.

And they did. The entire city was draped with flags, bunting, and banners, all with the traditional British colours of red, white, and blue. Three buildings stood out from all the others, each using floodlighting: Government House (RCMP headquarters), the Parliament Buildings (as they were called), and the stately residence of the Countess of Ashburnham on upper Brunswick Street (still standing).

Many stores promoted their products with a Jubilee theme, but only one had been chosen as the exclusive seller of the Jubilee mug. This was Shute's Jewelry Store, its Queen Street window filled with a huge display of the famous souvenir. Selected by the Fredericton Potters' Association, the mug was a special Spode design, selling for seventy-five cents, proving more popular than the Canadian Silver Jubilee dollar, which was in high demand and selling for $1.25 in some places.

In keeping with the dignity of the event, there was a Divine Jubilee Church Service on Sunday, May 5. All military units of the Fredericton garrison (in full dress with medals) paraded to Wilmot United Church on Carleton Street, the first ever garrison church parade held by the militia units. The sermon was given by Reverend J. W. Bartlett, pastor of the church, who preached from the First Epistle of Peter—"Honour all men! Honour the King!"

And the king did likewise. His amnesty for prisoners, a special concession on the occasion of the jubilee, was granted to ninety-one inmates serving terms in New Brunswick jails for violation of the Liquor Act. This affected ten prisoners in the York County Gaol in Fredericton. Those serving terms under the Criminal Code, excluding life sentences, were to be also considered for a reduction in time.

Monday, May 6, was proclaimed a public holiday in Canada by the governor general. In Fredericton, the festivities got under way at 10:00 a.m. sharp with the ringing of church bells, the blowing of factory whistles, and the sounding of automobile horns. It was the start of a memorable day.

Later in the morning, 1,700 school children from Fredericton, Devon, Marysville, Lincoln, and Barker's Point made their way to the Gaiety and Capitol theatres, where they were shown a patriotic film entitled *Soldiers of the King*. W. W. O. Fenety, owner of the theatres, provided this entertainment free of charge. Also free for each child was a jubilee medal, struck in aluminium for eight cents each and paid for by the central committee.

By noon, thousands of people from all over New Brunswick had arrived (because of reduced CPR and CNR rates) and lined the streets for the mile-long parade with its thirty-three floats, three bands, militia units, RCMP, veterans, Girl Guides, Boy Scouts, Wolf Cubs, and Brownies. Competition for the fifty-dollar prize for the first-place float was keen, the winner being the IODE battleship *Our Sovereign*. For the ceremony at Parliament Square, Dr. A. S. McFarlane, chief superintendent of education, was the chairman; music was provided by the Jubilee Chorus; several dignitaries delivered patriotic addresses. The afternoon concluded with the presentation of Fredericton's Silver Jubilee medals to sixty leading citizens in public service and seven military officers, each approved by His Majesty.

The Jubilee state dinner took place in the early part of the evening at Lady Beaverbrook's building on the UNB campus. Over one hundred invited guests included leaders in public life in the province, clergymen, members of the legislature, Supreme Court judges, military officers, and Fredericton city councillors.

The dinner was hosted by Lieutenant-Governor Murray MacLaren, who proposed the one and only toast—"Gentlemen, The King!" However, two responses were made: one from Premier L. P. D. Tilley, the other from Opposition Leader A. A. Dysart. Two more silver medals were presented to Chief Justice J. B. M. Baxter and Brigadier-General F. W. Hill.

Downtown, the crowds had gathered for $175 worth of patriotic fireworks along the south-side "green." On the north side, there was the brilliant illumination of the Boy Scout beacon on the Devon shore. The beacon, a major feature of the jubilee, was to be located originally on Poplar Hill on the Old Richibucto Road, but it was decided to move it closer to the city for all to see.

The final event of the day was the grand Jubilee Ball in the assembly chamber of the legislature; subsequently a midnight supper was to be served in the spacious corporations committee room. Everyone was welcome and over four hundred attended, all proceeds going towards the King's Silver Jubilee Cancer Fund in Canada. However, the Girl Guides, who were in charge of "checking," saved their proceeds for the upcoming summer jamboree.

When the party was over, there was just one complaint: why was Fredericton overlooked in the coast-to-coast hook-up of a national radio broadcast, whereby a brass band in each provincial capital played "O Canada" simultaneously? This was deemed a major slight, not only to New Brunswick but to the city hosting the provincial celebration.

The oversight was never explained and was eventually forgotten. On a positive note, a permanent reminder of the Silver Jubilee was established by naming a new Fredericton street after the occasion—Jubilee Street. Five years later (1940), the name was changed to Windsor Street, perhaps because King George V had changed the name of the royal house from Hanover to Windsor.

Today, only a few mementoes of the Silver Jubilee have survived and these are preserved in the Provincial Archives: a professionally-printed dance card from the grand ball, *The Canada Gazette* supplement listing all 10,000 Canadians who received Jubilee medals, the official souvenir program of the Jubilee review of the fleet at Portsmouth (England), and *The Daily Gleaner*'s special Jubilee issue.

Eight months following the event, King George V died on January 20, 1936. His death moved his granddaughter closer to the throne and to the long reign leading towards her own Golden Jubilee.

A Memorable First Visit as Princess

October 12, 2002

Following the twenty-one-gun salute at Union Station on York Street, Their Royal Highnesses inspected the military guard of honour. The full-length fur coat was a wedding gift from Canada.

Born in 1926, Queen Elizabeth II was a shy, young princess when she made her first visit to Canada in the autumn of 1951.

Twelve years earlier, her parents had made a similar cross-country tour of the Dominion, about which her mother often said: "The Canadian tour of 1939 *made me*!"

Perhaps Elizabeth II could also say this about her own month-long state visit over a half century ago. However, it was a royal journey that had dark overtones from beginning to end.

The princess and the Duke of Edinburgh were supposed to have sailed for Canada on October 2 but due to her father's failing health and subsequent removal of his left lung, the visit was postponed one week. They left England on October 8 and travelled by air instead of by sea, arriving at Dorval Airport (near Montreal) after 3,400 miles and sixteen consecutive hours.

It was the first time in history that the heir to the throne flew the Atlantic, the princess carrying with her a sealed envelope in case the worst happened while she was away. It contained her accession documents.

Three tons of luggage were transferred to the special train that was waiting to take the royal couple across Canada to the west coast and then back to the Atlantic provinces, almost matching the legendary tour of 1939. But there was one major difference.

Both the princess and her thirty-year-old consort had insisted on a simple program, with as many opportunities as possible to meet "plain everyday Canadians," especially the younger generation. They wanted their visit to be more informal than the elaborate schedule of 1939; for instance, Prime Minister Louis St. Laurent would not be accompanying them as MacKenzie King had.

Before they travelled east, there was Upper Canada and the West, each event on the itinerary representative of that part of the country: a hockey game in Montreal, the Dionne quintuplets in North Bay, a boat trip on the Rideau Canal, the Winnipeg Ballet, the RCMP Musical Ride at Regina, a special Calgary stampede with a chuckwagon luncheon, a lacrosse match in Vancouver.

Wearing the large diamond maple-leaf brooch that was a gift to her mother during the 1939 tour, the future queen met enthusiastic crowds wherever she went, even on the forty-five-hour side trip to Washington to meet President Harry Truman, her parents having made a similar visit to meet President Franklin Roosevelt.

CFNB Radio listeners in Fredericton had the opportunity to hear continuous detailed coverage of the tour in Ontario and Quebec. In fact, the entire Commonwealth tuned in to listen as the heiress presumptive to the throne of England made a memorable broadcast speech in response to a toast by Governor-General Viscount Alexander of Tunis during the state banquet in Ottawa.

In the meantime, the capital cities of the Atlantic provinces were immersed in preparations, especially Fredericton, the setting for New Brunswick's official reception. A representative planning committee from the province and the city had been organized as early as the summer of 1951 and consisted of the following: Lieutenant-Governor D. L. MacLaren, Premier J. B. McNair, Mayor H. S. Wright, Fred I. Haviland (city clerk), Muriel McQueen Fergusson (city councillor), Robert A. Tweedie (secretary to the premier), Major T. C. Barker (protocol officer), Dr. F. E. McDiarmid (superintendent of education), Superintendent E. H. Perlson of the RCMP, and David M. Dickson (president of the Fredericton branch of the Canadian Legion and the only member of the committee still living).

When Ottawa's undersecretary of state and the private secretary of HRH Princess Elizabeth arrived in Fredericton for a meeting on August 29, tentative plans were submitted for the five-hour royal visit in the capital city. The mayors of Saint John and Moncton were also present, arranging for their scheduled visits.

It was at this time that leading airwoman Roberta Richards of Fredericton was chosen from 1500 young women across Canada to be a royal secretary, a position that required her to travel on the royal train and to take dictation from Princess Elizabeth and Prince Phillip throughout the entire tour. After completing a secretarial course at Fredericton Business College, Richards had joined the RCAF and was stationed in Quebec, from where she was on loan for the royals.

Another young Frederictonian was chosen to present the royal bouquet. Her name was Sharon Green, an eleven-year-old student at Smythe Street School and the daughter of Blanche and Clarence Green. Her father, whom she never saw, had been a reporter for *The Fredericton Daily Mail* before he joined the army at the beginning of World War Two. He was one of the first casualties in London during the Battle of Britain.

Fredericton's royal bouquet underwent three major changes. At first, Mayor Wright decided that it was to be violets (the provincial flower). However, the majority of other bouquets across Canada were to be roses, so a switch was made in order to continue the trend. Finally, the princess was to be presented with a bouquet of New Brunswick orchids—the same flower presented to the Queen in 1939—from the greenhouses of Tom Ascroft of Moncton.

Ascroft shipped several varieties of his hybrid orchids (with various hues) to the flower shop of Everett Trites in Fredericton. At five o'clock on the morning of the royal visit, Trites selected twelve of the orchids and prepared the bouquet, allowing each member of his staff to add a personal touch to the unique floral creation before it was boxed and delivered to the legislature.

Another presentation, also involving a number of participants, was New Brunswick's official gift to the royal couple. It was a matched pair of automobile robes, with the RCAF tartan on one side and the province's coat-of-arms on the other. They were woven and presented by the Loomcrofters of Gagetown—Patricia Jenkins, Muriel Lawrence, and Enid Inch. During the two hundred hours of weaving, each citizen of the village had the opportunity to weave a few threads into the royal gift. When finished, the robes were displayed in the window of Madge Smith's Craft Shop on lower Queen Street.

As Tuesday, November 6 drew closer, Fredericton was ready: a civic holiday had been proclaimed; every house and business in the city had been decorated with flags and bunting, each competing for the top prize money; Police Chief J. D. O'Connell had driven slowly over the entire route, where crowds of seven and eight tiers deep would be standing; plans had been made for twenty thousand school children, who would be arriving by special trains to take up their position on the Green in front of the legislature, each child bringing a lunch and twenty cents for bus fare; several hundred veterans, IODE members, Air Force cadets, Boy Scouts, Wolf Cubs, Girl Guides, and Brownies had been assigned their locations at Parliament Square.

Five historic landmarks, all still standing, were directly involved in the Fredericton visit, the first being Union Station on York Street, where the royal train arrived at 10:00 A.M. sharp! After stepping onto the platform and meeting Lieutenant-Governor D. L. MacLaren and other dignitaries, the princess performed her first official function in New Brunswick—inspecting the one-hundred-man guard of honour, while the sound of a twenty-one-gun salute echoed in the background.

The visit had begun!

Entering a plastic-topped limousine, the royal couple were driven around the city and then "up the hill" to UNB, where the Bonar Law-Bennett Library (now the Provincial Archives) with its new Beaverbrook wing was waiting. The host for this part of the visit was UNB president Albert Trueman, who was caught completely off guard by the informality of Their Royal Highnesses and the unexpected departure from the rigid schedule, twenty minutes for UNB turning into an hour! (They took their time examining the exhibits and admiring the wrought-iron fiddleheads along the reading-room balustrade.)

Princess Elizabeth, chilled by the crisp morning air, requested a cup of tea, but the library staff had made no preparations for refreshments. However, they kindly obliged, using the unmatched cups and saucers they had purchased for themselves at the local five-and-dime, the handle broken on one. Water was hastily boiled in an old electric tea kettle; a quart of milk was quickly borrowed from the nearby kitchen of Mrs. Trueman. When everything was ready, spoons were at a premium, the royal couple passing theirs to the next person in line. (Amusing as it was, the entire situation was reminiscent of the famous 1939 tea stop at the Gilks House in Doaktown.)

At the request of the princess and the duke, it was to be a day of walking. When tea was finished, they strolled a considerable distance around the circular gravelled driveway, mingling with the students, inquiring about the crests on their jackets, looking up at the

Latin motto on the library building (translation: *Forsake Me Not, O Lord*). When the princess was told that the students had their own meaning (*Forsake Us Not, Your Lordship*, referring to Lord Beaverbrook), she threw back her head and laughed heartily.

The walking continued when the royal couple chose to stroll from Christ Church Cathedral to the legislative building, and then to the Lord Beaverbrook Hotel, stopping and chatting with the huge crowds every step of the way, the most walking they had done on the entire tour.

At the cathedral, they were welcomed outside the west door by Bishop W. H. Moorhead and Dean S. C. Gray. Inside, they were given a tour of the massive structure, built during the reign of Queen Victoria, the great-great-grandmother of the princess. The letters patent, sent by the queen to create the Diocese of Fredericton, was on display. Before leaving, they signed the 1860 Prince of Wales Bible beside the signatures of King George VI and Queen Elizabeth, who signed in 1939.

At the legislature, official addresses were delivered from the province by Premier McNair, and from the city by Mayor Wright, a framed and illuminated copy of each being presented to the princess. She also received a special souvenir from Fredericton—the collected poems of local poet Francis Sherman (1871-1926), beautifully bound in light blue morocco. When she began her response, fifty thousand spectators fell silent and listened to the soft, clear British accent that would become a familiar voice over the next five decades. Her concluding words: "Mr. Premier, I thank you and the people of New Brunswick for the welcome you have given us, and for your prayers for my father's health. And to you, Mr. Mayor, I also give my thanks, and through you to the people of Fredericton, who have greeted us today with so much friendship."

Following a tour of the assembly chamber (where the guest books for New Brunswick and Fredericton were signed) and the Legislative Library (where admiration was expressed for the Gothic architecture), the official government luncheon at the Lord Beaverbrook Hotel would be the last stop on the visit.

It had been a day of surprises, beginning with the royal train arriving at the station engine first, instead of backing in, according to the plan. Leaving UNB, the royal limousine suddenly developed engine trouble and stopped abruptly halfway down the hill, Prince Phillip and the chauffeur emerging to lift the hood and examine the situation before others came to the rescue. (Chrysler, Ford, and General Motors supplied sixty late models for the tour, six for each major city.)

However, the biggest upset occurred just before the hotel luncheon began, when Princess Elizabeth unexpectedly requested that all two hundred invited guests be presented formally! This switch in the program caused reporters to scramble for new leads for the stories they had already filed. It also caused a few tense moments for the organizers who thought that the royal couple would be too tired for a presentation ceremony. The princess, apparently, thought otherwise!

Two Fredericton women who were presented at the luncheon—Jean Snow and Irene Beairsto—still live in the capital city. Three well-known local musicians who were chosen to play chamber music during the luncheon, giving a command performance, have since passed away—Herbert Webber (violin), Walter McGinn (piano), Reid VanDine (clarinet).

At 3:00 P.M. sharp, Their Royal Highnesses returned to Union Station and boarded their train for Saint John. They stood on the observation platform and waved to the cheering crowds, just as Princess Elizabeth's father and mother had when they said farewell to Fredericton. As the train moved slowly away, they turned and entered the coach, the music of the 22nd Royal Regiment Band still playing.

In three months' time, she would be queen and, for the next half century, there would be many exciting visits from the new monarch, but there would be only one memorable visit when she was princess.

WHEN THE KENNEDY BROTHERS CAME TO VISIT

OCTOBER 14, 2000

John Fitzgerald Kennedy received an honorary degree from UNB during the fall convocation of 1957. Lord Beaverbrook was the chancellor.

FOR ALMOST A HALF CENTURY, the University of New Brunswick has held its annual convocation in October. Two of these degree-granting ceremonies have probably remained more memorable than all the others.

Forty-three years ago (October 8, 1957), Senator John Fitzgerald Kennedy was the guest speaker at a ceremony in which he received an honorary Doctor of Laws degree; ten years later (October 12, 1967), Senator Robert Francis Kennedy delivered the main address and he was honoured with the same degree.

Each of these affluent brothers came to Fredericton as a youthful forty-one-year-old aspirant to the American presidency. JFK made it but was assassinated while in office (November 22, 1963); RFK was making a successful bid for that same office when he, too, was assassinated (June 4, 1968).

Since the gunshots of Dallas and Los Angeles, scholars have been trying to assess the place in history of these two prominent politicians. However, it is unfortunate that critics and biographers tend to overlook the brief, quiet, autumnal visits that the Kennedy brothers made to New Brunswick's provincial capital.

Robert Francis Kennedy received an honorary degree from UNB during the fall convocation of 1967. Sir Max Aitken was the chancellor.

JFK was making his first visit to New Brunswick when he arrived alone at the Saint John Airport on Monday morning, October 7, 1957. He informed waiting reporters: "I'm interested in the Maritime provinces because my maternal grandfather, who was later to become mayor of Boston, had emigrated from this area, but I'm not sure of the exact locality."

The afternoon trip to Fredericton was made by car, JFK arriving at stately Somerville House, 238 Waterloo Row, to be greeted on the spacious front verandah by the mansion's owner, seventy-eight-year-old Lord Beaverbrook. There was a handshake and then broad smiles were exchanged between the young member of the United States Senate and the venerable magnate of England's Fleet Street. They were great friends, Beaverbrook supposedly having played a significant role in JFK's 1952 election to the Senate.

It was Lord Beaverbrook, chancellor of UNB, who had invited JFK to Fredericton. And he played the host with charming aplomb. That evening there was an elegant dinner at the Lord Beaverbrook Hotel, a momentous occasion with 150 distinguished people invited to pay tribute to the guest of honour. Among them were the three Maritime premiers: Hugh John Flemming of New Brunswick, Robert Stanfield of Nova Scotia, and A. E. Matheson of Prince Edward Island.

All spoke briefly, but it was Beaverbrook who introduced the Honorable Senator from Massachusetts, and in so doing, without hesitation, mixed a political comment with the now-famous prophetic utterance: "When he has become the President of the United States of America, I say to him, remember New Brunswick."

In response, JFK spoke with his usual quiet eloquence, beginning with a quote from the great New England poet Robert Frost: "Good fences make good neighbours, and I think the fences between Canada and the United States have always been well tended."

The next day the convocation ceremony commenced at 3:00 P.M. It was preceded by the academic procession from the historic Arts Building to the Lady Beaverbrook Rink, a thread of black gowns winding its way down the campus hillside, a sharp contrast to the blaze of autumn foliage.

For the first time, in the absence of the lieutenant-governor, Lord Beaverbrook filled the traditional role of visitor to the university on behalf of the queen. John Kennedy received his "first" Canadian degree, the citation being composed and read in Latin by Professor Robert Cattley. Professor Frank Toole read alternately in English, one of the lines echoing the omen from the evening before: "In the eyes of political friends and foes, he is destined for the highest office in the Union."

The biggest "first" was JFK's first major speech in Canada. Again, he was introduced by Beaverbook, but this time the chancellor displayed his reputation as a humorist, referring to the citation that had just accompanied the honorary degree: "The Senator has been introduced in both English and Latin. There is nothing left for me to do but introduce him in Greek."

There was much laughter and, when the cavernous auditorium fell silent, JFK stood to speak. With the UNB coat of arms bearing the motto *Sapere Aude* (dare to be wise) on the wall behind him, the dashing Democratic candidate and hero of World War Two began: "It is a very great honour for a New Englander like myself to come to this city and institution which represent so impressive a link between the New World and the Old. I am most grateful for the degree which you have seen fit to award me and am most honoured to receive it at the hands of your distinguished Chancellor, Lord Beaverbrook."

It was a stirring and provocative speech and it was printed in its entirety in *The Daily Gleaner* the following day; later it was published in handsome booklet format by the university. Its title: "Good Fences Make Good Neighbours." A copy can be found in the

University Archives, along with *Profiles of Courage*, JFK's 1956 Pulitzer Prize-winning book, which he autographed and presented to the library.

To make it possible for Kennedy to rest his aching back and to dine with Lord Beaverbrook that evening, UNB President Dr. Colin B. Mackay agreed to drive him to Harvey Station so he could catch the train.

There was a small lunch counter in the waiting room of the Harvey station and it was here that Kennedy asked for a bowl of tomato soup, one of his favourite snacks. It was prepared for him and, as he ate, he chatted with several of the local residents. When the Boston train came from Saint John, it continued on to McAdam, before taking the future president back to the United States.

When JFK's inauguration took place on January 20, 1961, UNB's scarlet, black, and gold flag, which is usually flown only for rare official events, was hoisted to honour its successful alumnus. And, instead of gathering dust, the famous convocation address was widely distributed and examined, being considered the best record of thoughts on American-Canadian relations by the thirty-fifth president of the United States.

In the fall of 1967, *The Daily Gleaner* carried this headline: UNB HONOURS SENATOR KENNEDY. On this occasion it was Robert Kennedy who, at the time, had a twelve-point lead over President Lyndon Johnson for political appeal.

It was to be a five-hour visit only, RFK arriving at the Fredericton Airport in the morning by private jet and leaving shortly after the convocation ceremony. Like his brother before him, it was a first visit to New Brunswick and a first major speech in Canada.

Many people were determined not to miss the tousle-headed, athletic senator from Massachusetts, the Kennedy who was the father of ten children, who had been a war correspondent for *The Boston Post*, who had gone on to write several books, and who wanted to follow his older brother into the White House.

In Fredericton, his schedule included the opening of the Lady Beaverbrook Gymnasium extension (where he was introduced as "Bobby"), the placing of a wreath at the President Kennedy Memorial in Officers' Square (since removed to the university campus), a noon interlude at the Lord Beaverbrook Hotel (where autograph seekers were waiting), and then the convocation ceremony at the Lady Beaverbrook Rink.

Dr. Colin B. Mackay was still the university president, but Sir Max Aitken was the new chancellor of UNB, his father, Lord Beaverbrook, having died in 1964.

Sir Max had been a long-time friend of the Kennedy family and this relationship was mentioned before RFK began to address the graduating class.

His speech was entitled “Different Paths of a Common Goal” and it brought a moment of stunned silence with its opening remark, a statement that was omitted from the university’s published version.

“Nouveau-Brunswick Libre!” he shouted. Then again, this time to laughter, “Vive Nouveau-Brunswick Libre!”

Ironically, in case someone had missed the point, he went on to say: “Before I came up here I thought I might find out what would go over well. So I got in touch with various world leaders, and got a telegram that said that’s the way I should start a speech. It said you would have immediate success and call great attention to your visit…signed Charles de Gaulle.”

Referring to the fact that the place was crowded to its steel-roofed rafters, RFK said: “I think it’s marvellous that we’re all here today. I think it shows how attached you are to the university…and I’m very appreciative.” Then, with piercing force, emphatic intonation, and the “Kennedy” finger-jabbing, he began his familiar warning about “a troubled and a turbulent world, a world full of a new kind of revolution.”

A photograph session with the other honorary recipients should have completed the day’s busy schedule, but outside the rink RFK was besieged by crowds of waiting autograph seekers and well-wishers. As Professor Cattley’s citation had said: “He was the *nonpareil* of American youth.”

Even with Sir Max waiting to drive his guest to the airport, RFK took a few extra minutes to give more autographs, to shake more hands, and to flash more smiles. Then, as he was climbing into the limousine, he waved and commented: “Come down and vote in the United States sometime!”

When citizens of Fredericton and graduates of UNB visit Washington, D.C., in this new millennium, they will probably be drawn to Arlington National Cemetery, where rows of white wooden crosses dot the rolling landscape.

One of these markers stands alone at the bottom of a grassy knoll and bears the name ROBERT FRANCIS KENNEDY. Farther up the hillside, surrounded by marble and granite and marked with an eternal flame, a slab of smooth, black stone bears the name JOHN FITZGERALD KENNEDY.

Two legendary visitors to Fredericton, who became distinguished alumni of the University of New Brunswick, are at rest.

Section Three: Historic Landmarks

REMEMBERING THE SCHOOL AT HAWTHORNE HILL

SEPTEMBER 1, 2001

The Hawthorne Hill School for the hearing impaired, circa 1895.

THE IDEA WAS CONCEIVED in 1881, the brainchild of Albert Frederick Woodbridge, a well-educated gentleman "of pleasant address," who came from England by way of Halifax.

At that time, the population of New Brunswick was 321,000. The number of hearing-impaired in the province was 344. Thus, a private school was urgently needed. On September 1, 1882, just such a facility became a reality when it opened in Fredericton.

The location was Hawthorne Hill, east of the city, where Forest Hill is today. It was here that a boarding school for the hearing-impaired was first housed—in the magnificent mansion on the 117 acres of the Botsford estate—this side of Forest Hill Cemetery.

Although the site was isolated, it was becoming well-known. Historic Hawthorne Hill was named after Colonel Hawthorne, who commanded the British fleet in its attack on Villebon's Fort at the Nashwaak.

George Botsford, who built the residence in 1863, was one of the first and finest equity lawyers in New Brunswick. When he became clerk of the Legislative Council, he sold the property to his brother, Senator Amos Botsford, who in turn leased it to Albert Woodbridge.

In his travels throughout the British Isles and France, Woodbridge, who became the principal of the school, had never seen a more delightful spot than Hawthorne Hill. The splendid views and the fresh country air would have a positive effect on his pupils, keeping them in good health and cheerful spirits.

At the opening, ten pupils—eight boys and two girls—from all around the province were registered. Among them were former students of Woodbridge when he taught in Halifax. Five more from New Brunswick and Maine were expected to arrive by the end of September.

There were several terms of admission, the main one being that all applicants had to be "deaf mutes of sound intellect, good moral character, and free from any infectious disease." The age range had to be between seven and eighteen.

Applications were to be addressed to the secretary of the school, the Reverend George Goodridge Roberts of St. Anne's Parish Church. These would be reviewed by a board of volunteer directors, including the Honourable Chief Justice John Allen (chairman), Professor H. C. Creed of the Provincial Normal School, Henry Chestnut (treasurer), the Honourable Judge G. F. Gregory, several clergymen and merchants, and two future mayors of Fredericton (William C. Crocket and George J. McNally).

The tuition was $80 per year, but only if the parents could afford it. If not, the child was still admitted and provided with instruction, lodging, laundry, books, stationery, and medical and dental care. The doctor on staff was T. Clowes Brown; the visiting dentist was B. H. Torrens. Both gave their professional services gratuitously. All medicines were donated by a local pharmacist; all shoe repairs were done free of charge by a local shoemaker.

In the beginning, there were five hours of instruction in the morning and one in the evening, all conducted by Mr. Woodbridge, the only teacher. Courses included several academic subjects, lip-reading, and single-hand and double-hand sign language. In time, there was hope for some trades and industrial pursuits.

During the afternoon, students were free to amuse themselves in various ways, but only after domestic and farm chores were done. Local women were hired to do the heavier housework, but the girls would make the beds and work in the kitchen, all under the supervision of the matron of the school—Mrs. Woodbridge.

A hired man looked after the farm animals, the gardens, and the odd jobs. The boys assisted him wherever possible, and a list of duties was posted in their sitting room. Some of the big boys got up early to get the fires started, but everyone carried in wood, keeping all the woodboxes throughout the building well supplied.

There would be several incendiary tragedies in the brief history of the Woodbridge school. The first one occurred at Hawthorne Hill on Easter Monday, March 26, 1883. The fire began in the barn at the rear of the main building, giving a chance to save all the children and the furniture before it spread. However, when the fire was over, the first Hawthorne Hill school was totally destroyed. The lease was to have expired in May of that year, at which time the board had arranged to purchase the building.

The cause of the fire was never discovered, but years later there was speculation that it had been set by either one of the students or by an adversary of Albert Woodbridge. The professor was in Charlotte County that particular night, soliciting funds for the school's support. He returned to start anew, hoping one day to return to the Hawthorne Hill site.

The following week, with help from volunteers who came from all over Fredericton, the school re-opened at the nearby "Uplands" estate—on the other side of Forest Hill cemetery. It was a few minutes' walk from Hawthorne Hill and unoccupied at the time. The main building was small when it was owned by Attorney-General Charles J. Peters in 1832, but it was enlarged when army captain William L. Scarnell bought it in 1865. In 1883, it became the home for New Brunswick's hearing-impaired for the next eight years.

Hawthorne Hill was not far away and was not forgotten. During the early summer of each year, picnics were held "at the old place"; Woodbridge and the Board were eager to build a large school on the site; Senator Botsford was ready to sell the entire property for the very reasonable sum of $1000. But where would the money come from?

Shortly after the school was established at Uplands, a new teacher arrived from England to take charge of the elementary class. His name was George Ernest Powers, a nephew of Mrs. Woodbridge and a former assistant to Mr. Woodbridge when he travelled throughout Britain as a missionary for adult deaf mutes.

After teaching for three years, Powers became a collector for the school, travelling around the Maritime provinces, Upper Canada, and Maine, accumulating an impressive list of financial subscriptions. He then prepared a master list for publication in the school's annual report, of which 1,200 copies were printed and distributed around the country.

Unfortunately, many of the financial pledges were never paid. Thus, if Woodbridge were to rebuild at Hawthorne Hill, he would need to convince the provincial government to assist him. He succeeded, the first step being that the grant given to the Halifax school be withdrawn and given to the Fredericton School. The annual amount: one thousand dollars plus an additional five hundred dollars for expenses.

The return to Hawthorne Hill had begun, but in the midst of this good fortune came competition. As a result, Woodbridge was unjustly accused of harassing the management of a new hearing-impaired school in Saint John. The provincial government investigated and found that there was no evidence for the charges made. However, the damage was done and the press had a field day with the story and the unbelievable details.

Undaunted, Woodbridge had only one goal in mind: his new school. He designed it himself, and in keeping with the beautiful hillside location, the main building, capable of boarding sixty students, would be an ornament for the eastern part of the city.

Joshua Limerick of Fredericton was awarded the tender with a total cost of $10,400. Construction began in the spring of 1889 and the school was completed for a total of $13,000 in March of 1891. Barns and other outside buildings were built at an additional cost of $4,000.

The entire Botsford estate was brought back to life, including the gatehouse, the carriage shed, the stables, the fowl house, the wood shed, the orchard cottage, and a new bridge over a little brook. In the background were a cricket field, lawns for croquet, flower beds, vegetable gardens, and the scenic beauty of Silver Falls.

The main building (school and residence combined) measured fifty-six feet by sixty-five feet and was entirely brick with stone trimmings, elegant porticoes, and a French slate roof. Inside the foyer, the main hall measured thirty-six feet by twelve feet and extended to a handsome staircase that led to the second and third storeys and the basement.

From the ornate cupola on the very top of the building there was an unmatched view of the city, the river, and the surrounding countryside. When two sleigh loads of legislators visited on March 25, 1891, they were able to see the dome of the legislature in the south and the Marysville Cotton Mill in the north.

The provincial representatives were also able to see twenty-two students perform regular class work under the guidance of three assistant teachers, one of them Ernest Prince, a former pupil at the school who became one of the best-educated deaf mutes in New Brunswick, having received all his tutoring from Woodbridge.

In September of 1895, fire struck again and destroyed a large barn, which contained the season's crop of hay. In September of

1897, fire broke out yet again, this time in a basement storeroom. An hour later, flames were bursting through the roof of the main building, making it impossible to save anything. The pupils were all in their classrooms, getting their evening lessons, but they escaped without harm and were taken in by members of the community.

As with the fire at the former Botsford estate, Woodbridge was away, this time in Oromocto, where he received the news the next morning. He and his wife, their two sons and two daughters were once again without a permanent home. They were not discouraged and began immediately to plan for another school on the same Hawthorne Hill site. But the loss was considerable, and the building was insured for only five thousand dollars, the furniture for one thousand dollars.

In the midst of public controversy, temporary "regal" quarters were found at Old Government House, although the former governor's mansion was in great need of repairs after its long vacancy since 1890. The government agreed to a new zinc roof and allowed free rent, the school being subject to removal upon three months' notice. Any interior renovations had to be done at the expense of the school.

After the entire place was cleaned from top to bottom, all the rooms on the first and second floors were put into use, the large dining room as a general eating area for both staff and students, the beautiful ball room as a classroom with new desks and blackboards, and the bedroom suites as dormitories. The former library room and the music room were used for articulation classes, held by Miss Irene Woodbridge, daughter of the principal.

Public visitation took place on Monday and Thursday afternoons from two until four. On March 11, 1898, Lieutenant-Governor Abner Reid McClelan and his wife arrived with their entourage. They were so impressed with Government House and the Woodbridge School that a half holiday was granted to the students, who showed their appreciation by the hearty clapping of hands.

During the five-year occupancy at Government House, the annual closing and graduation exercises every June 25 became a major educational event in Fredericton. Hundreds of spectators attended to see the students being examined in all their subjects. Everyone was pleasantly surprised at the accomplishments.

Ironically and tragically, as the ceremony for 1902 was taking place, the following charges were being laid against the school staff by *The Saint John Telegraph*: financial mismanagement, inconsistent teaching, harsh and cruel treatment of students, immoral conduct.

A lengthy investigation and subsequent inquiry (some in camera) took place during the summer of that year by a royal commission. Surprisingly, the charges were proved correct, although there seemed to be many conflicting stories about what really happened. As a result, the school did not open on September 1. Eventually, it was permanently closed and the provincial government paid the outstanding debts. The forty-two students were enrolled in a new school in Saint John.

Albert Woodbridge, in his final public address as principal, spoke about his dream to rebuild his beloved Hawthorne Hill, and about the school's bitter enemies, "who have caused us considerable trouble, anxiety, and regret, in the loss of our buildings."

After the board accepted his resignation, he returned to live at Uplands, which had become his private residence. He died in 1921 and was buried in Forest Hill Cemetery. A small cross of white stone bears the place and date of his birth: Birmingham, England, 1843.

Albert Frederick Woodbridge, founder and principal of the Hawthorne School.

THE ALMS HOUSE AND THE GHOSTS OF CHRISTMAS PAST

DECEMBER 21, 2002

In 1885, the Alms House on York Street hill was renovated and enlarged, becoming a handsome residence with a combination wire-and-picket fence surrounding the entire property.

IN THE BEGINNING, it was to be a home for paupers, but it was soon filled with the aged, the infirm, and the insane.

In the beginning, it was to be called the Alms House and Work House, but eventually everyone was saying, "Let's go over the hill to the poor house."

The location was "in the rear of Fredericton," completely isolated at the top of York Street hill, above the railway depot, on eighteen acres of land purchased from the estate of Lieutenant-Colonel Harris William Hailes (the provincial administrator in 1817). On the property there was an abundance of stone for the walls of the main building, and slate for the roof. The barn, stable, wash house, and sheds would be constructed of wood.

The idea for the Alms House was conceived 180 years ago, plans being finalized in December of 1822. William Franklin Odell, provincial secretary, had placed a notice for tenders in *The Royal Gazette* that fall. He then invited the citizens of Fredericton and the surrounding area to view the plans at his office in the old government building that still stands on the east side of the legislature.

A year later, in the fall of 1823, the Alms House was ready, and thirty-five men, women, and children of all ages moved in, crowding together in a building that would never be large enough, the ordinary decencies of life scarcely being preserved.

According to the census of later years, these charges of the parish, many of whom could neither read nor write, were listed as "lodgers"; according to the local papers, they were "inmates." (In 1830, "a house of correction for rogues and vagrants" was to be built in connection with the Alms House but the idea was abolished.)

When Fredericton was incorporated in 1848, the administration of the Alms House changed from provincial to municipal. A city council committee (with the mayor as chairman) took care of the finances and made rare visits; a commissioner (appointed weekly by the committee) inspected the premises and handled complaints; a keeper (selected from several applications) lived at the Alms House with his family and ran the place from day to day.

Unfortunately, the three levels of administration did not always work in harmony for the betterment of the poor. As a result, shades of Dickensian England emerged from time to time.

One of the main responsibilities of the Alms House committee was the annual distribution of contracts. During the 1820s and 1830s, notices were placed in *The Royal Gazette*, requesting tenders for the following supplies: corn meal, rye flour, ship bread, and mackerel, all by the barrel; tea, barley, and rice, all by the pound; molasses by the gallon; salt by the bushel; candles by the dozen.

In later years, the final contracts were published in various Fredericton newspapers, proving there were no conflicts of interest or patronage appointments. The following is the list for 1902 (one hundred years ago): "Groceries, W. H. VanWart, replacing the company of Hatt & Morrison; bread, William Murphy; meat, John Chase; drugs, Alonzo Staples; attending physician, Dr. B. N. Mullin, replacing Dr. J. W. Bridges; undertaker, Geo. Adams."

Good food was served regularly and abundantly, but the following bill of fare caused some to complain and others to say, "We live like lords": for breakfast, a half pound of bread (with butter on Sunday) and a bowl of tea for each resident; for dinner, fish and potatoes or beef and potatoes, or soup, alternate days; for supper, Indian or oatmeal porridge, alternate days, with molasses or milk.

The position of commissioner eventually went from an honorary weekly appointment to a full-time job with an annual salary of $100. Prominent gentlemen in Fredericton filled the position, starting with bank president Henry George Clopper (1822), and ending with Magistrate Richardson H. Boone in the early 1900s. All were responsible for "binding out" the pauper children as apprentices, Commissioner Elijah Clark placing this notice in *The Reporter* in the spring of 1884: "Good homes are wanted for several children now in the Alms House. Country preferred. Apply at the Institution."

The first keeper of the Alms House was Joseph Fleming who, with his wife, Martha, remained in the position for over twenty-five years. They had come from Ireland with their children and, when Martha passed away in 1841 at age sixty-three, Joseph continued as keeper, with the assistance of his daughters. In the mid-1850s, he retired, his son John leaving a job as master steward at UNB's Old Arts Building and succeeding his father as keeper.

John Fleming and his wife, Jane, were keepers until 1875, at which time, both John and his father passed away, within five months of each other, leaving Jane alone as the keeper for seven more years. She retired in 1882.

The two Fleming families were at the Alms House for over half a century (fifty-six years). They were respected by everyone and were very popular with the poor, working long, hard hours with little assistance, never complaining about the annual salary—$300! Both Joseph and John raised their families at the Alms House on this amount, paying for occasional hired help and other expenses themselves.

The Flemings set high standards, cleanliness being a major concern, every effort being made to see that the people under their care were clean. On being admitted, all were compelled to wash themselves and put on fresh clothing—under the personal supervision of the keeper and his wife. Regular weekly baths and changes of clothing were then insisted upon.

The Flemings also expected the able-bodied lodgers to work for their meals and accommodation, insisting that the young men help with the farm chores and the gardens, the young women with the laundry. However, during her seven years as keeper, Mrs. John Fleming requested and received an additional fifty dollars annually, subsequently hiring two servant girls and a washerwoman.

When Richard H. Phillips, a printer with *The Gazette*, became keeper in 1882, the fifty dollars extra was withdrawn and the hired help discontinued. As a result, Phillips and his wife found it impossible to give the care that was needed. The deteriorating conditions in the sixty-year-old building became a headline news story, emphasizing that the Alms House was overrun with bedbugs, lice, and rodents.

Throughout 1884, the local papers gave Phillips an opportunity to defend himself as keeper of the Alms House. He wrote letters to the various editors and appeared before city council on several occasions, always saying that he had done the best he could, under the circumstances, always presenting specific details: "I think it highly important that there should be separate wards for the sick of both sexes and that nurses should be furnished. To give an idea of how much a hospital this institution is, I would say that nearly four hundred prescriptions have been written the past year. We have the aged, the sick, the lame, and the blind; we have unidentified babies and attempted suicides. There is no one to assist, except one female inmate, and she has temporary fits of insanity."

When editorials began to appear in support of Phillips, city officials became agitated, realizing they had neglected their duty in not investigating the dilapidated and disreputable conditions and for not providing enough financial support. In order to save face, they agreed to make some changes. And they did!

During the renovation period (summer and fall of 1885), the old cholera hospital, located one hundred yards directly below the Alms House, was used for temporary quarters. It had been built for the 1832 Canadian outbreak, but the disease did not reach Fredericton until 1854. When the new Alms House was ready, the cholera hospital was overhauled for any smallpox outbreak that might occur.

The extensive improvements on the Alms House cost $8,000, the once dreary building now being compared with all the fine residences in downtown Fredericton. Instead of paupers dreading to be admitted, it probably became a pleasure for them. In a letter to the editor, one ratepayer had this say: "I think the paupers will rapidly increase when they find everything is to be so fine." Another wrote: "I had no idea the people of Fredericton were to pay for a palace to put the poor in."

The inside of the old building, with its stained, streaked, smoky, and sooty walls, was completely torn down, but the four outside stone walls were left standing. The remodelled interior went from basement to attic, with a first and second floor in between. All four levels were supplied with plumbing and heating systems, the former connected with the City Water Works at lower York Street, the latter connected to three hot-air furnaces in the basement.

The kitchen (also in the basement, along with the pantry and the wood cellar) contained an open fireplace and a large range, both used for cooking and for heating the wash water. The iron sink in the kitchen measured forty-eight by twenty inches; a dumbwaiter was installed to transport meals to the floors above.

The two dining rooms (one for men, the other for women) were on the first floor, along with the doctor's office and a washroom. The second floor was strictly for females, the attic for males, both floors divided into three wards (each eighteen by ten feet), along with a dressing room, a washroom, and closets, everything plain and neat, the walls papered, the ceilings whitewashed.

In addition to the repairs on the old building, a spruce-clapboarded annex (twenty-one by forty feet) was attached to the front, both the old and new sections having similar mansard roofs with cedar shingles. The keeper and his family were to occupy the new wing as their residence, there being a parlour and dining room on the first floor, three bedrooms on the second, open space in the attic.

When the time came to move back, there were a number of applications for the keeper's position, but Alderman Patrick Farrell got the job, replacing a very disappointed Richard Phillips, who never wanted to be relieved of his duties.

In 1888, Albert Duncan Thomas became the last of the Alms House keepers and, for the next twenty-one years, he conducted a model institution. He was "the most economical manager" ever to fill the position, saving the city about $200 a year. By improving the gardens on the property, he was able to provide all the vegetables that were needed. The committee rewarded him with a $100 increase in pay! When he resigned in 1909, the name of the Alms House was changed to the Municipal Home.

Over the years, the monotonous life at the Alms House was broken only on Christmas Day. During the last half of the nineteenth century, it became the custom for philanthropic gentlemen of Fredericton to provide a sumptuous and bountiful Christmas dinner with all the trimmings, and a Christmas tree.

In 1874, Lieutenant-Governor Samuel Leonard Tilley contributed the dinner; in 1883, it was Lieutenant-Governor Robert Duncan Wilmot. Wealthy businessmen Adolphus FitzRandoph and James VanBuskirk also took a turn, as did every mayor voted into office. They not only covered the cost personally, but each gentleman and his wife visited during the noon hour feast on Christmas Day. Three cheers would be given for the mayor and three for Queen Victoria.

It was a time of enjoyment. The two dining halls were decorated with evergreens, wreaths, and flags. The serving tables literally groaned beneath the weight of several turkeys, large roasts of pork and beef, gravies, vegetables, and condiments. In the centre, a huge plum pudding was surrounded by mince pies, apples, oranges, raisins, candy, and walnuts—"without stint." Gleaming white porcelain dishes took the place of the everyday tin utensils.

Various societies and church groups visited throughout the day, presenting every man, woman, and child with Christmas cards, little presents, items of clothing, and the ubiquitous handkerchiefs. There was also the traditional donation made to each smoker—a generous supply of tobacco!

In 1888, Commissioner Elijah Clark gave special Christmas gifts: for each male inmate, a vest, pants, undershirt, drawers, top shirt, socks, and braces; for each female inmate, a number of yards of swan's-down, cotton, and tweed, the two former to be made into underclothes, the latter into dresses.

In 1902, only one resident remained in his room during the Christmas festivities. At age 104, John McNamara could not walk down the stairs. Instead, Mayor William Crocket visited the blind centenarian and found him cheerful, talkative, and smoking. McNamara was the oldest resident in the province at the time. Born in Ireland, he had come to Fredericton as a young boy. He died just before Christmas the next year at age 105!

Another interesting inmate in the early part of the twentieth century was John Driscoll, a Fredericton butcher, who had been tried for the murder of Private John Brennen (22nd Regiment) in 1868, but who was set free because his sister perjured herself in order to save him. Driscoll became seriously ill in the fall of 1906, and passed away at the Alms House on November 4. He was buried in the Hermitage Cemetery, not far from the memorial marker that bears the name of his victim.

Many others who died at the Alms House and who were not claimed by next of kin were buried in a potter's field just below the main building near York Street. There were no markers and, as the city developed, no remains were ever exhumed.

By the 1950s, the Municipal Home became the Hillcrest Home, operating as a private nursing facility until the building was demolished in April of 1970 to make way for a new combined fire and police station.

If there are any ghosts of Christmas past, they can probably be found today in the vicinity of Dundonald and York streets, where the Alms House was once located. However, the old registers are all that remain to be seen, and they are now preserved in the Provincial Archives. Heavy and musty, with a formidable "do not disturb" appearance, they contain columns of neatly penned names—a lasting memorial for the hundreds of paupers who once lived over the hill at the poor house.

City's Symbolic Hand 150 Years Old

June 8, 2002

In June of 1852, Fredericton was still recovering and rebuilding as a result of the horrendous fire that swept through the downtown area nineteen months earlier.

On November 11, 1850, at two o'clock in the afternoon, a barn beside the Methodist Church caught fire. The flames spread and, in a few minutes, the wooden church with the steeple, situated on the northwest corner of King and Carleton streets, was enveloped and destroyed.

The fire continued north towards Queen Street and south towards the Old Burying Ground, the wind carrying the flames eastward as far as St. John Street. When it was over, half of Fredericton was gone—eighteen acres of residential and business properties with two thousand homeless. Total damage: £100,000.

In this Madge Smith photo from the 1930s, three of the four tower pinnacles (with wire bracing) can be seen at the base of the steeple, each terminating in elegant finials. The tower is sixteen feet square with supporting buttresses at each corner. One of the four Gothic chimneys (now removed) is at lower left.

A number of elegant brick buildings began to rise from the ashes but, according to one newspaper reporter in June of 1852, "there is still a great deficiency of roof and side ladders throughout the city, and this should be enforced in a wooden town like Fredericton."

The congregation of the Methodist Church decided against brick or stone because of the cost. They began to build another church (Phoenix-like) on the same site—and it was to be the largest wooden church in the province (eighty-six by fifty-eight feet). It was also to be a splendid example of Gothic architecture both outside and within. Seating capacity: 1,200.

By June of 1852, the exterior was almost finished, except for the final feature—an ornament for the top of the steeple. Should it be a weather vane? A globe?

That summer, 150 years ago, a carved wooden hand of huge dimensions and over seven feet in length, including a four-foot index finger pointing heavenward, was added to the top of the hexagonal steeple, giving a total of 205 and one-half feet from the ground. It would be the highest point in the city and, for years to come, the hand would be the centre of attraction for locals and visitors alike.

The driving force behind the new church was a young Supreme Court judge whose name was Lemuel Allan Wilmot. He would eventually become the first New Brunswick-born lieutenant-governor of the province. At the Methodist Church, he would become the Sunday school superintendent and the choir director for the rest of his life. He was devoted to children and music and, in 1852, he was even prepared to mortgage his beautiful Evelyn Grove estate (corner of Aberdeen and Regent) to pay for the new church.

Fortunately, the mortgage was not necessary because annual summer bazaars, held on the grounds of Evelyn Grove, helped to cover the cost. In 1852, over 1,000 people from various Christian denominations in New Brunswick attended and were able to admire for the first time the superbly carved hand (created from a single white pine log) before its ascent to the lofty perch on top of the steeple.

The thumb in the carving also pointed upwards, but the other three fingers, measuring twenty-two inches across the knuckles, pointed down (in the symbolic direction of Hell). Because of this particular design, the Imperial troops in the Fredericton garrison nicknamed the hand "Thumbs Up," a label that has never been forgotten.

It is believed that Wilmot was responsible for the hand, engaging one of the best woodcarvers in the province for the job. His name was Edward Charters who, as a young man, had immigrated to Saint John from Dumfrieshire, Scotland. He became a respected member of the port city before retiring to Dumfries (above Fredericton), where he died in 1882 at the age of eighty-one.

It has been said that the Methodist Church in Fredericton was the first in North America (perhaps the entire world) to have a symbolic hand on a steeple. However, four others followed: a Presbyterian church in Port Gibson, Mississippi; a Baptist church in Annapolis Royal, Nova Scotia; a United church in Twillingate, Newfoundland; the Steeves-Black Memorial Church in Moncton, New Brunswick.

When the new Methodist Church in Fredericton was opened for worship in December of 1852, Judge Wilmot, whose interest, skill, and generosity made it possible, gave the reason for the hand in a verse of his own composition:

Hope, with angel finger spired
And pointing to the starry sky
Speaks in tones with inspiration fired,
The soul's great destiny.

During the lifetime of the steeple, several elaborate wooden stagings had to be wrapped around the tower and the spire so that repairs could be done. All of these stagings were costly and, although solidly built, they tended to waver in the wind. But the view from the top was magnificent!

The first was in 1861, just nine years after the church was finished. There was a slight lean to the steeple, and an investigation uncovered cracks in the interior bracing network caused by the shrinking of the green lumber that had been used (there was no kiln-dried lumber in the mid-nineteenth century).

Contractor James Agnew, a trustee of the church, and his crew of men worked throughout the month of October, tightening the braces, reinforcing with additional screws, and giving the hand three coats of paint. At times the wind was so strong that they had to stop for fear they would be blown off the staging.

Charles Moffatt, the well-known city carpenter whose detailed diaries survive, was a member of the crew. Each evening, he would record his day: "The zinc roofing has cracked and corroded. Tinning the spire of the Methodist Meeting House. Mended the zinc around the base of the hand. Gave the hand another coat."

A quarter of a century would pass before any further repairs were done to the steeple and the hand. In April of 1887, seven thousand dollars worth of staging was erected by local contractor William Scarr. From the foundation on the tower to the tip of the finger, no part of the steeple escaped the hammer and the paint brush.

During the 1887 staging, which remained for a fortnight, hundreds of interested citizens were allowed to climb the twenty ladders to the top of the steeple. Both men (in their black suits and bowler hats) and women (in their long black dresses and heeled boots) wanted to experience the ultimate thrill—grasping the famous landmark hand. However, the number of adventurers was so great that the building committee had to place restrictions.

First, going aloft so high required a very steady head and a lightweight body; in fact, several heavyweights immediately went on a fish diet. Second, contractor Scarr wanted no accidents, but he said (amusingly) that he had no objection to newspaper reporters going up, "for if one of them did fall, he wouldn't be missed from the large city staff."

Among the first members of Fredericton's male population to risk their lives at the peak were Reverend William Dobson (the Methodist minister), Honourable Frederick Thompson (a prominent businessman and future senator), Berton Foster (a young schoolteacher who would become principal of FHS), Dr. George Coulthard, David Hatt (merchant), P. E. Cliff (UNB graduate), and L. W. Johnston (merchant).

At the top, their eyes swept the horizon and they noticed farmers leisurely driving their horses and wagons towards the city from all directions. They also took in all the dirty backyards below and could hardly wait to tell the health inspector. But the close-up of the hand surpassed everything, especially the great detail of the carving, the various folds and each clearly defined and life-like fingernail.

When the workmen were absent from the site, there was no security, and this gave young boys a chance to climb to the top, not for the view but to carve their names and initials into the soft pine wood of the hand, especially the forefinger. Over one hundred years later, these so-called "bad boys" continue to be immortalized through a simple act of mischievousness: H. Chestnut (was it Henry or Harry?), WEM (William E. McMullen, who eventually became the Sunday school superintendent), HFM (Harry Fulton McLeod (who became a Fredericton mayor and a member of parliament), Geo. Estey (surveyor), W. Mowatt (Wilbert, son of the Presbyterian minister), S. MacLean (?), and CT (either Charles Taylor, son of the famous photographer, or Charles Thomas, another future mayor of Fredericton).

When they returned to the ground, the men and boys were constantly interviewed about their bravery, but they could say very little because the first woman to make the climb outdid them all and set a dangerous precedent at the same time. The newspapers gave her the headline A PLUCKY LADY.

Her name was Louise Thompson, the twenty-year-old daughter of Alexander and Mary Thompson of Douglas. She was vivacious and daring and, when she reached the top, she grasped the wooden forefinger with one of her hands, leaned sideways and, with her other hand, waved her large white handkerchief "at the admiring Lilliputians assembled below."

In 1916, the staging went up again, this time inside the steeple. An opening was cut near the top, several feet below the hand, and, through this portal, a small exterior platform was built, from which ladders were hauled up the side.

The painting of the tower, steeple, and hand began, the tower in white, the steeple in black, the hand in yellow. Unfortunately, one of the steeplejacks, inadvertently let his bucket fall, causing half the length of the steeple to be spattered with bright yellow paint, leaving an artistic trail from the hand above.

During the early 1920s, lightning struck the hand twice in one storm, but there was no subsequent fire or damage. The next lightning strike would not be until May 7, 1930, and the result was fire.

It was one of the sharpest electrical storms ever experienced in Fredericton, reaching its peak at 3:00 A.M., at which time a severe flash struck the wooden hand, leaving a plainly visible mark, causing people within blocks of the church to be alarmed at the thunderbolt of noise and the possibility of fire.

Police Sergeant William Hughes and patrolman Kenneth Foster were on duty and were the first to notice the crack of lightning hit the hand, followed by thin wisps of smoke. They telephoned the fire station but, by the time ladders were in position, a blaze in the church tower was getting out of control. Fortunately, extinguishers were able to put out the flames before much damage was done.

The unstable and dangerous condition of the hand became the centre of controversy in Fredericton. Fire Chief Roy W. Smith said that it should be condemned as a hazard, not only to the church but to the pedestrians below.

However, the congregation and many other supportive citizens were against the removal of the hand. Reason: "The famous landmark has sentimental value; it is one of the city's distinguishing symbols, which always interests visitors."

As a result, the steeple was "staged" for the first time in forty-three years in order for the damage to be investigated and repairs made. There was no intention of removing the hand; instead, it received a manicure as well as the addition of a lightning rod and a new coat of paint.

During the 1930 renovation, two of the church members ascended the steeple from inside, climbing to the eight-foot beam that supported the hand at the top. An interior staging was constructed and Harry M. Clarke and William E. McMullen, with the aid of bright lights, were able to carry out a thorough inspection for the congregation. Their findings: "The steeple and its timbers are in good condition and damage by the weather entirely minor."

This was not the case after another forty-three years had passed. In 1973, congregation member John Schwartz ascended the steeple from the inside and found severe deterioration, decay, leaking, and instability. After 122 years, it was time for the hand (now twenty-five inches off vertical plumb) to be removed and for the steeple to be dismantled.

The high cost of restoration was beyond the congregation and the city, even though a "Save the Finger Fund" did its best to preserve the historic spire. On June 26, 1974, hundreds of spectators witnessed the end of a famous city landmark.

The bell tower was saved and repaired. And so was the hand. Today, it is on display in a glass case at the back of the church nave (southeast corner). Diagonally opposite, at the front of the nave, is a white marble bust of Lemuel Allan Wilmot, the man whose idea it was to have a symbolic hand on the steeple, and for whom the church was named in 1925 (following church union).

In this sesquicentennial year of Wilmot United Church, the hand will be admired for its history—how it was once the focal point for early land surveyors; how fledgling airmen in World War Two were tempted to "buzz" its soaring finger; how it was adopted and became well known symbolically by the Billy Graham movement; how it was eulogized in newspapers and periodicals across North America.

Because of its indigenous architecture, its unique history, and its 150-year survival in the middle of a growing city, the majestic wooden church itself has long been considered an important Canadian landmark.

Thus, this is the year to make it official and have the Wilmot United Church designated as a National Historic Site.

YORK COUNTY COURT HOUSE SYMBOL OF BYGONE ERA

JUNE 7, 2003

The York County Court House from Queen Street in the 1960s, showing the extensive renovations that had been made to the doors and windows over the years.

THE IDEA FOR THE AUSTERE Georgian-style building that still stands on lower Queen Street (directly across from Camperdown Lane and overlooking the St. John River) was conceived 150 years ago in the midst of controversy.

Although authorization was given, the city of Fredericton and the county of York spent the summer of 1853 locked in heated debate over the proposed architecture, the tenants, and the uses for a new York County courthouse.

However, the story really begins in 1814, when a Loyalist merchant by the name of James Taylor built a large wooden market house on the future site of the county courthouse. According to *The Royal Gazette*, "Taylor's Market House in front of a ferry landing is superior to anything of the kind in this or perhaps any other Province."

The two-and-a-half-storey structure was built with local lumber, and when finished, measured eighty feet by forty feet. The crowning feature was a tower with an iron railing, "a handsome ogee," and a fourteen-foot spire extending to an ornate weathercock. The view of the river and the surrounding landscape was magnificent.

In 1817, the York County Council purchased the Taylor building for the county's first courthouse, using the second floor as the courtroom, and leaving the ground floor for a public market. The original land grant (now preserved in the provincial archives) states that the site was to be reserved for a market in perpetuity. Thus, the name Market Square was born, but the amalgamation of court and market under one roof would soon create serious problems.

In the meantime, the spacious second floor would serve not only as a courtroom but also a school room, a meeting place, and even a ballroom. According to *The Gazette*, the garrison ball and midnight supper on January 27, 1836, was a grand success: "The Ball and Supper rooms were splendidly decorated, in a style that could not be surpassed, and the whole illuminated with wax lights....The delightful band of the 43rd was in attendance—the music was of the first order. Dancing of waltzes and quadrilles commenced at nine o'clock and continued without intermission until three o'clock in the morning."

During the disastrous Fredericton fire of November 11, 1850, the county courthouse was miraculously left untouched as every building across the street burned to the ground. A century later, local historians were still believing the rumours about the old wooden courthouse going down in the fire, but the first evidence of its survival occurred in a subsequent issue of *The Reporter* newspaper: "At a public meeting held in the Court House this 12th day of Nov., 1850, to take into consideration the means of relieving the sufferers by the fire of yesterday, His Excellency, Lieutenant-Governor Edmund Walker Head was in the Chair."

On November 23, a second meeting was held "at the County Court House in Fredericton" to continue with assistance for the fire victims. The lieutenant-governor was again in the chair and John Campbell Allen (a future chief justice) was secretary. The meeting was addressed by Judge George Frederick Street (the survivor of the famous duel with George Ludlow Wetmore), the Honourable John Simcoe Saunders (a future president of the Legislative Council), the Honourable Charles Fisher (a future Father of Confederation), His Worship John Simpson (the first mayor of Fredericton), Bishop John Medley, and several other gentlemen.

As Fredericton began to rebuild with brick and not wood, York County councillors began to consider a new brick building for the combined court and market at Market Square. There was also the growing competition from the popular market in City Hall at Phoenix Square.

As a result, the "uptowners" patronized the upper market and tried to influence the city council, the "downtowners" the lower market, supporting the county council. Each side felt there should be only one market in Fredericton. The issue turned into a heated debate.

By the summer of 1852, there was another problem: the old colonial building at Market Square was deteriorating so badly that there were calls for its immediate demolition. The presiding judges and the officers of the Crown agreed, having continually experienced heavy drops of rain falling on their heads from the cracked ceiling above. *The Reporter* was so ashamed of "this wretched old building" that it started a campaign to have it replaced: "Indeed, the individuals who occupy the lower and best flat of the Court House as a Butchers' Stall declare that it is getting utterly unfit for their purposes; but the effluvia which finds its way from the meat stalls renders the upper flat—the seat of justice—quite intolerable in warm weather."

On January 13, 1853, the York Bench of Magistrates voted unanimously for a new courthouse, stating "the *thing* which at present bears the name is not fit even for the Butchers' shambles which occupy its lower storey." However, they did not all agree with the proposed site, voting seventeen to fourteen in favour of the ground occupied by the old market house.

When Judge Street opened the 1853 summer session of the court, he began his remarks by emphatically condemning the building and then urging the members of the grand jury to use their influence with the proper authorities to get something done without delay "to relieve us all from the nuisance of this building."

The provincial legislature agreed and provided a grant towards the expense of a new courthouse—without the market. The city council hesitated to assist financially because it was in favour of having the market downtown to have more land. The county council debated the issue, but in the end, the plans once again incorporated a market on the ground floor, satisfying the original land grant.

It was not until 1855 that construction began. It was to be a two-storey, red-brick building, unpretentious and measuring 110 feet by 47 feet. It was completed two years later. It had three entrances on the front facade facing Queen Street and three at the rear facing the river. Thus, at each end there was a main double door flanked by smaller arched doorways with fanlights on either side.

With the market and council chamber occupying the ground floor, and the courtroom, jury room and judge's chambers on the second floor, the new building was unable to provide offices for the clerk of the peace, the county registrar, the auditor, the county treasurer, and the recorder. Unfortunately, they were located all over Fredericton and, according to *The Capital* newspaper, "those who had county business to transact had to plod from one end of the city to the other."

It would be twenty-five years before the combination of market and court in the same building came to an end. During that time, the grim conditions on the ground floor became progressively worse until the market ceased altogether in the early 1880s and was converted into six large offices for county officials and a vault for county records. At this time, the provincial courts were also accommodated in the courthouse because Province Hall at Parliament Square had been destroyed by fire.

The York County Court House would not undergo renovations again until the early 1950s, when glass bricks were placed in the windows of the upper storey, and the doors on either side of the main front and rear entrances were replaced by round-headed windows similar to those on the sides. The large rear entrance was eventually replaced by a window (later bricked in), and an exterior door was added on each side of the first floor.

In this unique building, magistrates, sheriffs, coroners, lawyers, and judges continued to administer justice and supervise local affairs. Elected county councillors continued to meet here for their week-long, semi-annual sessions, two each from the fourteen parishes of York County: Bright, Canterbury, Douglas, Dumfries, Kingsclear, McAdam, Manners Sutton, New Maryland, North Lake, Prince William, Queensbury, St. Mary's, Southampton, and Stanley.

In this building, grand balls continued to be given by local clubs, the large courtroom being transformed by elaborate decorations for various themes. The judge's platform was occupied by the orchestra; the barristers' room was used for card tables; the supper tables were laid in the grand jury room.

In contrast, the courthouse became the setting for bitter conflicts between the city and the county. Who was to have control of the former Market Square and the adjoining Court House Landing? Who was to protect the hay-weighing scales (in front of the courthouse) from constant vandalism and theft? Researching early legislation, members of the municipality of York discovered that the landing, the square, and the street were all under control of the county.

There were times when differences were set aside and the city councillors would host a dinner for the county councillors. Members of the provincial legislature would also be invited, and the reporters who were hired to cover the county council sessions were included as well. It was an all-male get-together where dozens of toasts were proposed and lengthy responses were given.

By the 1920s, the county was once again neglecting to maintain the entire Court House Square, as it came to be called. There was still a difference of opinion as to who should care for the property and make improvements, or even revive the outdoor market tradition of yesteryear. As a result, on October 3, 1927, the city council passed a motion to restore the square and maintain it perpetually—sending all bills to the county council!

The city and county councils would eventually join forces in 1964 for a history-making meeting in the courthouse to consider the matter of expanding the facilities at the overcrowded Victoria Public Hospital. Both councils pledged financial backing, hoping to alleviate the waiting list of 930 patients for 230 beds.

However, it was not the role of the York County Council that attracted the most attention. It was the courtroom drama that made the headlines as the courthouse continued to be the seat of county justice and sometimes unexpected tragedy.

In November of 1882, the infamous Lee brothers, George and Newton, were tried, found guilty, and then sentenced to twenty years in Dorchester Penitentiary for the shooting and wounding of Fredericton police sergeant Dow VanDine (with intent to commit murder), the crime precipitating one of the most dangerous chases throughout the city.

In December of 1916, Frederick St. John Bliss, judge of the York County Probate Court and secretary-treasurer of the York County Council, took his life at age fifty-four in a locked office on the second floor; the gun shot resounded throughout the courthouse, the city and the county. There was deep mourning for the unexplained loss.

At the end of World War One, Major Werner Von Horne, a spy for the German government, was tried and found guilty in the York County Court House. The charge: blowing up the international railway bridge over the St. Croix River at Vanceboro, Maine. The sentence: ten years in Dorchester Penitentiary.

The St. Croix bridge was Canadian property and, because of the damage done by the nitroglycerin explosives that were used, Von Horne's maximum penalty should have been life imprisonment. However, the York County judge was lenient, noting that the prisoner had waited until after midnight—when all passenger trains had passed over!

In the spring of 1949, the courthouse was the scene of a double trial, involving the Hamilton brothers, George and Rufus (of Barker's Point), for the grisly murder of Fredericton taxi driver

Norman Burgoyne. The separate trials were witnessed by packed courtrooms, and the two guilty verdicts led to the last hanging (the brothers back to back) in the capital city in July of that year.

The most dramatic event connected with the courthouse was yet to be. It occurred in 1966 when all county councils in New Brunswick were abolished as part of the centralization program known as Equal Opportunity, instituted by the Liberal government of Premier Louis Robichaud.

In July of that year, the York County Council met for the last time and unanimously approved a motion to investigate the possibility of having the courthouse turned over to the newly formed corporation known as York County Properties. Protection and preservation of the past became a priority as a political era, an honourable tradition, and a splendid institution came to an end.

In January of 1967, Canada's centennial year opened locally with a farewell dinner to honour all the York County councillors who had served for the past 111 years (the royal charter incorporating an elective council, having been established in 1855). The event took place in the capital city and almost one hundred councillors attended, including Stanley Dixon from McAdam (now living in Fredericton), who called the dinner the "Last Supper."

Various provincial government departments have since occupied the York County Court House; today, the departments of Public Safety and Information Technology have the entire building.

Inside, the huge doorways, the high ceilings, and the ornate woodwork from the early years are still plainly visible, as is the large courtroom and the council chamber, both now divided into small offices.

Outside, on the front wall, a distinctive plaque from the Historic Sites and Monuments Board of Canada recognizes the architecture, the heritage, and the symbolism of the old York County Court House.

FINAL CURTAIN: THE STORY OF TWO OPERA HOUSES

MARCH 31, 2001

Pauline Johnson, when she played the City Hall Opera House in Fredericton.

Oscar Wilde, when he played the City Hall Opera House in Fredericton. He is wearing the fur-trimmed coat that he purchased in Canada.

IN THE LATE 1800S, the small population of Fredericton supported two large opera houses and, according to the press of the day, there was never an empty seat.

These elaborate theatres were designed for travelling opera companies, local and visiting drama productions, musical concerts, lecture series, and special events.

Both "houses" were located downtown, just off Queen Street, one in the West End, the other at Phoenix Square. Although there was competition, each had its fair share of patrons.

On November 8, 1876, the City Hall Opera House opened on the second floor of the present City Hall. And what a grand opening it was, the program committee having planned months in advance for an inauguration concert.

Professor Edward Cadwallader of the Provincial Normal School wrote the words and music for the opening song—"We Greet you, Loyal Citizens." Published in Fredericton by the Charles Lawson Printing Company, a copy of this sheet music is preserved today at the Provincial Archives.

No expense was spared for the new hall, which measured 60 by 115 feet, including the foyer and the stage. The plastering and the cornice work were done by a large crew of master artisans; the heavy moulding on the ceiling was enhanced by two reflectors, instead of the chandelier that was planned originally.

The stage, framed with an ornate proscenium, was twenty-two feet deep and twenty-seven feet wide. The orchestra seats and the horseshoe balcony provided accommodation for eight hundred. It was one of the largest and handsomest auditoriums in the province and, for the next sixty years, some of the best talent from North America and abroad would perform there.

On October 4, 1882, Oscar Wilde "drew a large audience" when he lectured on the decorative arts. "The reserved seats were all taken, and the body of the house well filled." The celebrated Irish playwright, poet, and essayist did not mind that a group of boisterous UNB students in the front row had fun as they agreed with his aesthetic philosophy.

Under the patronage of the lieutenant-governor and the mayor, some of the world's leading theatre companies arrived in Fredericton to perform at City Hall. Each troupe would remain several days and would present a different production each night. *The Reporter* and *The Capital*, the two major newspapers at the time, provided top billing space and then gave lengthy reviews.

The 1883–84 season alone included the Kellogg-Brignoli Opera & Concert Company, the Egleston English Opera Company, the New York Windsor Theatre Company, and the Stafford-Foster Grand Shakespearian Revival Company. Tickets were sold at three Queen Street bookstores—McMurray's, Fenety's, and Hall's. Each had floor plans for reserved seating; the prices ranged from fifty to seventy-five cents.

However, some of the first-class touring companies were giving Fredericton the cold shoulder because the City Hall Opera House had a small "packing-box" stage. There was no money in the treasury, but taxpayers requested improvements. A large stage meant more revenue and better entertainment.

In the fall of 1884, alterations to the stage and gallery began and were completed for a citizens' re-opening concert on December 30. The packed house was disappointed with the fifty-member chorus from the city but not with the renovations.

The stage was now the full width of the hall and ten feet deeper; a staircase in one corner led to new dressing rooms in the storey below. The ends of the gallery were removed and the remaining seats raised, affording a full view of the performers. Four drop curtains, made especially for the new stage, each with a different scene, were ordered from a Chicago company.

The City Hall Opera House was ready once again to be the major venue for live entertainment. But it would not be for long.

On April 11, 1887, Lee's Opera House opened on the second floor of a large livery stable on Westmorland Street. It was the brainchild of Alexander Lee, a local boy who returned home after twenty years in New York, bringing grandiose plans for Fredericton's operatic and theatrical future.

Inside, the entire space over the livery coach house (but not the stable) was transformed into the seating area, measuring seventy by forty feet. The six hundred seats were elevated on a gradual incline from the front of the hall to the back.

To provide a stage that would not be surpassed anywhere in Canada, a section was added to the building. It was forty feet wide and twenty-six feet deep, with a twenty-two-foot proscenium opening. It contained modern dressing rooms, six drop curtains (painted by Fredericton artist John Eggar), and a control panel for the entire gas-lighting system throughout the hall (overhead globes, gasoliers, side reflectors).

Outside, over the main entrance, there was an eighteen-foot-long balcony where the Fredericton Brass Band, under the direction of J. W. Williamson, would greet theatregoers and provide background music until curtain time. Over the balcony, there was a ten-foot-long sign with LEE'S OPERA HOUSE in gold letters.

For the grand opening, Lee engaged James J. Campbell's Comedy & Specialty Company from New York, including the celebrated clog dancing of Gilson and Miles. The performance was to run every evening for a week but, on the third night, Lee closed

LEE'S OPERA HOUSE, - F'ton.

MONDAY EVE'NG
March 26th

BOSTON
COMEDY CO'Y

H. PRICE WEBBER, - - - - MANAGER

MONDAY EVENING, March 26th, '88,

Will be performed the World's Famous Drama

FANCHON
The Cricket!

FANCHON, The Cricket, ... EDWINA GREY
FATHER BARBEAUD, a Rich Farmer, ... EUGENE J. SULLIVAN
LANDRY, } Twin Brothers, ... H. W. FARISH
DIDIER, } .... H. PRICE WEBBER
FATHER CAILLARD, ... J. K. MILLS
ETIENNE, ... OWEN CARROLL
MARTINEAU, ... W. H. BEDELL
COLIN, ... PAUL CARROLL
MOTHER BARBEAUD .... MRS. SUMMERS
OLD FADET, the Witch, ... Mrs. H. C. HILLMAN
MADELON CAILLARD, ... BLANCHE HILLMAN

Act 1.--The Shadow Dance.
Act 2.--St. Andoche Festival.
Act 3.--The Will-o'-the Wisp.
Act 4.--The Witch of Cosse.
Act 5.--One Year Later.

PEOPLE'S POPULAR PRICES:
Admission 15, 25 and 35cts.
Seats Reserved in advance, WITHOUT EXTRA CHARGE, at the usual place.
Doors open at 7 1-4. - - - - - - To commence at 8 o'clock

Change of Programme Nightly

Located in the UNB library archives, this is one of nine different handbills preserved from Lee's Opera House.

the show and refunded the ticket money when city council demanded a five-dollar tax for each time the curtain went up.

The people of Fredericton were angry and severely condemned the city's action. As a result, the problem was settled immediately and Lee's Opera House re-opened to become one of the finest theatres in Canada, even superior in ambience and entertainment to the City Hall Opera House. Unfortunately, it was to have a life span of only six years.

At two in the morning, on August 12, 1893, arsonists set fire to the three-storey building. The entire population of Fredericton turned out to witness the most disastrous blaze in the city since the establishment of the water works ten years earlier. Lee's Opera House was levelled. Because it had not been in operation for some time, it was not insured.

Several other public buildings went with it, including John Palmer's Tannery, Parson's Hotel, Dunphy's Hotel, and the Gaunce Livery Stable. Private dwellings and barns were also destroyed. Total loss: $16,000.

There appear to be no surviving photographs of Lee's Opera House and the only memorabilia seem to be nine handbills in the UNB Library Archives. Five are from Brennan & Quinn's Star Theatre Company, three from the Boston Comedy Company, and one for the Irish melodrama "More Sinned Against than Sinning" as performed by Fredericton Home Talent.

The City Hall Opera House never had to compete with a similar theatre again, but this good fortune was not taken for granted. Although the lessees changed over the years, the high calibre of entertainment remained.

On June 3, 1897, the great march king John Phillip Sousa and his forty-six-member band arrived in Fredericton by special train at 6:00 P.M. Two hours later, one of the world's most famous composers and conductors directed a brilliant program before a packed house. A great part of the pleasure was in watching how Sousa remained nonchalant and happy, flinging sheets of music from the podium into the mouths of the instruments in front of him.

At the start of the twentieth century, two improvements were made regarding fire safety. The opera house was wired for electric lights and, at the same time, a steel fire escape, leading from a window, was attached to each side of the building. But, in order to climb down the escapes, patrons had to climb up to the window sills. Better protection for the stage involved the installation of a water pipe with fifty feet of hose attached to it.

Poetry readings were major events, an entire evening of entertainment for the large audiences. When William Henry Drummond recited from his best-seller *The Habitant and Other French-Canadian Poems* on March 29, 1901, Winters' local orchestra and the College Glee Club shared the program.

On April 20, 1908, the Mohawk poet Pauline Johnson stood on the stage and gave a passionate two-hour recital relating to her native background and the beauty of the Canadian wilderness. Understanding the theatrical appeal of her ancestry, Johnson appeared in a buckskin costume with bear-claw necklace and beaded moccasins. "The audience was delighted and greeted her again and again with hearty applause."

The most successful week's run in the history of the opera house was that of the Myrkle-Harder Drama Company in March of 1909—setting the record at $1,200. Manager William Harder was so enthusiastic over Fredericton as a show town that he expressed a willingness to take two-thirds interest, with local capital, in building a new theatre. The offer from the wealthy showman was never accepted.

On its own, the opera house proved to be a profitable proposition for city council. Top attractions continued to be booked months ahead, and there was something for everyone.

Comedy was always a winner, whether it was the Billy Van Minstrels or a one-man show with Arthur Lloyd, the celebrated British comedian. He was a favourite of the Prince of Wales and appeared regularly at Marlborough House before his successful run in Fredericton.

Two of the world's leading violinists made separate appearances before fashionable audiences: Mary Hall came from England, bringing a Stradivarius that had been played by the great Paganini and that had been purchased for £1,600 from the royal collection; Princess Lily Dolgorouky was a member of Russia's royal circle and, following her performance, the sad story of her personal life read like a soap opera on the pages of *The Daily Gleaner.*

A spectacular underwater act from the New York Hippodrome featured a bevy of bathing beauties in acrobatic, swimming, and diving feats. They brought with them a tank that covered half the stage and was filled with 4,500 gallons of water.

Although some of the performers missed their bookings, the major problems were with the local audiences. It was a house rule that all ladies had to remove their hats after taking their seats. Some refused, especially when the spring millinery openings encouraged the pleasure of exhibiting the latest styles in head-gear.

Another situation began exactly one hundred years ago when the controversial drama *A Bachelor's Honeymoon* made it to the stage without censorship. According to the review, "There are a few coarse suggestions and one or two vulgarities in the farce that a refined audience does not enjoy."

When the first motion pictures came to Fredericton, they were shown at the opera house. Curious crowds were fascinated with outdated news events that included the Spanish-American War, President McKinley's funeral, the coronation of Edward VII, the death of Pope Leo XIII, and the Jeffries-Sharkey boxing match (which Fredericton was the first to present in Canada).

As film improved and movie theatres were built, the opera house could not compete. The travelling companies stopped coming; the Empire Day programs, the temperance rallies, and the political gatherings moved elsewhere. The last big event was a combined band concert in 1938. The grand old hall began to deteriorate.

In March of 1942, the opera house was closed until after the war. In February of 1944, it was officially condemned by the fire marshall as being unsafe for public assemblies. Following a fire at the back of the stage in 1948, part of the hall was made into offices. In 1975, the opera house became the current council chamber.

Today, it is difficult to imagine that this same room was once the centre of Fredericton theatrical life, where command performances were given on a number of occasions: on August 15, 1887, the Redmund-Barry Company for Sir John and Lady Macdonald; on June 2, 1893, the Tyrone Power Company for Prince Roland Bonaparte, grand-nephew of the great Napoleon.

As with Lee's Opera House, very few artifacts have surfaced from that particular era. The Provincial Archives does have an original program for the Swiss Bell Ringers, who performed on December 4, 1883, and one for John Phillip Sousa. There are also six surviving tickets, each stamped CITY OPERA HOUSE—three for balcony seats, three for orchestra.

THE RISE AND FALL OF THE BARKER HOUSE HOTEL

SEPTEMBER 28, 2002

The Barker House lobby with the hotel clerk in the background behind the counter and the famous Coleman frog in the foreground inside the case.

IN ITS DAY IT WAS ONE OF THE MOST POPULAR and colourful hotels in North America and an essential feature in Fredericton's commercial and public life.

According to legend, gangster Al Capone once stayed there; President Grover Cleveland was supposed to have been a guest; and, in the lobby, a giant green frog was stuffed, mounted, and preserved for all to see.

For over one hundred years, passengers arriving in Fredericton by stagecoach, steamship, or railway heard the familiar greeting, "Stay at the Barker." They did, and the reasons were evident.

The location was one of the best on Queen Street, directly across from Officers' Square and the St. John River. On the west side, the Barker House Lane (later Alley) ran between the hotel and the Sharkey building and led to the well-equipped Barker House stables near King Street. In time, the adjoining Grosvenor building on the east side would become part of the hotel.

Spafford Jedediah Barker was the builder and first owner, acquiring the lot in 1834 at age twenty-four and constructing a small wooden hostelry. After it burned in the great Fredericton fire of 1850, he started to rebuild the next year, this time a four-and-one-half-storey structure entirely of brick, the main part fifty feet square, and a large wing in the rear fifty-eight feet by thirty feet.

When the doors of this major hotel opened in May of 1853, the gentlemen's front entrance from Queen Street led up a flight of stairs (seven feet wide) to the first landing. On one side was the gentlemen's parlour, on the other an elegant dining room, both furnished in black walnut and mahogany.

The ladies had a private entrance on Queen Street, leading directly to the second floor and the ladies' parlour. The third floor had small private parlours and bedrooms; the fourth, bedrooms only, giving a total of sixty-seven rooms throughout, each with ornate plaster mouldings outlining the high ceilings. There were thirteen fireplaces.

The wing in the back contained the kitchen, pastry room, pantries, keepers' rooms, and several bedroom suites. The entire building was supplied abundantly with gas (for the ceiling lamps) and water (for the porcelain basins), the latter being conveyed by pipes "into the most intimate parts of the premises." Each floor had one public bathroom.

City council was so impressed that it presented Barker with a silver tea service for his beautiful home on upper George Street. Thus, the grandson of a Loyalist lieutenant in the King's American Regiment had become one of the city's most prominent citizens. He was also president of the local Gas Light Company, and a director of the British North America Bank.

However, a year after the hotel opened, it became the setting for a political controversy that went down in history as "the Barker House Conspiracy," the result of a major power struggle between the members of the legislature and the lieutenant-governor, the rallying cry being "responsible government." A large number of politicians stayed at the Barker House, where they planned their strategy and signed a document that would bring down the government with a vote of non-confidence following the Speech from the Throne.

Undaunted, Spafford Barker continued to attract Fredericton's finest to his hotel, and all visiting dignitaries were representative of the educated and wealthy upper class. The hotel also became the headquarters for many local organizations, the Society of Saint Andrew holding its annual dinner during the last half of the nineteenth century and into the twentieth at "the Barker."

Although the hotel was built to endure (the outer walls were 20 inches thick; the inside partitions were lined with brick), improvements and additions were eventually needed. In 1861, city council granted permission to lay a sewer from the hotel to the river; in 1867, Spafford Barker opened a separate dry goods and grocery store on the ground floor, facing Queen Street, next to the alley.

General maintenance was another challenge and, as a result, local carpenter Charles Moffitt was hired as one of the regular handymen. Each evening he kept a detailed diary (preserved today in the UNB Archives) and commented on his work of the day. During the 1860s, he "stopped" the rat holes, cleared snow off the roof, rebuilt stalls at the stables, mended chairs, cleaned ice from the gutters, repaired blinds, and fixed the stage of the flag pole.

On April 19, 1865, Moffitt wrote: "Flag at Barker House half mast high in respect for President Lincoln who is to be buried today." This gesture was very important to Barker, who was the American consular agent in Fredericton.

On March 7, 1867, Moffitt wrote that he was "at Barker House, putting up partition to form pantry for Mrs. Orr, and shifting nest of drawers and pot closet." Mr. and Mrs. Robert Orr worked and lived at the hotel; she was the matron in the kitchen, he was the manager of the stables. Their dedication helped to establish the hotel as one of Fredericton's famous and profitable landmarks. But it did not last.

During the 1870s, Spafford Barker lost on a major investment and was forced to mortgage the hotel to the Central Fire Insurance Company. In 1880, this company took over the Barker House. Spafford died six years later and was buried in the Old Burying Ground beside his first wife and their infant son.

During the 1880s, a young businessman from Saint John, Fred B. Coleman, managed the hotel and, in 1889, purchased the business from the insurance company for fourteen thousand dollars. The name Barker House remained but many other changes took place as the hotel began to grow once again.

The interior was painted, varnished, carpeted, and refurnished throughout. When a hot-water heating system was installed, the Barker House became one of the best-heated hotels in the Maritimes. Every room was provided with a radiator, by which each guest could regulate individual temperature. Total cost: $3,000!

Coleman was determined to push the hotel business as he never had before. He made a new departure by fitting up one portion of the Barker House expressly for permanent boarders, among the conveniences, "a gorgeously furnished sitting room for their special use." The advertisement read: "Moderate terms. The best of satisfaction guaranteed."

At the same time, the well-known Barker House stables entered into a new era of prosperity under the management of A. N. LaForest. The livery stable keepers were prepared to furnish any kind of "trap" that might be needed by hotel guests or the trade of the city. The large barns at the end of the alley housed twenty-eight horses and stored hacks, buggies, spindle wagons, and sunshaded phaetons for summer, and the best line of sleighs and pungs for winter. A new coach, richly upholstered, with hangings about the windows, was acquired for family ventures.

In 1885, Fred Coleman leased a large property at Heron Lake (probably named for Scottish settler William Heron), four miles north of Fredericton and built a well-appointed summer hotel. He spent thousands of dollars beautifying the property, stocking the lake with fish, and planting orchards, and named his proposed resort—Killarney. However, it was not as successful as he had anticipated, but the name stayed and so did the Killarney Lake legend of the Coleman frog.

The frog, according to Coleman, jumped into his boat while he was fishing and became a well-fed pet for the next eight years, eventually weighing in at thirty-eight pounds! When the frog died, it was sent to a taxidermist in Bangor, Maine, and was returned to be exhibited for many years in the Barker House lobby, becoming an attraction for the locals and the tourists as the amusing story spread throughout North America. (In 1961, Coleman's daughter-in-law donated the frog to the York/Sunbury Museum, and the legend continued.)

Another story about Fred Coleman was not as flattering and might have led to his early demise. In the late 1880s, a local clergyman accused the Barker House proprietor of "rumselling" in a Fredericton newspaper called *The Religious Intelligencer.* Coleman fought back with letters to the editor in *The Capital* newspaper, but he could not deny the fact that he had been charged with four offences in relation to the Canada Temperance Act (which made it illegal to sell intoxicating beverages at hotels).

He was subsequently arrested in June and served a two-month sentence in the York County Gaol during the summer of 1890. Because the Barker House could not operate without his expert administration, the hotel was closed until July 28, at which time an OPEN sign appeared in the window, and a circular distributed by Coleman announced the re-opening: "During my visit in the Palace of Retribution, I have caused my agents to have the Barker House thoroughly renovated, adding many modern improvements which will tend to the greater comfort and convenience of my patrons."

It had been a summer of sympathy for the popular Barker House Hotel, the New Brunswick railway even dropping a coach from all its passenger trains to Fredericton. But the affable Fred Coleman continued to gain respect and admiration; the community even presented him with new flags for the front of his building.

When he died suddenly on July 20, 1901, at age fifty-four, all Fredericton mourned, especially the poorer children of the city, over one hundred of them having looked forward to his annual dinner on New Year's Day, a feast that reflected "the highest credit upon one catering to a company of most distinguished persons."

His funeral began at the Barker House and then moved to St. Anne's Parish Church, the mile-long procession being led by the 71st Regiment Band (playing "The Dead March in Saul"). Crowds lined both sides of the streets and along the road to the Rural Cemetery, where he was buried in the Coleman plot.

He left behind a wife, two sons, and a daughter. The oldest son, Chauncey, at age twenty-two, became the capable new proprietor and manager of the Barker House, his only experience being that of the hotel's clerk. For the next six years, this youthful engineer, musician, athlete, and inventor managed the business.

In 1907, Chauncey leased the hotel to Fredericton alderman Terence Vincent Monahan for eighteen years and then returned as manager himself until 1949. At that time he sold to Joseph Arthur Cain, a Fredericton hardware merchant and the last major owner of the Barker House.

The Monahan years experienced big changes, beginning with additional rooms by leasing floors in the adjoining buildings. Doors were cut through the brick walls of the (Samuel) Grosvenor House, and a catwalk was constructed across the alley to the (James) Sharkey Block. The result was a total of eighty-six guest bedrooms, each with fumed oak furniture, half with private baths.

A double suite of rooms in the new annex was immediately occupied by Lieutenant-Governor Josiah Wood and his family during his term in office (1912–1917). "Neither pains nor expense" was spared in fitting up the private gubernatorial suite with mahogany furniture and solid brass beds. The handsome state barouche was kept nearby in the Barker House stables.

Premier James Kidd Flemming and members of his cabinet occupied various other suites in the annex. (As a rule, the Conservatives patronized the Barker House; the Liberals, the Queen Hotel farther down the street.) Following the openings of the legislature, official receptions would take place in the governor's rooms, 175 ladies and gentlemen generally attending; state dinners would take place in the brilliantly decorated dining room, with about 30 gentlemen as guests.

A new brick addition at the rear of the main hotel, sixty feet long and two storeys high, provided for a gentlemen's writing parlour, a smoking and reading room, a barber shop, a conference hall, sample rooms for commercial travellers, and an extension to the dining room. When everything was finished, 1,600 yards of Brussels carpet and a complete system of electric lights, bells, and telephones had been installed throughout the Barker House complex.

By the 1930s, the automobile had invaded Fredericton and, as a result, the old Barker House stables were used mainly for storage, housing such items as the barouche sleigh used many years ago by Sir Leonard Tilley, and the early stagecoach that was driven between Fredericton and Newcastle. Unfortunately, in the early morning of May 26, 1939, fire broke out in the stables, and the city awoke to one of the worst disasters in years. Flames spread to the Gaiety Theatre, several businesses, and sixteen family dwellings. Estimated damage: $200,000.

The Barker House complex was saved, but fire was to strike the main hotel years later on a Sunday afternoon, June 8, 1975, resulting in a four-hour blaze. The old hotel had been converted into apartments and the ground floor had become the location for the Four Seasons Realty and the Seven Seas Restaurant.

Fighting the flames and smoke caused extensive damage; because of smouldering sawdust insulation, fire-fighters were forced to rip open the entire structure in order to hose everything with water. They also had to chop and tear up the floor and walls of what was once the hotel dining room.

In the end, only a brick shell was left and, the next year, after fire destroyed the Sharkey building, the old hotel annex was also left vacant. Demolition did not take place until 1982, leaving two gravel parking lots, divided by the Alley.

In the 1990s, the Greenarm Corporation began to build the huge Barker House Office Complex, which stands today on the site of the hotel and the Sharkey property, the former alley having been located directly under the new clock tower.

Overlooking Officers' Square and the St. John River, the view is still one of the best in Fredericton, Spafford Barker having picked the right spot 168 years ago.

York Street School Once Home for FHS

June 22, 2002

A rare photo of York Street School, taken before York Street was paved in 1925, showing the stately tower with the Gothic turret.

The little assembly hall was overflowing with parents and friends of the FHS graduating class. There was an atmosphere of excitement and anticipation. However, when the principal stood to give his opening address, he began by telling everyone that King Edward VII was gravely ill, that the next day's coronation was postponed indefinitely, and that Fredericton would be cancelling all celebrations. That was one hundred years ago, the morning of June 25, 1902. The place was York Street School. The principal: Dr. Berton Caleb Foster. Number of graduates: thirty-one.

Fredericton High School is the oldest English high school in Canada: for 217 years, it has been sending forth students to take their places in the world. But the graduation exercises were not always big affairs; there was a time when the closing ceremony was small, intimate, and memorable.

The origins of FHS were Tory, Loyalist, military, Anglican, and Baptist, but the school outgrew these early influences long ago. It also outgrew its accommodations, having been housed in various buildings within the city, each with its own unique history—from the

Collegiate School on lower Brunswick Street to the George Street School on the old Park Barracks property, and the sprawling complex at the top of the hill.

Perhaps the most interesting of all the FHS locations has been the York Street School—still standing at the corner of York and George streets. For thirty-two years, a total of 925 graduates called the handsome brick building, with copious trimmings of olive freestone, their high school.

It was built on the site of the old Baptist Seminary, the excavation beginning in July of 1891. The building was completed two years later. Total cost: $27,000!

The contractor was Joshua Limerick; the superintendent, John Hodge. Both were from Fredericton, but they worked from plans by J. C. Dumaresq of Halifax, who had already designed the following for Fredericton: Charlotte Street School, the Legislative Building, St. Paul's Presbyterian Church, the Randolph Block (now the Greenarm office complex).

The architectural drawings for the York Street School (each signed and dated by Dumaresq) survive and are preserved today at the provincial archives. Besides the various floor outlines, there are sketches for the decorative finials over the three main entrances and the dormer windows, the latter projecting from the mansard roof of the third storey.

The first and second storeys were the same, each with four large classrooms (thirty by thirty-five feet), each classroom with an attached cloakroom for students and a raised platform for teachers. On the third floor (or "upper flat"), there was an assembly hall, and two more classrooms. In addition, there were several smaller rooms for a library, a laboratory, private study, and storage. Five wood furnaces in the centre of the basement provided the heat throughout.

During the first year of operation, five hundred students were enrolled from grades one to eleven. The primary department (one to six) was on the first floor, the intermediate (seven and eight) was on the third, and the high school (nine, ten, and eleven) was on the second. Letters were used to label the high school grades, the students affectionately calling themselves the Crazy Cs, the Busy Bs, and the Stately Seniors (Class A).

Each department was restricted to its own floor, and students were restricted to entrances leading into the building, the boys using the George Street side, the girls, the Baptist Church side. Teachers and visitors entered through the main door on York Street.

Last-minute additions to the building included majestic granite steps for all three entrances and an electric bell system, the latter installed in every room by local resident Henry White. Unfortunately, the yards and grounds had to be left in their rough state for the grand opening in September of 1893.

The first and only high school principal at York Street was Dr. Foster, who, after thirty-five years in the top job (three years at the Collegiate School), remains the longest-serving principal in the history of FHS. He not only taught mathematics to every high school student at York Street but, at the same time, he was also the principal of the other departments, the superintendent of all the city schools, and the first president of the New Brunswick Teachers' Association.

From the beginning and over the years, Foster had a strong and dedicated support staff of only three other teachers in the York Street high school department, one of them being the second master (or vice-principal). Another was Ella Louise Thorne who, when she retired in 1920, had taught for fifty years in New Brunswick schools, forty-six of them in Fredericton, twenty-seven at York Street. She not only fostered a love of English literature, but she organized the long-running Golden Rule Circle for female students and was honorary president when she died in 1927.

Major John E. Page, who was involved with the school Cadet Corps and who taught Latin and Greek at York Street, achieved a remarkable attendance record during his forty-seven years in teaching: only five days of absenteeism and not one for illness! He resigned in 1946 and enjoyed his retirement to the age of ninety-three, passing away in 1968, his wife predeceasing him by four days.

Major Frank A. Good (science) and Dr. A. Sterling McFarlane (history) had organized the Cadet Corps, training the boys to such proficiency that they won the Strathcona Cup (a trophy for excellence in drill) successively and permanently when competition ceased. In time, both of these teachers would leave for higher positions: McFarlane to become chief superintendent of education in New Brunswick; Good to become vice-principal of the Provincial Normal School.

Whenever a teacher resigned from the York Street high school, the departure became a major part of the graduation exercises. At the school's first graduation on June 26, 1894, the nineteen graduates presented James M. Palmer with a long address of appreciation, accompanied by a valuable gift (a set of field glasses).

There was no valedictorian or special speaker that first year. Instead, the graduation was confined to the regular classrooms in half-hour periods, the teachers conducting their subjects under the watchful eyes of parents and visitors.

After the routine work was finished, the high school classes marched up to the assembly hall for the presentation of prizes. Just before noon, the secretary of the Fredericton School Board presented the graduates with their certificates, reading the list in the order of accomplishment (first, second, and third division).

The class of 1894 left two traditions that continue: the name Fredericton High School and the school colours of yellow and black. The class was also unique in that every member continued on to institutions of higher learning. One student Lilian Mary Beckwith, would graduate from UNB, marry James Brown Maxwell, and become a well-known Fredericton historian and author.

At the 1895 graduation, Principal Foster announced that each of the graduates had been requested to write a graduation essay and that several of the students would be reading their results. Fanny Hoben wrote about "Alcohol" and Ethel Brittain attempted to answer the question, "Do Circumstances Ever Make Men Great?" They split the three-dollar literary prize with Lizzy Doherty.

In 1895, the tradition of having a special speaker address the graduates was started, Canon George Goodridge Roberts (father of Sir Charles) being the first of a long line of local clergymen to do the honours over the years. He finished his speech by noon, after which the graduates and their high school teachers embarked on a steamer cruise and picnic down the St. John River.

By 1896, the school motto had been chosen and, along the wall facing the assembly hall's wide doorway, the graduates suspended a large black banner with the following words in gold letters: *Palma Non Sine Pulvere* (no success without work). Fred McNally won the silver medal for Classics that year (always the most important prize since it was introduced by Lieutenant-Governor Howard Douglas in 1829 in conjunction with the gold medal for Classics at UNB).

The year 1897 was a Victorian graduation in honour of the queen's sixtieth anniversary on the throne. Each of the fourteen graduates took part, singing "The Diamond Jubilee Hymn," reciting "Ode to the Queen," and reading their essays on different aspects of the Victorian Era. "Music and Art during Queen Victoria's Reign" was delivered by Lemuel Allan Wilmot Lemont, who himself would become a celebrated North American musician.

By the end of the nineteenth century, the word "diploma" was being used for the twenty-two graduates in 1898 and the twenty graduates in 1899. The exercises were still in the morning and the last Saturday in June was the most popular day for the occasion. The deliverance of scholarly essays and the presentation of highly competitive prizes in the various academic disciplines continued to dominate the program.

With the year 1900 and a new century approaching, Gertrude Coulthard delivered the first valedictory speech in the history of FHS. Unfortunately, she was overshadowed by William Shakespeare and the twenty-three graduates who gave a synopsis of *The Merchant of Venice*, followed by a dramatization of the trial scene. When a departing teacher was honoured, the graduating class presented him "with a beautiful set of Shakespeare in 25 volumes."

By the time Wilfred Estey did his valedictory in 1906 and Lillian Corbett hers in 1907, their speeches were almost an hour in length, covering in detail the history of their three high school years, including accomplishments of the Debating Society, the Literary Club, and the sports teams. *The High School Echo* was published professionally each month (but in later years at York Street, it would be succeeded by *The Yellow & Black*, *The FHS Monthly*, and *The Chanticleer*).

Both Estey and Corbett paid individual tributes to their many classmates who had "dropped out" over the three years in order to find work at the Hartt Boot & Shoe Company, the Marysville Cotton Mill, or a dry goods store on Queen Street. "Why did they not finish their education? Are non-academic courses needed?" they asked.

From 1909 to 1914, graduations were held either at the Normal School or the opera house (City Hall). The assembly hall at the York Street School had been converted into a manual training room, and one of the first-floor classrooms was being used for domestic science. When the Smythe Street School opened, more room became available and, as a result, the assembly hall was changed back to its original condition, this time with electric lights. The first evening graduation in the history of FHS was held there on June 29, 1915. Because of the war, there were only eighteen graduates.

When the war was over, the twenty-six members of the 1919 graduating class joined with the reunion class of 1899 in unveiling a memorial tablet to honour the FHS graduates who made the supreme sacrifice for their country. Major (Reverend) F. S. Porter, a former graduate, had just returned from overseas and was the guest speaker. Leo Cain was valedictorian. The class leader was Lillian Machum.

As FHS entered into its last five years at the York Street School, there would be challenging times ahead. For the first time in his career, Principal Foster was confronted with grooming and truancy situations. The senior girls wore tissue-paper ribbons in their hair because of the high cost of silk; the senior boys played "hookey" to attend the afternoon harness races. All were reprimanded severely.

Because evening audiences had become too large for the assembly hall, the 1921 graduation was scheduled for the morning. However, the forty-two graduates protested and won. They convinced the school board that their gowns and suits were only for evening wear, and reminded them that a dance would be following the ceremony.

The worst of the post-graduation pranks included the painting of the letters FHS on downtown doorways and across the sides of moored river steamers. In a lighter vein, the senior boys of the 1922 class climbed to the top of the Legislative Building and placed a lighted lantern in the hand of the Britannia statue.

When "the family skeleton" was removed from its closet in the science lab, following the 1924 graduation, it was discovered by passers-by the next morning—hoisted to the top of the school flagpole. The next year, a police officer had to stand guard all night in the lab with the skeleton as his companion.

By 1924, only three hundred visitors were able to be seated, while three hundred more stood in the corridors. The sixty-six graduates and special speakers packed the stage, the temperature being so uncomfortably warm that the chairman of the school board declined to deliver his address. Hopefully, the new $100,000 composite high school being built at the corner of George and Regent streets would be ready for the next year.

But it was not, and so the last graduation at York Street was held on June 29, 1925. There were sixty-nine graduates, the increase being the result of the new commercial department (established in 1922 by Harry W. McFee) and the enlarged history department (with former graduate Esther Clark in charge).

Two Boone brothers (Maurice and Charles) and Arthur McFarlane Limerick were double prize winners in 1925, the school's regulation of "two prizes only" preventing them from receiving a third and even a fourth. John David Babbitt, the valedictorian, called for a student council, an alumni society, a yearbook, and a better sports program in the new school. He concluded with this comment:

"I must admit that we were all sorely disappointed that the honour and pleasure of being graduated from the new school was not to be ours. However, there is a slight consolation in the thought that hereafter no other class will have to graduate from this small, hot, overcrowded room."

The York Street building continued to be an elementary school for forty more years. In 1965, it was sold to the Brunswick Street United Baptist Church, renamed York House and, following very few renovations, used for Sunday School classes and various church organizations.

Gone are the slate blackboards, the elegant arched hallways, and the turret on the tower. But the ten spacious classrooms and "the dear old assembly hall" are much the same.

It was, and still is, an educational landmark that played an important role in the lives of so many Fredericton students.

DOMINION EXPERIMENTAL FARM BEAUTIFUL AND USEFUL

JULY 5, 2003

The Dominion Experimental Farm—summer, 1963. The superintendent's residence (built in 1926) is at far right, with the flower gardens and ornamental hedges in front, and the orchards at far left. During the early years, the twenty-one acres of lawn were maintained by horse-drawn mowers. The large administration and laboratory building (built in 1960) is in the centre. In 1973, a new wing was added, creating a 130-member staff from both federal and provincial agriculture departments.

WHEN A CPR FREIGHT TRAIN ARRIVED in Fredericton from Ontario on Friday evening, July 3rd, 1903, dignitaries and local citizens had the opportunity to see some of the best livestock ever brought to New Brunswick—one hundred years ago!

The centre of attraction was a carload of twelve head of cattle, all shorthorns, all raised by the top stock breeders of Ontario. As a result, it was hoped that the breeding of livestock in New Brunswick would be encouraged and be successful.

The man who had made the trip to select the cattle was William Woodbridge Hubbard, New Brunswick's agricultural agent for the CPR at the time. Ten years later, in July of 1913, he would be the first superintendent of the Dominion Experimental Farm (or Station) that was being established a few miles below Fredericton. However, his life and career had already been impressive.

William Hubbard grew up on a farm (on the St. John River at Burton) that had been granted to his Loyalist grandfather Nathaniel Hubbard. After attending the Ontario Agricultural College at Guelph, he returned to manage the Lincoln farm (Belmont) which belonged to his maternal grandfather Robert Duncan Wilmot, a Father of Confederation and a lieutenant governor of New Brunswick.

Because farming was in his blood, William devoted the rest of his life to agriculture and its improvement. Besides being involved with a number of associations, commissions, and exhibitions for farmers, dairymen, and stock breeders, he was also editor of two publications—*The Maritime Farmer* (Sussex) and *The Homestead* (Halifax). Following his position as an agent for the CPR, he became secretary for the agriculture department of New Brunswick in 1909.

By the end of the nineteenth century, the Dominion government had begun to establish experimental farms (or stations) across the country in order to improve the agricultural methods of farmers. The central or principal one was near Ottawa, while others were situated in Brandon (Manitoba), Agassiz (British Columbia), Indian Head (Northwest Territories), and Nappan (Nova Scotia). Eventually, there would be eight in the west, and two more in the east (Prince Edward Island and New Brunswick). In the fall of 1912, W. W. Hubbard was chosen as the superintendent for the potential location in New Brunswick.

The position came with an annual salary of $1800 and a yearly increase of $100 (up to $3000), together with a new residence on site (heated and lighted) and such farm produce as needed to feed his family (wife and son). He would also have an assistant—Isaac Peabody of Nashwaaksis, one of the best-known farmers in York County and a veteran breeder of standard-bred horses.

The task ahead was phenomenal, but for the next ten years Hubbard met the challenge every step of the way, starting with the selection of a site and the acquisition of land. From the beginning, New Brunswick newspapers gave him continued support: "We hope the time is not far distant when we shall have an experimental farm in the fertile upland country on the River St. John"

Hubbard accompanied the federal minister of agriculture around the province, looking over various locations. He was attracted by the Charles Smith farm at Woodstock, but finally decided to secure 460 acres on the riverbank below Fredericton (now within the city limits). The road to the site was poor, but the view from the top of the hill was (and still is) breathtaking!

Originally, the proposed site was a small section of a large 10,000-acre, pre-Loyalist land grant called the Morrisania estate, located on the east side of Mill Creek and extending along the St. John River in the area of Fredericton towards Lincoln. This grant had been made to Charles Morris Jr. who, with his surveyor-general father, laid out the land and eventually sold it all in 1770 to James Simonds, the first New Englander to settle on the river.

The land obtained by the federal government in 1912 consisted of several adjoining farms that were once a part of the Simonds property but then owned by John Adams, Dell Gunter, H. C. Jewett, A. H. Waterhouse, Wesley McConnell, and W. W. Boyce (110 acres on the Wilsey Road). The purchase price totalled about $18,000, making the cost per acre a little less than $40. (Some five hundred additional acres would be purchased by 1960, of which 105 were from the farm of Dell Hossack.)

Unfortunately, only one hundred acres were ready for the plough; thus, during the spring and summer of 1913, an extensive land-clearing program was necessary. Fourteen men were hired; as a result, 150 acres were cut over and the brush burned, fifty acres of this being cleared for crops, oxen and horses being used for stump pulling and ploughing.

Twenty-four acres at the front of the site were reserved for orchard work, and an additional acre was put in shape for a nursery. Over 12,000 seedlings (ornamental trees, shrubs, and hedges) and 119 varieties of perennials (for flower beds and borders) were ordered from Fredericton, it being the practice to have artistic landscape effects on the farms of the Dominion Experimental Farm system.

Although plans were made to construct all new buildings at the site, existing structures on the purchased farm properties had to be used for almost two years, even though the farmhouses and the barns were in considerable disrepair. The Gunter barn was the first to be restored, in order to house the fourteen work horses used to clear the land. A one-storey frame office (twelve feet by thirty feet) was built in a hurry, and it was here that a telephone was installed to serve the entire project.

A humble farmhouse on the Waterhouse property became the superintendent's residence, having been built by Lord Ashburnham of Fredericton when he owned the property in the early 1900s. According to Hubbard, "It was comfortable enough, though not designed for the entertaining which the superintendent was sometimes supposed to do for distinguished visitors."

During 1913, Hubbard worked closely with Dominion agricultural officials by visiting them in Ottawa or hosting them in

Fredericton. The layout of the new farm was finally approved and it called for the main road (sixty feet wide) to run through the middle of the Gunter property from the river road to Doak Station. A second entrance, from the Fredericton side of the farm, was to begin where the railway line crossed the highway, the road winding its way up the hill (approaching where the public picnic grounds and barbecue area are today).

In the form of a quadrangle, the following farm buildings would be constructed alongside the main road: two cattle barns, 50 feet wide by 100 feet long, (both destroyed by fire in 1936); a dairy barn, 41 feet wide by 102 feet long, for milk production; a horse barn, 30 feet wide by 90 feet long, equipped for breeding purposes; an extensive piggery (for the study of pork production); several poultry houses, and a dairy and ice-house building, where butter and cheese would be made.

These buildings and a small house for the herdsman would not be started until September of 1913 and would not be completed until January of 1914. The successful contractors: Smith-Merrithew & Company of Fredericton. Total cost: $40,000.

In the meantime, the clearing continued and Hubbard began to make the Fredericton Experimental Farm (as it was unofficially called by local citizens) one of the leading livestock stations in the Dominion Farm system. He acquired all kinds of animals, including one hundred head of cattle, thirty young cows, and a flock of Shropshire sheep, to consume the forage and grain crops from thirty acres of the land.

It was proposed that the water supply would be provided by Mill Stream, a short distance from the site, but by the end of 1913, it was decided that a pneumatic water supply plant would be installed in a new building instead. The five thousand gallons of water required each day would be pumped from a bored well.

Unfortunately, the water pumping plant became the site of the first tragedy when, on March 11, 1915, a terrific explosion awakened all the employees at 3:00 A.M. A large drum of paraffin oil, placed too close to well-drilling equipment, ignited and spread to the wooden pump house and fifteen tons of coal in the attached shed, creating a spectacular blaze that could be clearly seen in the capital city.

A bucket brigade was organized immediately but the water plant and the drilling equipment were destroyed, the total loss (with no insurance) estimated at $8,000. It was definitely a setback, but the following year a concrete-block pumping station was built, of which only rare photographs survive today.

The impending war was another unexpected challenge for Hubbard. During the summers before the conflict occurred, he had from eighty to one hundred men on the payroll. They were divided into squads, each with a foreman, and their work consisted of land clearing, ditching (11,500 feet), underdraining (96,000 feet), fencing (8.6 miles of woven wire), road building, crop and fruit growing, gardening and harvesting.

When World War One began, Hubbard made it a rule not to employ any man fit for enlistment, the result being that the labour situation became difficult. He had to rely on girls, boys, and old men. He was to recall later: "Some of the girls were not very helpful, but others were wonderfully efficient and stuck by me into the late Fall, when the last of the crops were gathered."

After a wonderful summer of 1916, when the corn ripened, the watermelons grew large, and there were thirty varieties of grapes on the vine, there followed the reverse in 1917, when the weather was continually poor. However, Ottawa gave the order to grow one hundred acres of turnip for seed production experiments. When it came time to thin this large acreage, the only way to obtain enough help was to call on the merchants and manufacturers of Fredericton to send all the people they could for Sundays. Hubbard had to provide the transportation, the meals, and the wages, the last being three times what the workers were worth!

It was also during those early summers that visitors requested guided tours of the grounds, gardens, and buildings. Students from UNB and the Provincial Normal School would spend an afternoon, but agricultural groups would arrive for the whole day. The Farmers' and Dairymen's Association held their annual conventions in Fredericton and then every delegate "remained over for the big field day at the Experimental Farm." There would be inspections and demonstrations, and at noon "a sumptuous dinner was served by Superintendent Hubbard."

Some of the visitors were on official business. After the apiary was established in 1914 with five colonies of black bees, the chief apiarist of Canada (F. L. Sladen) came and conducted an inspection of all the beehives; acclaimed pathologist Gilbert C. Cunningham carried on experiments with two hundred varieties of potatoes in 1915 but could find no widespread incidence of a disease that had caused the Canadian government to place an export embargo on New Brunswick potatoes.

With his boundless energy and kind-hearted nature, W. W. Hubbard welcomed everyone who drove up the main road of the farm, but, by the early 1920s, his differences with Ottawa officialdom became so acute that, according to him, the work of the Fredericton farm threatened to be seriously damaged. He resigned to become the Maritime representative of a Toronto fertilizer company and, upon retirement, returned to the family farm in Burton to continue with agriculture on a smaller scale. He died in 1955 in his eighty-ninth year.

During Hubbard's ten years at the farm, the superintendent's residence was never built, although one was promised year after year. Ottawa presented a grandiose plan for a brick colonial at the top of the hill on the Jewett lot, where it would command a magnificent view and be in plain sight of the city.

In 1926, four years after the first superintendent had left, the residence was finally built, but with a touch of irony. Hubbard had presented a modest plan for a $12,000 cottage, but the Federal minister thought it was too expensive. The building eventually cost $40,000, even though it was constructed with natural stone found on the farm property.

In the meantime, the farm continued to grow in all other areas, the first major construction under the new superintendent (C. F. Bailey) being a long-awaited agricultural school at the site, supported by both the federal and provincial governments. The proposal called for a two-storey building (eighty feet by fifty feet) of concrete block. A main feature was to be a central judging area for livestock, where removable seats were to be positioned for the convenience of classwork.

In July of 1923, Lieutenant-Governor W. F. Todd laid the cornerstone for the $25,000 school building, and Premier P. J. Veniot was the special speaker at the ceremony. Both returned in November for the official opening and to greet the first class of fifteen male students. The first principal (M. A. MacLeod) had an apartment in the new school, but the students stayed in a makeshift dormitory (the machinery building) during their six-week course.

When a brick school was built in the mid-1930s (and burned in 1941), the old concrete school building became a carpentry shop. It still exists today but is almost an anachronism as it stands across the road from the modern new Potato Research Centre.

There have been many changes at the Experimental Farm since a hillside near the capital city was chosen for the site ninety years ago. New structures have been added, older ones demolished. The superintendent's residence was closed in 1987 and stands empty today. No longer do any of the employees live at the farm; livestock research ended in the mid-1990s; the splendid gardens and the ornamental hedges have diminished.

But there has been one constant: the public picnic site has remained much the same, with its wonderful view of the St. John River. For the thousands who have enjoyed this spot, followed by a leisurely walk around the grounds, the old Dominion Experimental Farm will be more than just an agricultural memory. It will be a part of Canada's unique heritage at Fredericton.

William Woodbridge Hubbard (1866–1955) was the first superintendent of the Dominion Experimental Farm at Fredericton. He was later made a member of the Agriculture Hall of Fame for the Maritime Provinces.

Section Four: Natural Disasters & Human Folly

GETTING AWAY WITH MURDER IN 1868

OCTOBER 13, 2001

This memorial stone in the Hermitage Cemetery bears the name of John Brennen, an innocent soldier who was brutally murdered in 1868. The original marble tombstone disappeared in 1910 when the Catholic cemetery was moved from Regent Street to the Woodstock Road.

OCTOBER IN FREDERICTON is one of the memorable months of the year with autumn, Thanksgiving, and Halloween. There is also the haunting memory of a senseless crime that took place many years ago and then went unavenged as a miscarriage of justice.

It happened on a Thursday evening, October 8, 1868. A soldier's battered body was found beside a fence on the green area at the corner of George and Smythe streets. The beating had been quick but vicious, leaving the skull crushed, the face beyond recognition. Blood soaked the ground and, during the days ahead, hundreds would come to see the scene of the murder, trying to imagine what had really happened.

Ever since Fredericton became a garrison town in 1784, the soldiers and the civilians appeared to live on friendly terms, but beneath the surface, there was dissatisfaction with the military presence. The main complaint was the negative influence upon the local youth.

Timothy Driscoll (age thirty-seven) and his wife Catherine (age thirty-five) were concerned parents in 1868. They operated a butcher shop at the corner of Queen and Westmorland streets, where they lived and raised their seven children: John (eighteen), Patrick (sixteen), Elizabeth (fifteen), Helena (thirteen), Johanna (eleven), Louisa (nine), Timothy Jr. (eight).

The Driscoll family also had a boarder by the name of John Shaughnessy, a tall, stout, twenty-one-year-old who always wore a straw hat. He came from King's County to be the hired hand on the Driscoll farm at Kingsclear. The oldest son, John, worked with him, the two travelling back and forth each day, spending their evenings in Fredericton.

Since his arrival in May of 1868, Shaughnessy had become infatuated with the oldest Driscoll daughter. However, his intentions were not encouraged or returned. The beautiful young Elizabeth was interested in someone else. Unbeknownst to her parents, she had been attending the military dances at the Exhibition Barracks (located back of town) and it was here that she met a dashing young soldier who would capture her heart.

His name was John Brennen, a private in the 22nd Cheshire Regiment. He was twenty-five, and had been born in Newtown, near Mount Kennedy, County Wicklow, Ireland. He was handsome, with a touch of grey in his dark sideburns. He was popular and well-liked, especially by his commanding officers and fellow soldiers.

But John Brennen had one great misfortune: he fell in love with Elizabeth Driscoll, although the subsequent relationship would be totally forbidden by her parents. Thus, in the beginning, it was a clandestine affair with contrived meetings supported by close friends. Brennen never went to the family home or farm.

Many Fredericton families welcomed the gallant soldiers of the 22nd, since their arrival in the spring of 1866. The hopeful prospects of a marriage for the young women of Fredericton pleased most families, even though it meant the daughters would have to leave home and travel abroad to wherever the regiment was stationed.

A military marriage for Elizabeth Driscoll would have had an ulterior motive—escape. She would be free from Shaughnessy, the jealous suitor, for whom she did not care; there would no longer be the family who tormented and stalked her, threatening to burn all her clothes, locking her out of the house, forcing her to plead with fearful neighbours to take her in.

Her brother John, a short, slight boy with a hateful personality, became obsessed with his sister's relationship with Brennen, making every attempt to locate her hiding places. In a rage, he would knock on doors and search through woodsheds. On one occasion, after he found her, he was about to strike her, but ordered her home instead, his parting words being heard throughout the neighbourhood: "If I ever meet you with that damned soldier, I'll kill him and murder you too!"

Another threat came on a Monday morning, October 5. Shaughnessy was having his breakfast at the Driscoll home when, in the course of the conversation, he yelled: "So help me God, I will leave John Brennen a corpse!" Elizabeth was present and heard the comment. Her next rendezvous was planned for Thursday evening, October 8.

The couple met at the corner of King and York a few minutes after seven and walked out to George Street, where they turned and started towards Smythe. It was overcast and extremely dark, there being no gas lamps on the back streets and the candles that illuminated various front windows providing very little light. Other than Brennen greeting a few soldiers, the only sounds were Elizabeth's long skirts brushing against the picket fences and the distant bell of the Baptist Church (which would soon be stopping at its regular time of 7:30).

When they reached Westmorland Street, they were observed by Sergeant Joseph Moore of the 22nd, who was having a smoke and leaning on the gate of his rented house. Moore also saw two shadowy figures lurking along the street, stopping and starting whenever the couple did. The followers, a tall person and a short one, eventually crossed at St. Anne's Chapel, concealing themselves behind a pile of lumber.

Before Elizabeth and Brennen reached Smythe Street, the two figures caught up and passed by, reaching the corner, where they stood waiting. Elizabeth recognized the straw hat and knew at once that it was the boarder Shaughnessy and her brother John. She told Brennen to run: "They are going to kill you." He replied, "They can't kill me," and kept on going.

At this point, Elizabeth turned and ran back down George Street for help. But it was too late; she had already heard a blunt instrument hit Brennen's skull. Passing three soldiers of the 22nd (privates James, Rolfe, and Greely), she cried, "For God's sake, go up to the corner. They're killing Brennen and he has no one to help him." Then, reaching the home of Mary Watters, whose husband John was also in the 22nd, she flung open the door and gasped, "My brother John and John Shaughnessy have murdered Brennen."

As the traditional eight o'clock gun was sounding at Artillery Park (corner of George and Regent), John Brennen was found—unconscious and badly beaten about the head. He was carried to the little military hospital inside the garrison compound (corner of

York and Queen), where the regimental doctor examined the fractured skull and the deep facial wounds. There was no hope. Death came at half-past the hour.

Shaughnessy returned to the Driscoll home where he was arrested later in the evening; John Driscoll left town and could not be found. As they both fled from the scene of the crime, they dropped the weapon—a thick, three-foot wooden stake with points at each end. When a young boy by the name of Chalmers Turner discovered it at dawn, it was partially covered with blood and clumps of black hair.

On Friday morning, a postmortem examination took place and, in the afternoon, the coroner's jury held its deliberations in the council chamber of City Hall. Coroner S. D. MacPherson and Mayor William Needham presided. Based upon the evidence of Elizabeth Driscoll, which she gave while under oath, the verdict of the jury was as follows: "That the said John Brennen was maliciously and wilfully murdered on the night of the eighth day of October by John Shaughnessy and John Driscoll."

Elizabeth Driscoll was declared the principal witness and was placed in protective custody until the preliminary investigation was over. Unfortunately, an unprecedented lapse in the justice system allowed her mother to have a private visit with her daughter. It was this visit that would alter all future proceedings.

On the Friday evening, the tension between the soldiers and the "town rowdies," which had been developing for some time, erupted into street riots and physical confrontations. Feeling deeply aggravated at the loss of a comrade in such a violent manner, the military had reason to seek revenge. One of the sergeants said that, if he had his way, the regiment would sack the whole bloody town. Instead, he formed his men in a line, gave the command to charge, and rushed down Queen Street, breaking store windows as they went.

On Saturday, the anger had subsided as the citizens of Fredericton and the entire 22nd Regiment (led by Colonel Francis Pym Harding, who was also the lieutenant-governor at the time) marched in the funeral cortege that carried John Brennen to his grave at St. Dunstan's Cemetery on Regent Street (where the school building is now located).

He was buried with full military honours, including a gun carriage upon which the casket was placed, a firing party with arms reversed, and the band playing "Dead March in Saul." As the procession passed near the York County Gaol, Elizabeth Driscoll and John Shaughnessy sat in their cells and heard the muffled sounds of the drum.

On Sunday, John Driscoll was found hiding in a barn near the family farm at Kingsclear. His father and Sheriff Thomas Temple brought him back to Fredericton, Bishop John Medley saying that the father demanded and accepted the $500 reward or else he would take the city to court.

The preliminary investigation began on Monday, October 12, in a private dwelling on Queen Street. Standing in the midst of the crowds that lined the route from the gaol was Juliana Horatia Ewing, a prominent British author whose husband, Alexander, was a captain in the 22nd. Her keen powers of observation resulted in interesting details that were written home to her family.

Mrs. Ewing was surprised that the prisoners were on foot, the brother, whom she had heard "has always been a *bad lot*," walking first, doing the jaunty, the other looking very sad. The mayor and the city's two policemen were the escorts. Elizabeth came last, "a *very* sweet looking, ladylike girl."

Both Driscoll parents were present and showed no reaction when their son pleaded, "Not Guilty, most decidedly." However, when Elizabeth was placed on the stand, her mother motioned and her father stood. At this point, the girl revoked all testimony she had given at the coroner's inquest, pausing at first, and then continuing in a mesmerized manner. She testified that she saw no one and that she could remember nothing about the fateful night of October 8.

When the case came before the Supreme Court in November, it continued to fall apart. The presiding judge, Charles Fisher (a Father of Confederation), admitted that he had not read the depositions; Timothy Driscoll swore that his son John and his hired hand Shaughnessy were with him all evening on the night of the crime; younger son Patrick supported his father's testimony.

By the time the defence called the father of John Shaughnessy, the trial had lost all credibility. Dennis Shaughnessy spoke highly of his oldest son and of his seven other children. He presented letters from clergymen and prominent people, all testifying to the "unimpeachable character" of John Shaughnessy.

The jury retired for seventeen minutes and then returned with a verdict of "not guilty." The two prisoners waited in the box until the Crown dispersed and then they stepped back into the world and became a part of society once again. Each was escorted out of town in his father's horse and wagon, Driscoll travelling to Carleton County, Shaughnessy back to King's County.

When Timothy Driscoll returned, he discovered that the house and barn at his Kingsclear farm were burned down, the result of an incendiary fire. He had no insurance; his loss was heavy. After the insurance on his Fredericton property was cancelled, he and his family moved to Kingsclear and began to rebuild.

According to the census for the next twenty years, there were ten children in the Driscoll family, the names of John and Elizabeth among them. Both had returned to live with their parents. There was no John Shaughnessy on the list.

Elizabeth Driscoll had been indicted for perjury and was committed to stand trial in the Supreme Court. Due to missing documents and inadequate preparation on the part of the justice system, her case did not appear until early May of 1869, at which time the grand jury failed to find a true bill against her.

In late May of 1869, she stood on the wharf and watched the 22nd Regiment leave Fredericton, the last of the imperial troops to be stationed in the city. They were on their way to Ireland, the homeland of John Brennen, and she might have been going with them, along with the eighty young brides from the city. Instead, the strains of "Auld Lang Syne" would remain with her for a long time.

Before the departure of the Cheshire Regiment, the officers and soldiers placed a monument over John Brennen's grave—an eight-foot shaft of Italian marble. In 1910, this impressive tombstone disappeared when the St. Dunstan's Cemetery was moved to the Hermitage on the Woodstock Road.

In the year 2000, a common memorial was unveiled at the hermitage to honour all those who had been buried at St. Dunstan's. John Brennen's name appears on the first tablet with the year of his death—1868.

SCANDAL & TRAGEDY TOUCHED UNIVERSITY CENTENARY

MAY 27, 2000

For the UNB centenary, six Venetian poles, covered in red, white, and blue bunting, were placed at intervals in front of the college. The students hung festoons of greenery and flowers from these poles along with banners, flags, and shields.

IT WAS MAY 1900, and the city of Fredericton and UNB were joining forces on the eve of a week-long centennial celebration. The citizens expressed a desire to do their part by opening their homes to visitors; many of the historic buildings would be hosting a memorable event; all entertainment would be free.

Planning had begun in January and a month later a general invitation was issued to all graduates of the university. Delegates were invited from the leading colleges and academic institutions in North America and the United Kingdom. The invitation card, which appeared on the front page of *The Daily Gleaner*, was signed by the chancellor (Thomas Harrison), the Senate President (James Inch), and the alumni president (Douglas Hazen).

The response was overwhelming. Distinguished guests were to arrive from Oxford, Cambridge, Dublin, and Glasgow; from Cornell, Princeton, Yale, and Harvard; from McGill, Dalhousie, Toronto, and Manitoba.

The festivities began on Sunday afternoon (May 27) with the centennial service at Christ Church Cathedral, Mr. H.M.M.

Hackett, principal of Montreal's Theological College, preaching the university sermon. He encouraged the students to be true to their College, to its teachings, and to its traditions.

The next evening (May 28), one of those traditions received unexpected and unfavourable attention when a large gathering filled the library on the second floor of the Old Arts Building (then called the college, now known as Sir Howard Douglas Hall).

It was the sixty-seventh encaenia and the program included the usual Founders' Day address, the awarding of medals and prizes, the reading of winning essays, and the presentation of bachelor degrees to the twelve graduating students—eleven young men and Lena Sherwood.

"Gus" Crawford was the valedictorian and it was his speech that captivated all those present, but not for its routine review of college life during the freshman, sophomore, and junior years. "The beginning of our Senior year was marked by a wide difference of opinion concerning the carrying out of some of our customs. The breach grew wider and wider, and finally an event occurred which is familiar to everyone."

The main custom in question was "initiation." It had met with opposition and was abolished for that year. But not all upper classmen agreed and, a week after the college opened in the fall of 1899, the first-year students were intercepted one night as they came on campus to attend the annual reception.

The hostages were escorted to the little wooden-frame gymnasium, in a grove on the west side of the college, where their collars and neckties were removed and their shoes taken off their right feet. These personal items were then carried away and the door locked.

Those responsible continued their pranks by holding up a student driver and his team of horses, taking two freezers of ice cream and a quantity of cake from his carriage, then sending him on his way to the Great Hall to report the mischief. When the refreshments and the new students failed to appear, Chancellor Harrison, accompanied by the college porter and a lighted lantern, started upon a tour of investigation that took them directly to the gymnasium.

They could hear strange noises but were refused admission. Sending the porter for an axe, the chancellor remained on guard until the door could be broken open. The ties, collars, and shoes were found and the reception continued; however, the missing ice cream and cake were never recovered.

The aftermath came the next morning when five of the most popular seniors on the campus and about the city were summoned before the seven-member faculty and expelled. Eleven sophomores and one junior, who had also taken part in the "hazing" ritual, were suspended.

It was feared that the remaining seven seniors might resign in support of their classmates, indicating that there would be no centennial graduation. And there was a further difficulty: the college had to graduate some students each year or forfeit its charter!

However, the students were divided on the issue and so was the faculty. Three professors were ready to hand in their resignations if the punishment was reversed. A number of students threatened to leave for other universities.

Thus, the remainder of the fall term was filled with tension and confrontation as the senate and the faculty met endlessly in an attempt to settle a scandal that had become well known throughout Fredericton and beyond. Eventually, the penalty was changed to a brief suspension for those involved, and all students and professors agreed to stay.

Unfortunately, relationships were strained for the rest of the year but, on graduation night, the valedictory offered the last word: "Nothing can be said in favour of one student trying to bring about the expulsion of another, especially a classmate; even if he is not in accordance with the actions of a fellow student, and so feels that he cannot help him when he has got into trouble, he should at least refrain from interfering in any way, and allow the faculty to deal with the matter in the way they think best."

The centenary continued on Tuesday afternoon (May 29) with a grand procession from College Hall, along University Avenue, to the legislature. The official guests, the senate, the faculty, the alumni, and the students were in full academic robes. The 71st Battalion Band led the way.

For the centennial event, Premier H.R. Emmerson and the provincial government placed the assembly chamber at the disposal of the university. Inside, the galleries were filled with spectators and the combined choirs of all the city churches. The floor area was reserved for those directly involved and that included Reverend Canon W. H. DeVeber, the oldest living graduate at that time (class of 1843), who opened the event with the Lord's Prayer.

As the conferring of forty-two honorary degrees began, one of the candidates fell to the floor. Before a shocked crowd, the unconscious gentleman was carried to an anteroom to be treated, and the names of the other recipients continued.

One name on the list was not called and everyone's worst fears were confirmed when the chancellor came forward and announced the sudden death of Dr. Theodore Rand, a published poet, a former chief superintendent of education for New Brunswick, and a founder of the free school system in this province.

In the midst of disbelief, the Honourable George Foster, the alumni orator and a former UNB classics professor, was called upon to give an impromptu tribute. He began: "Mr. Chancellor—truly, this is a heavy task you have imposed upon me. That tears lie very close to joy in this old world of ours has been shown by the sudden cloud that has darkened the exceeding brightness of our Centennial Day."

The program resumed with each visiting delegate bringing greetings from his university. Their addresses were written in Latin and in old English script, and they were accompanied by official wax seals in tiny gold boxes. The impact of the tragedy had passed and all returned to the legislature in the evening to enjoy a reception tendered by lieutenant-governor and Mrs. McClelan.

Wednesday (May 30) was Students' Day and the university procession marched to City Hall in the morning to be welcomed by Mayor Harry Beckwith. The visiting delegates, who were given the key to the city, were called upon again, but this time each one addressed the students with words of wisdom and advice.

After three rousing cheers and a "tiger" for the queen, the students proceeded to College Field for an afternoon of competitive sports. The others were invited to the Windsor Hall Hotel for an elaborate luncheon tendered by the city. In the evening, everyone returned to city hall for the UNB Glee Club concert and drama production at the opera house, a "full dress" occasion and a fitting close to a day that belonged entirely to the students.

On the final day, Thursday (May 31), the festivities returned to the campus, where the chancellor and his wife hosted an afternoon garden party on the terraced lawns in front of the College, the oldest university building in Canada (1826). By 1900, there were just two other buildings: the Brydone Jack Observatory (1851) and the gymnasium (1863).

But many more buildings were in the future and the cornerstone for a new science hall was laid that afternoon, completing the centenary with a permanent memorial. The college calendar, the centennial issue of *The University Monthly*, local newspapers, and a collection of coins were placed inside the time capsule.

In the evening of the last day, the Alumni Society hosted a brilliant event at the College—"At Home." Over four hundred ladies and gentlemen in their finest danced to an orchestra in the Main Hall and a band in the library. An elaborate late supper was served in the basement. At midnight, as the lights in all the windows were extinguished, one coach after another rolled away from the great doorway and proceeded down the college path towards the city.

It was over. The centenary had passed into history.

For the next one hundred years, UNB's growth was phenomenal. However, as one of the oldest colleges in the country took its place on the world stage, memories of the centenary remain: the letter of apology, signed by the five seniors, is still preserved in the university library archives; the addresses and seals from the visiting delegates have also been saved and some have been on exhibit this month; the wooden gymnasium burned on February 6, 1902 and was replaced by a brick structure, which is now part of the Head Hall engineering complex; the first science building is also part of the same complex; the remains of Dr. Rand were returned to his home town in Nova Scotia, after a Fredericton funeral at Brunswick Street Baptist Church, May 30, 1900.

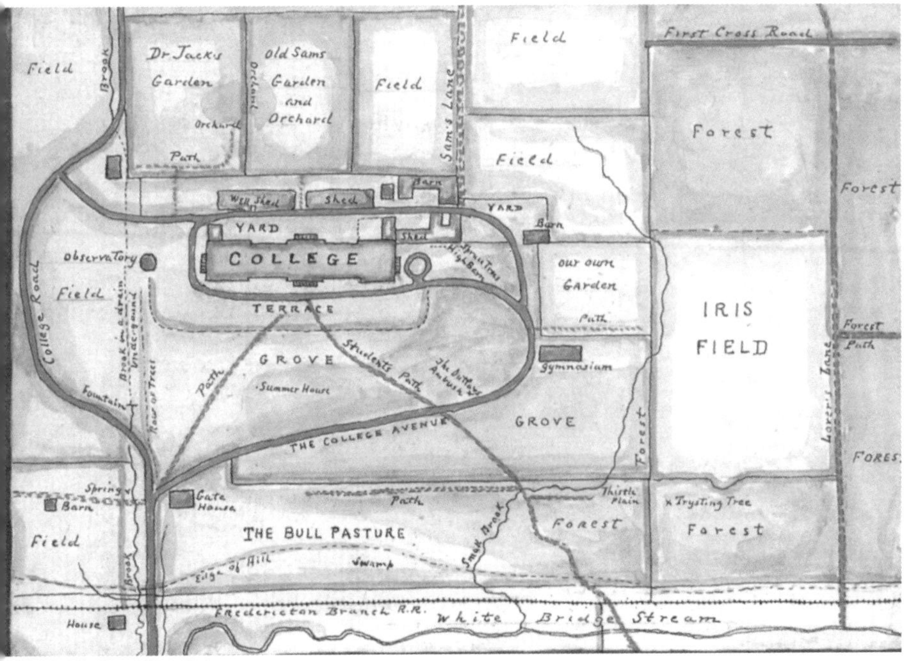

This sketch of the UNB campus was drawn in the late 1880s by Joseph Whitman Bailey, who was born in the Old Arts Building (the College) and who graduated from there in 1884.

June 24, 2000

Middlemore Children Provided with Homes

Middlemore children aboard *S. S. Newfoundland* en route to Canada in June of 1928. Annie Fereday is third from left, second row, and on her right is Amelia Reason. Both girls settled in Fredericton. The matron is in the centre of the second row. Upon departure, each child was given a Bible and a shilling from the mayor of Birmingham.

For New Brunswick's Middlemore Home children and their descendants, the summer of 2000 meant a twentieth get-together, which happened on the last Saturday in August.

The capital city is an appropriate site for this reunion because the Middlemore orphans started coming to New Brunswick 115 years ago and Fredericton was the "distribution centre" during the early years. The British Child Emigration Movement began even earlier, in 1869, and twenty years later there were more than fifty philanthropic organizations bringing street children from the industrial cities of Great Britain to Canada.

Those under nine years of age were placed for adoption; those ten years and older were contracted out for farm labour or domestic service. Unfortunately, many of the 100,000 destitute children brought to Canada until the 1930s (when child immigration ended) never received any of their promised wages.

The Middlemore child-care venture started in England in 1872. The place was Birmingham; the dedicated organizer was Dr. John T. Middlemore, a twenty-eight-year-old surgeon and a Member of

Parliament, who was later knighted for his work. His chief objective was to prepare orphans, paupers, and delinquents for foster families in Canada. Before he travelled across the Atlantic with a new group of children every year in the month of June, he did all the administration and the training.

The first reception house was established in London, Ontario, in 1873, but Middlemore was informed that good homes could be found in Fredericton as well. On one of his crossings, he met Colonel George Maunsell, commander of the new infantry school in Fredericton, and Mr. Thomas Morris, a former Fredericton alderman. Both gentlemen wanted to know why the well-mannered children on board the steamer were not coming to New Brunswick for placement.

Upon returning to England, Middlemore wrote a letter to Mayor George Fenety, as well as Maunsell and Morris, requesting their assistance in locating homes in and around Fredericton. The letter was published in *The Evening Capital* (February 24, 1885) and the search began.

The first party of twenty Middlemore boys and girls arrived in Fredericton in June of 1885; in 1886, there were twenty-four more. After disembarking at Halifax (another distribution centre), they took the train to Saint John, where a river steamer brought them to the Union Line Wharf at the end of Regent Street. The children walked down the gangplank in pairs, and at the head of the line was John Middlemore himself. Spectators who had gathered saw a middle-aged man with a benevolent bearing and a facial expression indicative of authority.

They were met by Colonel and Mrs. Maunsell and marched to the Officers' Quarters in the Military Compound, where the successful applicants were waiting. Goodbyes were said; siblings were separated, and several broke down and wept. The horse-drawn carriages then departed for Keswick, Maugerville, Douglas, Prince William, Tay Mills, and Upper Nashwaak and many of the children were never to see each other or Dr. Middlemore again.

During the early 1890s, the children arrived in Fredericton by train from Quebec City (another distribution centre) and were met at the railway station by the Barker House coach. By the late 1890s, the Maunsells had returned to England and The Very Reverend Francis Partridge, the first dean of Christ Church Cathedral, volunteered to be the contact person. By then, placements were being made in the Woodstock and Miramichi areas, as well as York and Sunbury Counties.

In 1898, Dr. Middlemore and the matron of the Birmingham Home brought fifty boys and girls to Fredericton, ranging in age from three to sixteen years. According to the local press of the day, "They were located at Long's Hotel until they could be disposed of." In this group, there was a nine-year-old lad, Norton Clayton, whose short life in Canada met a tragic end.

After being placed on a farm in York County, Norton ran away and returned to Fredericton. He was then taken to the Miramichi but serious trouble developed with the new family. In December of 1899, he ran away again, this time hiding for three days in the hay loft of a cold barn. He was asleep when found and when awakened he was unable to walk because of frostbite. He was admitted to the Victoria Public Hospital in Fredericton where both of his feet were amputated. On January 1, 1900, he died at eleven years of age.

An inquiry was ordered into the circumstances preceding the death of Norton Clayton and it was held in the old Supreme Court court room of the Legislative Building, a coroner's jury of seven men in attendance. Witnesses testified that the boy had been severely beaten on several occasions. However, the verdict, after an hour's deliberation, stated "No Person Blamed."

Situations like that of Norton Clayton were rare in New Brunswick, but various forms of abuse did exist. Thus, by the early 1900s, a Fredericton committee of seven prominent citizens was set up to look after the Middlemore children and to recommend good Christian homes within the city and beyond.

In Birmingham, the affable Mr. George Jackson was assigned to work with the new committee when he brought the children to Fredericton. He was to remain for a week and visit with the boys and girls whom he had placed in previous years. Some of the older ones even travelled to Fredericton to see him; he was their only link with "the old country."

As the Middlemore groups became larger, two matrons and two male assistants began to travel with Mr. Jackson. The gentlemen always registered at the Barker House, the matrons and the children at the various other hotels, such as the Lorne, the Exchange, and the Empire. The next morning, after breakfast, the children were marched to either the York County Court House or City Hall, where large crowds of curious spectators had gathered to size them up.

Jackson and the committee were soon dealing with six hundred applications annually, only a small portion of which could be filled. There were also the critics, who had serious doubts about the selection of homes and the follow-up visits. Although the local newspapers published complete lists after everyone was placed, only the children themselves knew what really happened as the years went by.

Happily, in 1902, Annie Clements of Birmingham came out with the group as the betrothed bride of Benjamin Rollston, himself a Middlemore child who came over years earlier and who eventually bought his own farm in Kingsclear. They were married in St. Peter's Church, Springhill, on June 7 that year and took in one of the home children.

Sadly, in 1903, the Bagley family of four brothers and one sister were all separated, Annie, William, Richard, and Walter having to leave five-year-old Leonard in Fredericton, since his young age prevented him from being readily placed. One reporter wrote: "The boys were brave lads and fought to keep back the tears."

Since the beginning, over five thousand Middlemore children were sent to Canada, the majority becoming good citizens, giving much to their adopted country. One New Brunswick story symbolizes this success.

In 1926, twelve-year-old Annie Fereday entered the Birmingham Home after the divorce of her parents. During library class, she read *Anne of Green Gables* and realized that Canada was where she wanted to live.

On July 11, 1928, Annie stepped ashore at Halifax Harbour and was eventually taken to Petitcodiac, New Brunswick, where she waited alone on the station platform for someone to come for her. She clung to a small sackcloth bag, which held all her possessions, including a little sewing box from her father. When the farmer finally arrived, he was driving an old Model-T and Annie had her first ride in an automobile.

Four years later, she came to Fredericton and worked in several homes, trying to finish her education while coping with poor health. During this difficult time, her one joy was writing letters to her mother and waiting for the mail.

Eventually, Annie met James Cairns, who had come out from Scotland. When he returned to Canada after the war, they married and raised two children. James worked as a caretaker at UNB and Annie provided meals for university students. In 1958, they built their own home on Beaverbrook Street, from where they were able to watch the encaenia procession each year. In time, two grandsons would be among the graduates.

At age eighty-six, Annie Cairns was a widow still living in her own home, her backyard blooming with lilacs and bedding plants. "It's my little bit of heaven," she said proudly, although she had made seventeen trips back to England!

She initiated the first Middlemore reunion in 1980 has and never missed a year; her scrapbook of clippings attests to the memories. Looking forward to the twentieth in the summer of 2000, she knew that only a few of the original children were left, but that there are many descendants to keep the story alive in the new century.

Fredericton's Link with the *Empress of Ireland*

Ada Driver (right) and an unidentified woman (left) aboard the ship that brought them to Canada in the spring of 1914.

IT HAS BEEN ALMOST NINETY YEARS since the tragic sinking of the *Empress of lreland* in the St. Lawrence River. Now the famous luxury liner is back in the news again and this time at the centre of controversy.

On January 2, 2003, an export permit was granted and, as a result, a large private collection of *Empress* artifacts currently housed in Quebec, and considered to be of great national interest, could be sold to a prospective buyer in Florida who, in turn, intends on selling then "to the four corners of the world."

However, one item of memorabilia from the *Empress* has been preserved in Fredericton and, along with several other links, will remain a part of the city's cultural history for all time.

It is a letter and the story of this letter begins in the early spring of 1914 when an advertisement was placed in a British newspaper by Bishop and Mrs. John Andrew Richardson of Fredericton. The Richardsons were living at Bishop's Court, 806 George Street, and had done so since he was ordained in 1907. They had a family of five children, one boy and four girls, and were subsequently in need of "a hired girl," preferably one from the Old Country.

The advertisement for domestic help was answered by a young lady from London who lived on Marylebone Road near Regents Park. Her name was Ada Driver and she was twenty-two years old when she came to Canada to accept the position at the Bishop's residence in Fredericton. To pay for her passage over, she secretly saved small amounts from her babysitting money, giving the remainder to her parents to assist with family expenses at home.

Being independent and completely liberated, Ada Driver travelled across the Atlantic alone, probably third class, on a liner much like the *Empress* ships, arriving in Saint John and then taking the train along the valley railroad to the capital city.

Immediately after she and her trunk were transported from the station to Bishop's Court, she was interviewed over tea by Mrs. Richardson.

Besides leaving her family behind, Ada Driver also left a boyfriend. On May 26, 1914, she wrote the following letter to a Fred Griessen of 85 Charlotte Street, London, England:

My Dear Fred,

I can hardly believe we are so far apart. I expect you will have received my first letter alright. I quite enjoyed the boat. Had a lovely voyage but the trains are to awfull for anything. This is a lovely place. Some beautiful shady walks. Don't you wish you were here? Well how many places have you visited since I saw you? Write and tell me all about it. Never mind if it is bad English.

How did the photos turn out. Don't forget me. I think I like this place. It is rather a nice house, quite large in fact. We have some pictures here so that makes it a bit more cheerfull.

Write to me soon dear. I have only your photo to look at now. I will have some small ones taken very soon and will send you one. Please remember me to the "Thaises." Must close now. With all kind thoughts, kindest regards from yours, very sincerely,

Ada Driver XXXX

The letter was mailed at Fredericton (May 27, 4:30 P.M.) and then travelled by train to Quebec City, where, during the afternoon of May 28, the mail for the Old World was placed on board the great passenger liner the *Empress of Ireland*, one of the sister ships built for the CPR in 1904, the other being the *Empress of Britain*. Both were commissioned to handle the massive migration from Europe to Canada, both becoming the pride of the Canadian Pacific's transatlantic fleet, the first round trip of the 1914 summer setting sail from Quebec on May 29.

Besides Ada Driver's letter, there was one other link with Fredericton on board and that was a young first-class passenger, David Johnston, who was returning home to Scotland after living in New Brunswick's capital for over a year. When he first arrived in Fredericton, he purchased the W. Thomas Murray property at Kingsclear, a thriving estate originally owned by Colonel Edward Winslow, and one of the finest properties in York County.

The son of one of the Law Lords of Scotland, David Johnston made many friends in Fredericton. Thus, when he fell heir to an estate in Scotland and sold his Kingsclear property, including livestock and farming implements, for $9,000, his departure was very much regretted.

A total of 1,057 passengers plus 420 crew members were on board the *Empress*. Joining Johnston in first class, there were eighty-six others, including the famous British actor Laurence Irving and his beautiful actress wife, Mabel Hackney; Sir Henry Seton-Karr, a British parliamentarian; Leonard Palmer (and his wife), a noted British journalist who had been visiting Fredericton; Major Henry Lyman (and his wife), a prosperous businessman; Dr. Alexander Lindsay of Halifax, a well-known pathologist; Ted Fitchett, the celebrated English boxer; Alfred Ernest Barlow, a prominent professor from McGill University; Mrs. F. H. Dunlevy, a Denver socialite; and Mrs. Ella Hart, an author and the wife of the British colonial secretary in the Bahamas.

Second class was just over half filled with 253 passengers, including 176 members of the Salvation Army, one of five Canadian contingents (400 members in all) on its way to the Great Salvation Army Convention to be held at Albert Hall in London. Among the Salvationists were Commissioner David Rees, his wife and three children, and the thirty-nine members of the Salvation Army Staff Band.

Among the Salvation Army officers (and their wives) on board, two had close ties with Fredericton: Major David L. Creighton of Creightonville (near Sussex) had been stationed in Fredericton in 1900, formerly in charge of the local citadel; Adjutant Everett S. DeBow of Forest Glen (near Petitcodiac) had become a member of the Fredericton Corps while he was attending the Provincial Normal School in 1899–1900. The Creightons left their five small children with friends in Toronto; the DeBows left their little boy with her parents at Armstrong's Corner (near Welsford).

Third-class quarters were nearly full—717 men, women, and children, many of them former immigrants who belonged to the working class and who were returning home. Ada Driver herself would have travelled to Canada with a similar group, spending most of the crossing time far below the decks in overcrowded steerage. With the arrival of thousands of immigrants to Canada during 1913 and 1914, the fare for third class dropped as low as six pounds (second class costing ten pounds; first class, fourteen pounds).

Along with 1,100 tons of general cargo, the *Empress* was carrying in the strong room a large quantity of bullion—bars of silver and gold amounting to millions of dollars. In the ship's mail room, there were four railway wagonloads of mail sacks, most of the letters being registered because they contained money orders on their way from Canadian settlers to European relatives. Ada's tiny envelope, with her letter to Fred inside, would have been in one of these sacks.

In the early hours of May 29, the *Empress* approached the port of Rimouski, where the last bags of mail and dispatches were exchanged with the tender *Lady Evelyn*. One more stop farther on was at Father Point, where the cutter *Eureka* came to pick up the St. Lawrence River pilot who had guided the ship from Quebec.

However, as the huge liner headed back out across the river, a low bank of dense fog closed in, causing the captain to stop the engines immediately. This proved to be disastrous because it put the *Empress* directly in the path of an oncoming boat—a six-thousand-ton Norwegian collier known as the *Storstad*, which was carrying 11,000 tons of Nova Scotia coal to Montreal and which, apparently, had altered course in the fog.

A collision was inevitable, the *Storstad* slicing twenty feet into the *Empress* on the starboard side and then pulling away, leaving a gash that soon filled with water, causing fourteen thousand tons of steel and Edwardian elegance to list quickly and sink to the bottom of the St. Lawrence River in just fourteen minutes—only four miles from the shore! It rolled over with such speed there was no time to launch lifeboats.

A total of 1,012 lives were lost (men, women, and a heavy child mortality): 51 from first class, 205 from second class, 584 from third class, and 172 crew members. Among the victims were more than 150 Salvationists, including Commander Rees and his entire family, the Creightons, the DeBows, and 30 members of the Salvation Army Band.

Among the distinguished passengers who drowned, there were the Irvings, the Palmers, Sir Henry, and David Johnston of Fredericton, the last whose remains were never found. The stateroom which he occupied had been situated in that portion of the *Empress* which the *Storstad* struck and, in all probability, Johnston was one of those killed by the sudden impact. (Lord Johnston of Scotland sent instructions to spare no expense in efforts to locate his son; he also sent $10,000 for the relief fund for the *Empress* victims.)

The Creightons were to be buried in Toronto, a brother arriving from Sussex to identify the bodies and to bring home the five orphaned children. The DeBows were to be buried in New Brunswick, friends from Fredericton arriving in Quebec City to identify the bodies and to accompany them home. The two caskets were placed side by side in a railway baggage car for the journey back.

When the train stopped at the little station in Welsford on the morning of June 2, a sorrowful mother and father and a little boy (Eldon Percy DeBow, age four) were standing on the platform. However, only Mary DeBow (the former Mary McKim) was taken from the train for burial that afternoon at Armstrong's Corner, her childhood home. After the final separation took place, Everett DeBow (age 33) was taken to Petitcodiac, where his parents were waiting. Two days later, he was laid to rest at Forest Glen (now Pollett River), his childhood home.

For eight hundred of the victims whose remains were never recovered, the sunken *Empress* became their final resting place, a buoy, bobbing in the middle of the St. Lawrence marking the exact spot. It was not until 1999 that it was declared an historic site.

Shortly after the sinking, salvage divers went down and dynamited a hole in the hull, enabling them to retrieve the purser's safe, the silver and gold bullion, and the sodden bags of mail from the ship's strong room on the main deck, an easily accessible area. According to press releases, there were 155 bags of newspapers, 51 bags of letters, 301 parcels, and 1,905 registered articles.

The Canadian post office wanted each item returned to its sender but only after a drying-out process, with each letter being opened and placed on tables, under the strict security of local postmasters. Unfortunately, most of the stamps on the letters could not be saved, many peeling off due to the dampness.

Return addresses were located on inside headings, such as the one that Ada Driver had written: c/o Bishop Richardson, Bishop's Court, Fredericton, N.B., Canada. When it finally arrived, there were two green-coloured imprints on the front of the envelope: "Recovered by divers from wreck of S. S. Empress of Ireland" and "Returned December 6, 1914."

She never sent it again. By 1918, Ada Driver had met a young Fredericton widower with three children and became Mrs. George Wandless. They lived at 360 Church Street and had two daughters. Over the years, she never parted with the letter that sank with the

Empress; in time, it was passed on to her daughter Mona MacMillan, who later placed the prize possession with the York-Sunbury Historical Society. The letter is now preserved under proper temperature control in the society's collection at the provincial archives.

Ada (Driver) Wandless passed away on June 7, 1958, and was buried in Forest Hill Cemetery. Bishop Richardson, who was responsible for her immigration to Canada, died in 1938, his wife in 1972. They were buried in the close of Christ Church Cathedral. The Bishop's Court at 806 George Street is now "a Victorian Bed & Breakfast."

With the declaration of World War One during the summer of 1914, the ill-fated *Empress of Ireland* was soon forgotten, the official inquiry in June having concluded that the *Storstad* was entirely to blame. The Honourable John Douglas Hazen, a former mayor of Fredericton, was a member of the investigating commission. Due to the death of one diver during the initial salvage operation, all early attempts at salvage were discontinued. In time, the CPR abandoned title to the ship and, with no explanation, destroyed all records and files pertaining to the *Empress*!

In the mid-1970s, Philippe Beaudry, a young man from Montreal, became interested in exploring the wreck of the luxury liner at the bottom of the frigid waters of the St. Lawrence. By the mid-1980s, he had made 195 dives to the sunken hull (at his own expense), retrieving over five hundred artifacts. His final goal: to bring up all the Salvation Army Band instruments.

When an American collector offered Beaudry 1.5 million dollars in 2002, the application for an export permit became public, many concerned Canadians hoping that Heritage Canada or Canadian museums would intervene and purchase the historic collection before March of 2003, at which time the artifacts will probably leave the country. National news reporters are following the proceedings closely.

In the annals of maritime tragedies, the sinking of the *Empress* ranks with the *Titanic* (1912), the *Lusitania* (1915), and the Halifax Explosion (1917), especially in loss of life. These are disasters which should never be forgotten and, with memorabilia like Ada Driver's letter and Philippe Beaudry's artifacts, hopefully, the *Empress of Ireland* never will be.

OCTOBER 27, 2001

SURVIVING THE TERRIBLE EPIDEMIC OF 1918

Dr. William Francis Roberts, New Brunswick's first minister of health, was appointed at the end of World War One and the beginning of the Spanish Influenza epidemic.

Mrs. Katharine Black (née Robb) led the appeal for volunteers in Fredericton during the great epidemic of 1918.

BEFORE THE SPREAD OF AIDS and before the fear of anthrax, there was another killer disease and it endangered the world in the autumn of 1918. It was called Spanish Influenza or "la grippe" and there was no October flu shot at the time to prevent it. Tens of millions died! How did Fredericton prepare and subsequently react to this deadly pandemic, a catastrophe similar to the one which last swept the country in 1889?

Momentous as it was, the outbreak of 1918 never once made the front pages of local newspapers. The final days of World War One received all the headlines; items about a developing plague were buried in the middle and at the back.

The first news arrived in several letters from friends in Boston. People there were being attacked with severe colds and dying within a few days, some in twenty-four hours with pneumonia. Doctors and undertakers could not cope.

The advice was to stay at home and that is what Margaret Crowe and Florence Holder did. These two young women were scheduled to leave Fredericton for Boston on September 17, Crowe continuing on to Rhode Island to study nursing. On that particular day there were eighty-one deaths in Boston alone.

It was a warning and, as a result, the local board of health began to take precautions. All people coming into the city, especially those from infected areas, were to be observed closely. Prompt action would be taken to prevent an outbreak.

The board did not have to wait long. By Monday, October 7, ten cases of influenza had been reported. Fredericton was under siege and its population of 7,500 was about to fight a war at home. The enemy: a mysterious virus.

In the meantime, Premier Walter Foster and his Liberal government moved with haste, passing a new health act, creating a Department of Health and appointing Dr. William Roberts as the minister. Lieutenant-Governor William Pugsley proclaimed these measures in the legislature the first week of October 1918.

Dr. Roberts, who laid the groundwork for the new department, was to have the distinction of being the first health minister in the British Empire. However, with the onset of a contagious disease, he had no time to think about the honour.

He was ready for the task before him, but he was fortunate to have a chief provincial medical officer, three district health officers, and a number of capable administrators on the local board of health of every village, town, and city. In Fredericton, John M. Wiley was chairman and George Y. Dibblee was secretary.

Large "Public Notice" posters began to appear. The subtitle: SPANISH INFLUENZA. A list of points regarding prevention followed: realize that the disease is contracted by direct contact with an infected person; when seized suddenly with chills, headache, muscular pain, and fever cough, remain in bed; avoid all crowded places and stay away from all public meetings; use daily an antiseptic spray or gargle for the nose and throat; report all cases immediately .

In view of the threatening epidemic, Dr. Roberts wanted each local board to take steps to procure a suitable building for use as an emergency hospital for those cases such as strangers, or those who were unable to be treated at home. For cases remaining in their own homes, the board was to placard the house at once with the word QUARANTINE, and place the patient in strict isolation.

The first place to be placarded was on Westmorland Street, when one of the ten cases reported on October 7 was a soldier who was visiting the home. He became suddenly ill and was so sick that he could not be taken to the Victoria Public Hospital. Upon his eventual removal, the house would be fumigated.

The other nine cases were at Old Government House Military

Hospital on the Woodstock Road. Four nursing sisters and five soldiers were "down," having been placed immediately in an isolation ward. A quarantine was attached to the institution, all staff and patients being denied their usual freedom.

In the spring of 1918, Old Government House had been remodelled and expanded to become a major convalescent centre for returned soldiers in the Maritime Provinces. The massive interior, including the historic rooms and the spacious vestibules, was changed into a well-planned set of wards, offices, and quartermaster closets. Three wooden units were added on the down-river side, all connected to each other and to Government House by wide corridors.

The three additional wings were devoted to hospital wards, recreational areas, dining rooms, kitchen space, and sun parlours, the last being located at either end on both floors. There were also quarters for the male and female help and the attendants. By the fall of 1918, the five hundred beds were fully occupied, but no one expected the unforeseen setback of an influenza epidemic and the quarantine order.

The military hospital was off limits for civilian patients, but military doctors would eventually be called upon to assist in the city and they did. Thus, when the Fredericton Board of Health met on October 10, they realized the necessity of having an isolation facility and the search began for an empty building.

Ironically, on October 11, there would be many empty buildings because of a proclamation issued by the new Department of Health: "All schools, theatres, churches, dance halls, billiard parlors, lodge rooms, and bowling alleys to be closed until further notice, and all public meetings to be prohibited, in view of the danger of an epidemic of severe Influenza." As an extra precaution, the by-laws which prohibited loitering and spitting on sidewalks were to be strictly enforced.

Prior to the proclamation, other places in the province were having serious problems, but Fredericton was recording very few incidents. Fred Hatt of Brunswick Street was reported to have the disease, his home being placed under quarantine, and Vesta Ruth Brewer of Devon had died in Rhode Island from the disease, her remains arriving at York Street Station and being taken immediately to the Rural Cemetery for a brief committal service. (Caskets could not be opened under any circumstances and only two people could accompany them.)

When the city fell silent on October 11, there was still no major outbreak. The managers of all public amusement centres drew their blinds, realizing there would be a loss of revenue. Trains, loaded with UNB and PNS students returning to their homes for the enforced vacation, slowly pulled away from the station.

When another case was reported on George Street, people were afraid to go to work, so stores and offices had to operate on reduced hours. Tension mounted. To make matters worse, there was a diversity of opinion among the doctors. Some did not agree with what the influenza symptoms were; others were against quarantining. The Board of Health felt powerless because many of the illnesses were not reported.

In certain cases, just as the influenza patient was recovering, pneumonia developed and the illness took a serious turn, the chief mortality being due to this complication. It happened in Fredericton on October 12 when nursing sister Agnes Alpaugh and Sergeant Major Roland Richards died at the military hospital. She was twenty-two and from Quebec; he was twenty-eight and from Fredericton. His brief funeral service, with military honours, took place in front of Old Government House, after which the remains were conveyed to the Rural Cemetery.

By October 15, the disease had spread throughout the entire city, with an equal number of cases being reported in Devon, Marysville, Nashwaaksis, and Morrison's Mills (near Forest Hill). Several households had the entire family infected and no one to care for them. Nurses were not available, many being stricken themselves, and some homes could not bear the expense. Fredericton's seven physicians were kept constantly on the move, tired out from the demands made upon them, trying to check each case before it developed into pneumonia.

By October 21, the situation in Fredericton was serious. Over 250 cases of influenza and 24 of pneumonia were reported to that date, but there were many more left unrecorded because there were not enough doctors or nurses to make house visits. No matter whether the patient was rich or poor, even ordinary help could not be obtained. In many homes small children were caring for the sick.

With the loss of two important services, the city became paralyzed. Firstly, only a few of the two dozen operators at the local New Brunswick Telephone Company office were able to remain on the job, trying to handle 15,000 calls a day. Secondly, the Victoria Public Hospital was forced to shut down, owing to the collapse of almost the entire staff with influenza. It was necessary to refuse the admission of new patients and to part with all those who were at all able to go back to their homes.

At this time, one woman came forward and took on the task of organizing all volunteer help, visiting many homes herself, delivering special meals, and preparing pneumonia jackets. Her name was Katharine E. (Robb) Black, a local resident who had already achieved national celebrity when she organized the first IODE chapter in 1900 in order to provide services for the soldiers of the British Empire who were fighting in the Boer War.

In 1918, Mrs. Black was a high-ranking officer in the St. John Ambulance Brigade. She was the person in charge of the Fredericton-area division and she had direct contact with the Minister of Health. Part of their correspondence survives today and is preserved in the provincial archives.

When young women without any medical background volunteered, Mrs. Black enlisted them immediately, gave them a few simple directions to study, and told them to learn all they could about nursing pneumonia. She then encouraged the volunteers to provide themselves with warm clothing so they could sit up at night without discomfort.

When she joined forces with Dr. Roberts, they went to the press regarding the various needs in a desperate situation. They appealed to men as well as women to come and nurse the sick. They asked for Boy Scouts to carry in wood, tend furnaces, and run errands. They informed the public that automobiles, which were loaned to carry supplies and volunteers to the afflicted homes, would bear the Red Cross sign, giving the chauffeurs freedom from strict observance of the traffic laws.

The volunteers went into homes and met many pitiful cases and witnessed scenes that were appalling. They worked continuously and, because of the care and attention given, saved lives during the epidemic crisis.

On October 24, there were 23 new cases of influenza, taking the city total to 450. In addition, there were 75 cases of pneumonia and 24 deaths. This showed a big spread in a short time, proving that the disease was by no means checked.

By Halloween, which was not a festive occasion that year, the epidemic reached its crest with a total of 585 cases of influenza and 92 of pneumonia. The 34 deaths for the month of October were considered a low rate of mortality in view of the duration and the seriousness of the disease. At that time, all doctors agreed that there was no need for an isolation hospital, although there would be over 700 recorded cases of influenza by the end of November and over 100 cases of pneumonia.

On November 14 the ban on public meetings was lifted; the eighteenth was set for the re-opening of schools and the twentieth for colleges. Dr. Roberts required each student returning to university,

Normal School, and business college to present a certificate of good health before entering the classroom.

When the city schools re-opened, the attendance was greatly decreased, especially since those coming from homes where there was still influenza were not permitted to return. Many parents and some doctors thought the ban should continue until the danger of contagion was absolutely past. The ban still applied to Morrison's Mills only, but Marysville, Devon, and Nashwaaksis refused to open their schools and churches because several new cases were still developing.

It was certainly not over and, on December 18, another health ban had to be imposed when there was a definite re-occurrence of the disease. This time an emergency hospital was set up at the corner of York and King streets and, before the ban was lifted on January 13, 1919, there were ninety-six new cases of influenza, twenty-five of pneumonia, and sixteen deaths. Christmas was not a joyous season that year.

Many were against the second ban, including restless soldiers who, when they returned to find no amusements, demonstrated in the streets. The president of UNB, the bishop of Fredericton, the theatre manager, and the city undertaker all wrote to the Minister of Health asking if he would relax the regulations.

Dr. Roberts did not give in, probably because he himself came down with the illness and knew what it was like. He survived and continued as Minister of Health for several more terms. After his death in 1938, he was honoured with a monument that still stands in front of the New Brunswick Legislature.

During her crusade against influenza, Mrs. Black became one of five people in Fredericton who contracted diptheria and was quarantined to her home. She survived and continued to organize Empire Day programs for the schools and the city until her death in 1936.

One of the positive outcomes of the epidemic was the discovery in Ontario in the late fall of 1918 of an experimental vaccine that might have cured the disease. The honour fell to Dr. W. Reginald Jaffrey, formerly of North Devon. However, when interviewed, Dr. Jaffrey stated to the press that whiskey was also an excellent remedy to use, especially in the very early stages!

Another gain was the formation of the Fredericton branch of the Victorian Order of Nurses (VON) in 1919, whereby home visitation of the sick has continued, especially during the next Spanish Influenza outbreak in 1957.

THE NIGHT THE RAILWAY BRIDGE WENT OUT

MARCH 18, 2000

A long piece of rail in the foreground snakes along Waterloo Row after the 1936 freshet destroyed the railway bridge.

THROUGHOUT NEW BRUNSWICK, historical markers and splendid memorials assist tourists and researchers with the highlights of our province's heritage. One miniature brass plate, obscure and unpretentious, never ceases to attract attention, causing amazement at what it must have been like on that fateful Thursday night in Fredericton sixty-four years ago—March 19, 1936.

Spring came early that year, with the ice in the St. John River breaking and running over several days, the earliest break-up since records began in 1825. There was only one other occasion in 111 years when the break-up was early and that was March 28, 1921.

Disastrous floods had occurred over the years, such as those in 1831, 1887, 1913, and 1923, but the "Rhine of America," as the St. John has been called, was never more intimidating than it was during that early freshet of 1936, the year Fredericton's first railway bridge "went out" and three-quarters of a mile of steel disappeared to the bottom of the river bed!

Alexander "Boss" Gibson and Senator Thomas Temple had formed the Fredericton Bridge Company in 1885 in order to erect a structure that would carry the rails of the Canadian Eastern Railway into the capital city, the contract being let to Lachine Construction of Quebec. Eventually, the bridge accommodated both the CPR and the CNR and, when it sank, all rail service in and out of Fredericton was completely cancelled.

The Westbound Express from Newcastle had crossed the bridge around 1:00 P.M.—the last train to do so. Constable Hazen Perry of the CNR Police was the last person to cross the bridge, about a half-hour before it was carried out at 9:25 on that dark and rainy evening.

Perry had placed Constable Harry McNeill at the Fredericton end to prohibit sightseers and then crossed to take charge of the Devon end. When the time came, hundreds of interested spectators stood on the river bank and witnessed the destruction of the nine spans as they were lifted off their granite piers by the crushing surge of ice, following one another into the water with a grinding crash.

It was over in a few minutes and there were no injuries. Several large trees on the shoreline formed a bulwark to hold the twisted track as it was pulled from its base, shrieking and groaning, free from the sinking bridge. As the steel rails were torn up for some distance along the embankment, they cut off utility poles, leaving the upper parts hanging, supported only by telegraph and telephone wires.

Earlier that day, the run-off in the Fredericton area had been checked due to the ice jamming against the islands in the Oromocto section of the river. But jams that had formed in the St. John River west of Fredericton, at Long's Creek and McKinley's Ferry, had already broken, giving a rapid rise in the water at points below.

With the demolition of the railway bridge came the breaking of a jam that flooded the entire east end of the city, as well as areas all along the river, producing conditions unknown before 1936 and causing two million dollars in damage. The ice and water reached a level of 30 feet, four feet higher than the level of 1887. During the late afternoon, water had risen at the rate of four inches per hour; just before the jam broke, the water increased its height at one foot per hour.

The water was a fraction of an inch from entering the lobby of the old Queen Hotel, but Lemont's Furnishings, also on lower Queen Street, received considerable depth; Phoenix Square was flooded to the extent that the basement of City Hall was filled two-feet deep; the provincial legislative buildings were entirely surrounded; and the Automobile and Boating Clubhouse on "the Green" at Parliament

Square was heavily damaged when cakes of ice crashed into it, smashing the railing and pillars of the outer veranda.

Mountains of ice were piled high into the west end of the city, private boat houses and stables being crushed and then strewn along the river bank. Miraculously, a large barn belonging to the Grand Hotel was moved down river by the ice but was not greatly damaged!

When the water receded, huge blocks of ice, sixteen to eighteen inches thick, were left on Queen Street and as far back as Brunswick, forming a traffic hazard for curious citizens who thronged to inspect the site where Fredericton's first railway bridge once spanned the St. John River. The next day, school was cancelled, giving children a chance to marvel at the ice cakes littering the lawns of Christ Church Cathedral.

For the first time in the history of the New Brunswick Legislature, flood conditions interfered with the progress of the session, a projected night sitting having been cancelled. The next day, there was an adjournment and a delay of the budget debate because there was no heat, and motors that were being used to pump water out of the basement sent fumes throughout the building.

The low-lying districts of Sunbury County, chiefly in the parish of Maugerville, were also flooded to the greatest depth in recorded history. When the water started to recede, help was on the way: six hundred loaves of bread were rushed to the Sunbury area from Fredericton, and even Premier A. A. Dysart inspected the scene by boat, but he became stranded on an island and was marooned for twenty-two hours!

A new Fredericton railway bridge had to be built. The CNR decided on the same location, but only after some of the wreckage was removed by the Garson Wrecking Company of Halifax. They found the first span on the Fredericton end half in the water and half on the bank; the second span was completely submerged, dynamite having to be used before it could be placed in an upright position, thus facilitating navigation between the piers.

The nameplate on the cornerstone of the bridge was removed and presented to local historians for safekeeping. Unfortunately, this important artifact has been misplaced over the years and, although an extensive search has been made, the nameplate has not been found.

Did a similar fate occur with the time capsule that had been placed inside the cavity of the bridge's cornerstone and laid in place at the excavation site on the river bank, just at the beginning of Waterloo Row? Lady Macdonald, the wife of Canada's first prime minister, did the honours on August 15, 1887, subsequently spreading the opening with mortar and then watching the granite block being lowered into place. Her husband (Sir John A.) and other dignitaries observed from a nearby platform.

The tin box used for the time capsule contained recent issues of *The Saint John Sun, The Fredericton Capital,* and *The Maritime Farmer*, along with English, Canadian, American, and Chinese coins, and a copy of the stone-laying ceremony. It is not known what happened to the tin box when the piers were dismantled a half century later.

The new railway bridge was to be six feet higher than the former, in order to safeguard it from floods, and subways constructed at each end were to replace the former level crossings, with Waterloo Row, University Avenue, and Queen and Brunswick streets converging at the southside underpass. The materials: steel and concrete. The cost: $1,250,000. The opening ceremony: June 1, 1938.

Today, this impressive architectural structure is a link in the Fredericton walking trail system, with the metal tracks removed and a wooden floor and guard-rail installed. Now relatively safe from flooding, the bridge will remain as an historic monument, spanning the St. John River and echoing the tragedy of its predecessor.

To remind future generations of the 1936 flood, a permanent twelve-inch by six-inch brass marker was securely fastened to the stone of the right-hand pillar at the entrance of the provincial government's Departmental Building on St. John Street. Major A. A. Dodge of the Bridge Engineers' Department prepared the blueprint, which indicates the height of water that covered the eastern portion of the city in that disastrous freshet.

The marker states the date, and arrows point to the actual indentation made by members of the provincial public works department when they measured the height of the water, well above the three marks which had already been there as a result of previous floods—twenty-seven inches above the 1887 record!

Official water markers were also placed on the stonework of Fredericton City Hall and the stone base of the wrought-iron fence of the old Provincial Normal School (now the Justice Building). These two markers have been removed some time during the last sixty-four years and have not been found to this date, but the unique brass plate on the Departmental Building is still there, the little arrows and simple inscription symbolizing the once-destructive power of the mighty St. John River.

MAY 13, 2000

THE MYSTERY OF THE MISSING MURAL

IT ALL BEGAN OVER A HALF CENTURY AGO—May 21, 1948. It was Empire Day and thoughts of patriotism were most appropriate, especially at 9:00 P.M., when a brilliant and fascinating wall mural, measuring twenty feet square and divided into two spectacular scenes, was unveiled before a packed auditorium in the old Fredericton High School on George Street.

It was undoubtedly a memorable moment in the history of the oldest English high school in Canada, a moment that CFNB Radio helped to share with its many listeners, who were waiting with anticipation to hear the description of the mural, the name of the artist, and the special relevance that this work of art was to have for Fredericton.

The chairman for the ceremony was Dr. O.V.B. Miller, principal of the high school who, in his introductory address, said that Empire Day, 1948, "has been selected as the day on which we recognize the great service that has been performed for humanity by so many of those young men whose voices were raised in song in this auditorium such a short while ago."

According to reporters at the time, "the ceremony was outstanding in its simplicity"; according to surviving documents in the FHS Archives, "a number of distinguished guests took part," including Lieutenant-Governor D. L. MacLaren, Premier J. B. McNair, and Bishop W. H. Moorhead. John Clark, 1948 president of the Student Government Association, read the sixty-three names inscribed at the base of the mural; Ralph Hay, 1946 president of the students who planned for the project, presented the memorial to the Fredericton Board of School Trustees. Mr. Justice P. J. Hughes accepted.

The mural was unveiled by Robert Corbett, a 1946 graduate whose brother was one of the brave boys from FHS who had given their lives for their country in World War Two. Like all war memorials, it was an impressive list, especially since the names belonged to former classmates.

The program concluded with the introduction of the talented young artist who had devoted two years of his life to the FHS mural. His name was Fred Ross and he had already gained national attention for a mural in the Saint John Vocational School. In the spring of 1946, the nineteen-year-old artist was approached and, shortly after, his preliminary drawings were presented and accepted by the Fredericton School Board.

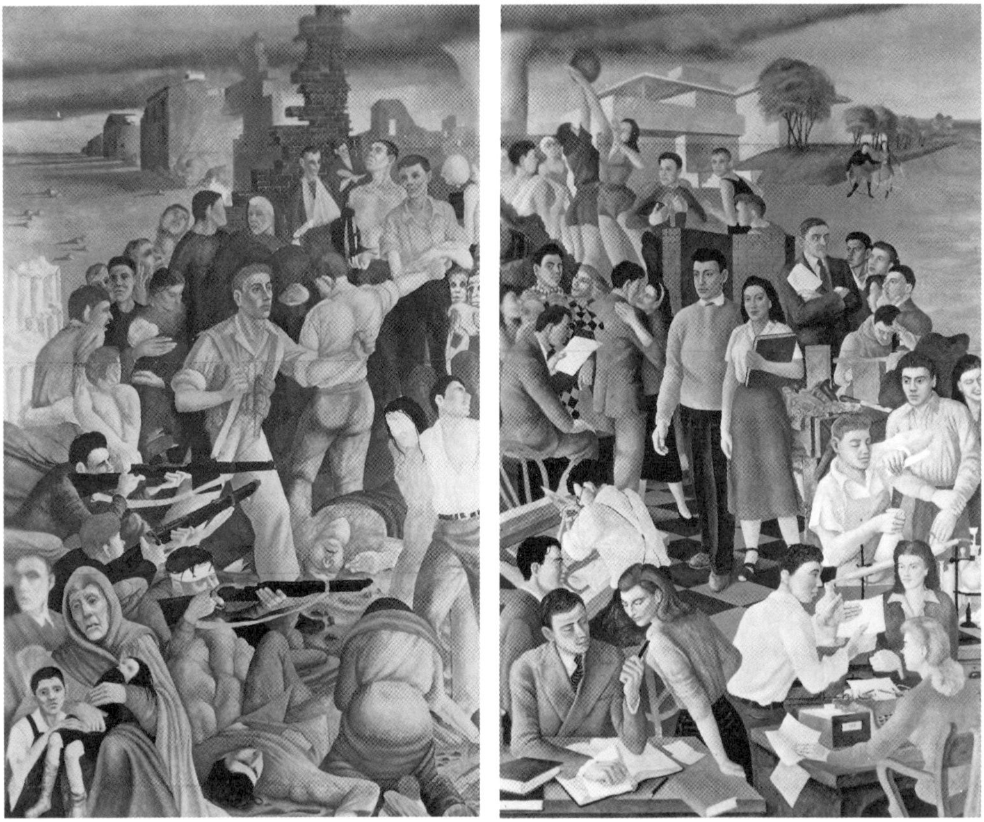

The left and right panels of the FHS memorial mural by Saint John artist Fred Ross. The late Mrs. O. V. B. Miller (wife of the principal) was present when the mural was unveiled in 1948: "It was large and colorful, and now it is gone; the black and white photographs that remain will never do it justice."

At his parents' home in Saint John, Fred Ross made many sketches before he decided on the final design. When he did, he chose atomic energy as the motif that would unify the two panels, using the explosion of the bomb as the visible symbol of that power. He wished to stress no special religion, race, or country, but rather the idea of the brotherhood of man breaking down all international barriers.

In the first panel, the one to the left, he depicted the horrors of war, its destruction, and the misery and suffering it inflicts on mankind. In the second panel, he showed the better life through education. The dominant figures here are a young man and woman stepping out from their various school experiences into a world where the sun is setting on a distant future that is bright and happy.

Before Fred Ross started the actual painting, full scale drawings, known as cartoons and done in black, white, and red, were made on toned paper, the artist working from direct observation, using his friends and acquaintances as models. These cartoons took about one year and when they were finished they were transferred to ten horizontal sections of masonite boards, the final painting being done in casein tempera on a gesso ground, a technique that gave a flat finish in sympathy with the surface of the auditorium wall.

It was a small but proud staff of twenty high school teachers who attended the unveiling; three of them still reside in Fredericton: Glen MacKenzie, who had come forward with the proposal that a mural be placed in the assembly hall; David Coughey, who had been the liaison person with Saint John; Edwin Allen, who had been involved with the fund-raising efforts of the students.

In the fifty-two years since the unveiling, Frederick Joseph Ross has gone on to establish himself as one of Canada's best realist painters. During preparation for a major exhibit of his work in the 1980s, an inquiry was made about including the FHS memorial mural. However, after much deliberation and subsequent embarrassment, a school official made the quiet announcement that the long-forgotten painting of 1948 was now missing!

As the news spread among teachers and students, the same question was asked over and over: "How could a twenty-foot-square painting disappear without a clue?" As the search began, several red herrings surfaced, but the mystery unfolded slowly but inevitably.

In 1954, a gymnasium/auditorium was added to the old George Street High School and, as a result, the antiquated assembly hall at the head of the stairs from the main entrance was changed into several classrooms. In the process, the mural was dismantled, the two large panels being separated into six sections (instead of the original ten) and stored in the FHS bookstore, a small room at the end of one of the corridors. Fading into oblivion, the mural remained there for a number of years, since no other walls in the old school were high enough to display such a large work.

Unknown to new administrators, an ever-changing staff, and continuous generations of students, the six sections were eventually moved from their standing position to become an overlay for the floor of the bookstore, the entire painting facing down.

The desecration had begun and it was not until 1967 that this horrendous situation was discovered when the bookstore underwent renovations, the mural being quietly collected together and shipped to the storage area of Charlotte Street Elementary School for safekeeping. When this school was closed in 1972, the mural, still intact but badly damaged, was removed to the Doak Road Elementary School for further storage. It was at this location that a young maintenance employee with the district was in desperate need of a piece of wallboard, so, without realizing the future consequences, he reached for one of the mural sections standing nearby and put it to another use. The desecration had continued!

Fortunately, the remaining five sections were returned to the empty Charlotte Street School and remained there until the new Fredericton High School on Priestman Street was finished. In 1974, the severely damaged and incomplete mural was moved to its new home at the top of the hill. For the first time in two decades it was assembled on the spacious basement floor and examined. Because of the deterioration and the missing section, it was decided to contact the artist about possible restoration.

Fred Ross was interested but the project would involve considerable time and work. Because there was no immediate money, the mural was again forgotten, the five remaining sections being placed in a corner of the basement against a wall. In time these sections were covered and surrounded with colourful backdrop sets from annual Glee Club stage productions. In another decade the once-famous painting would eventually lose its identity altogether.

That is, until the retrospective exhibition featuring Fred Ross was being planned for the UNB Arts Centre in 1984. It was the wish of the organizer that the FHS mural be a part of this exhibit. Although the five remaining sections would definitely not have been in any condition to be displayed, the sad fact was that the five sections could not be located anywhere in the basement storage area.

Exhaustive searches were made but those concerned soon realized that the mural was no longer on the premises. Assessment of blame was difficult to arrive at, given the passage of time and the fading memories. However, certain revelations indicated that the painting became a part of one of the annual clean-ups and was taken away for disposal.

Although FHS staff and administrators over the last decade were not involved with the mural mystery, they have shown deep concern and serious consideration for what has happened, establishing guidelines to see that the situation will not occur again. All valuable paintings, photographs, and memorials have been framed and mounted along the many hallways, stairwells, and foyers, this having been the responsibility of a diligent photo-restoration committee.

In 1993, an enlarged black and white photograph of the FHS mural was mounted in the main entranceway of the school, the sixty-three names of the young boys listed at the base once more.

In 1995, the life-size sketches of the mural completed a North American tour, along with a number of other works by the renowned artist. When the inauguration for this exhibit took place at the Beaverbrook Art Gallery, the case of the missing mural surfaced, about which one FHS student was heard to say: "We should see to it that our war memorials last forever."

In 1997, Fred Ross donated the cartoons of the memorial mural to the National Gallery of Canada, where they were placed on exhibit a year later to mark the fiftieth anniversary of the Declaration of Human Rights.

The Bryan Priestman Tragedy

November 11, 2000

Bryan Priestman is remembered by his students as a tweedy personality with a sharp wit, a decided accent, a quick mind, and a sense of humour beneath it all. He was an intense professor who inspired students.

PEOPLE WHO VISIT FREDERICTON are intrigued by the various street names, especially the one called Priestman. Located on the South Side at the top of the hill, Priestman Street, which has an elementary school and an office building with the same name, is an extremely busy artery in the city today. It is easy to see that many of our street names emanated from members of royalty, political giants, and historical figures. But who was Priestman and why is there a street in his honour?

A few inquiries will provide the basic facts of the story: a physics professor, Dr. Bryan Priestman lost his life while attempting to save a boy who had fallen into the St. John River. However, a closer look at this tragedy reveals compelling and dramatic details.

Priestman's youth was spent in England; he was born in London in 1897. He was the eldest of five children, having four sisters. The father was an acclaimed landscape artist. The family was Quaker.

After attending a Quaker boarding school, Bryan went on to Cambridge, where he received a BA (with honours in physics) in 1923. He then came to Canada to attend McGill, where he obtained two more degrees in physics—an MSc in 1926 and his PhD in 1929. Before he finished his Doctorate, he had already come to Fredericton to be a one-man physics department at UNB's Memorial Hall.

During the 1930s, there were only seventeen professors on the UNB faculty, one of them being Dr. Frank Toole, who shared an apartment with Priestman on the second floor in the west wing of the Old Arts Building.

"Putting in" large quantities of apples and walnuts, eating them for breakfast, the two professors spent long hours talking about education, religion, and politics. When Dr. Toole married and went to live at 824 George Street, Dr. Priestman took rooms upstairs in the same building.

Early in 1940, renouncing the Quaker pacifism of his youth, but still an enemy of "militarism," Priestman offered his services to His Majesty's forces and joined the RCAF. "I'm not going to miss this one," he said, having spent World War One on the sidelines as a conscientious objector in the Friends' Ambulance Unit created for Quakers.

By 1943, he had been promoted from pilot officer to flight lieutenant to squadron leader. The great enterprise of ferrying bombers from Canada to the war theatres was just under way when he saw an opportunity for even more brilliant war service.

By the time he was forty-eight, he had navigated thirty-five bombers from Canada to the battle zones, setting a record in accurate performance probably unequalled in an air force or flying organization. According to the departments of National Defence and Veterans Affairs, Priestman was the navigation pioneer of the North Atlantic. He saved twenty-four of his flight plans and thirty-two of his flight charts and these were eventually placed in the UNB Archives.

He was a modest senior officer who would dash into side streets to avoid being saluted. He refused to wear medal ribbons and badges and, when he was honourably retired, he would not wear his uniform to social functions.

In the fall of 1945, he arrived back on the UNB campus in Fredericton, ready to re-organize the Physics Department and to renew old acquaintances.

Then came Remembrance Day.

Under clear blue skies of a Sunday afternoon, November 11, New Brunswick's capital city was reposed in a perfect autumn setting. Earlier in the day hundreds of citizens had gathered at the Cenotaph on lower Queen Street to pay homage to men and women who had given their lives in two great wars. It had been the first peacetime Remembrance Day service held in Fredericton in seven years.

Eight-year-old Ronald Dempsey and eleven-year-old Edward McLean from Barker's Point had hoped to be there to see the parade. To save time, they took the popular short cut across the railway bridge that spans the river below the cenotaph. But they were too late; the parade had already made its way to Officers' Square for dismissal.

Deciding to stay "over town" for a while, it was not until four o'clock that the two boys proceeded back toward the railway bridge and the shortcut home. There were several other people present, not for a shortcut but for a Sunday afternoon walk (gasoline was still rationed and few people were driving cars).

Unfortunately, no provision had been made for pedestrians in the construction of the bridge, and regulations prohibited people from walking the railway ties. But this did not prevent one hiking enthusiast who had walked the bridge many years before the war and who was now using it again.

Bryan Priestman had just started to stroll along "the Green" toward the bridge, his maroon Royal Canadian Air Force (RCAF) beret pulled tightly over his slightly curly, light-brown hair, a blue scarf tucked inside his well-worn blue jacket. He had not attended the morning ceremony at the Cenotaph but had, instead, planned his day around an afternoon hike to the Devon side of the river, almost forgetting that he must return for an early evening dinner invitation with friends.

The railway bridge had often been his route for "jogging" before the war, because others were mildly amused at the typical Englishman who actually enjoyed getting out of breath but did not like being ridiculed. The only problem was the railway ties; they were so spaced that he could neither run nor walk on them evenly. It took time for his low black shoes to get used to that part of the trestle extending from the rail toward the girders.

The heavy, black leather boots which came up around Ronald Dempsey's ankles were also having trouble with the railway ties. To make his walking easier he placed his feet on top of the wooden guard rail or beam which was fastened to the ties with large, projecting bolts. McLean was not as brave, so he stayed in the middle of the tracks, walking a few feet ahead of his chum.

When the boys reached the last pier on the Devon side, McLean was aware of an abrupt sinister silence and, turning around quickly, noticed that Dempsey had fallen through the opening between the wooden guard rail and the steel girder, dropping thirty feet to the river below.

The lean figure of the forty-eight-year-old Bryan Priestman moved quickly. Doffing his gloves, shoes, beret, scarf, and jacket, letting them fall on the flat part of the steel girder and, telling McLean to go for help, he dove, without hesitation, from the great height. Within seconds man and boy were one, Priestman's arm tightly around Dempsey's body. But then there was a slight struggle and they both disappeared into the icy water, never again to surface alive.

Early the following morning, thin slivers of ice broke away from the river's shoreline as the grappling parties continued operations from the Sunday afternoon before. Later in the evening of the second day, one of the hooks of the grappling irons caught the boy's clothing, lifting the pair to the black surface of the water just about nine feet from the Devon shore (in front of the Irving oil tanks, not far below the spot when the accident had occurred). Caught on the mangled metal of the old railway bridge that gave way in the 1936 freshet, they were carried no farther.

Dr. Priestman's body was taken to Memorial Hall, where it lay in state until the funeral. At Forest Hill Cemetery, his grave is marked with a small, unpretentious stone, which reads: "Greater love hath no man than this." Ronald Dempsey was buried on the north side of Fredericton in Sunny Bank Cemetery. (Edward McLean grew up to be the owner and operator of the same Carleton Street barber shop that had been frequented by Dr. Priestman.)

At the close of 1945, a commemorative plaque to Priestman was placed in Memorial Hall by the UNB Veterans' Club but was moved later to the Memorial Student Centre, now the Alumni Building. On October 24, 1946, the *UNB Journal of the Air* delivered a Bryan Priestman Memorial Broadcast over Radio Station CFNB. Among those taking part were Dr. Frank Toole (fellow professor), Squadron-Leader W. Munro (fellow airman), and students Robert Lawrence, Douglas Rouse, and Dalton Camp. The fifteen-minute recording is now located in the UNB Archives.

Also in 1946, Bryan Priestman was posthumously awarded two medals: a gold from the Royal Canadian Humane Association, and a bronze from the Carnegie Hero Fund Commission. In 1952, Lord Beaverbrook delivered the medals to Priestman's mother in England. In 1977, the Priestman sisters returned the medals to Fredericton to be permanently housed at UNB.

During the early 1950s, the York-Sunbury Historical Society brought forth the idea of having a street named in Bryan Priestman's honour, minute books and the daily press indicating that the society never gave up on this particular memorial idea until it was finally realized in 1956. To this date, it is the only street in the city of Fredericton which bears the name of a local hero!

The University of New Brunswick also wanted to establish a memorial, something that would respect his wishes but would not be an elaborate monument. Thus, "The Bryan Priestman Memorial Lectureship" was set up, the first lectureship at the university. Since the academic year 1951–52, outstanding authorities in one or other of the natural or social sciences have been brought to the campus, the annual visitor spending several days and delivering three formal addresses.

Perhaps Francis Reginald Scott, Rhodes Scholar, Canadian poet and Priestman's close friend during their McGill years, said it best when he wrote an elegy in 1954 entitled "For Bryan Priestman." The poem shows that the Englishman/Canadian who adopted Fredericton for his home lived and died by his creed, his faith, and his upbringing:

This was a formula he had carried from childhood,
That can work but once in the life of a man.
His were the labels of an old laboratory,
And the long glass tubes of the river.

June 23, 2001

Rioters and Revellers and the Local Constabulary

The Fredericton Police Force one hundred years ago. From left to right: John O'Neill, Paul Phillips, Zebedee Wright, George Rideout. The forage cap was similar to that of a railway conductor or a soldier's informal cap.

In June, 150 years ago, city council passed a law that made the front page of *The New Brunswick Reporter & Fredericton Advertiser*:

"To establish a Police and to punish vagrants, beggars, drunkards, idle and disorderly persons in the City of Fredericton."

Five "fit and able" men, one for each ward, would be appointed annually to act as constables for preserving the peace, preventing all crimes, and apprehending offenders. The salary would be "not less than twenty pounds."

Although Fredericton was growing rapidly, there was another reason for the establishment of a small police force. In 1847, a major riot had broken out between the Protestant-Orangemen and the Irish-Catholics. The local citizens never again wanted to witness such confrontations.

It happened on the "glorious" twelfth of July, Orangemen's Day. As early as eight o'clock in the morning, a considerable number of Catholics, most of them strangers from the outlying areas, had assembled on the sidewalk under the windows of the Orange Lodge Hall at the corner of Queen and Carleton streets. There were loud, defiant cheers towards the Protestants, who were inside celebrating and preparing for their march through Fredericton.

Several magistrates appeared, but the boisterous crowd ignored the pleas for peace. Instead, both sides continued to exchange insults and to wave their firearms. Even when Lieutenant-Governor William Colebrooke arrived in the evening, the mob remained as turbulent as ever. Unfortunately, the Riot Act was never read.

The Orangemen's procession was cancelled and a number of special police were sworn in to walk the streets during the night. However, attempting to break up several intense skirmishes, the constables became the victims of multiple beatings. At that time, serving as constable was a civic duty—without pay!

When it was all over, many of the 350 rioters had fled; only fourteen Irish-Catholics were taken into custody. There was one fatality and it occurred when Thomas Welch (a Catholic) was shot outside the Carleton Street home of William Armstrong (an Orangeman). Although Welch was standing on the street and unarmed, Armstrong was never charged.

Following the Religious Riot trials and the subsequent constabulary law, it was decided to have eight special policemen always waiting in the wings for any emergency that might develop. The choices were made by Sir John Campbell Allen, Fredericton's second mayor, and the names were listed in the city council minutes for July, 1851, now preserved in the provincial archives: "Henry A. Estabrook, George Coulthard, George Todd, James W. Tower, Robert Wiley, George Coulter, George Hatt, John Mullin."

Ironically, Orangeman William Armstrong became the policeman for Queen's Ward, but no one else could be found to join the permanent force for the other wards (King's, St. Ann's, Wellington, Carleton). As a result, more auxiliary constables were appointed: Thomas Sweade, John O'Connor, Phillip Brannen, Benjamin Creighton, and William Payne.

By the time the next riot broke out, the city still did not have a full complement of five permanent policemen. But there was an addition. On May 3, 1871, Colonel John Lothrop Marsh was sworn in as the first police magistrate, a position he held for almost forty-five years. His first major challenge was the unexpected circus riot of 1874, which resulted in one of the most bloodthirsty confrontations that ever degraded Fredericton.

Involved was the "Great and Only New York Circus," which was to appear in the barrack yard of the Military Compound on a Monday evening, July 6. The performance concluded at 10:30, at which time the outside canvas around the big tent was mysteriously and quickly flapped down, forcing the audience to clamber over seats, getting out the best way they could. This angered the circus hands, who immediately lowered and extinguished the large circular gaslight in the centre of the tent.

The spectators began to panic; a circus man shouted, "Shoot the damn rascals"; and several pistol shots were fired into the crowd. Four young male citizens fell to the ground with serious wounds. Their names: Samuel Macauley, David Carr, William McLean, Armstrong Lowry.

Someone rang the fire bell and this brought hundreds from all over the city to the scene of the riot. Alarmed at what they saw and heard, they demanded that the gate to the compound be closed. When one of the circus wagons tried to get through, the horses were unhitched and the wagon taken down to the river and thrown over the wharf.

There were only two policemen on the force, John Woodard and Phillip Mulligan, and they had been on street patrol that evening. When they reached the tent, they worked like heroes, but could not bring the situation under control. Mayor Edward L. Wetmore and Police Magistrate Marsh were summoned and lost no time in swearing in twenty-five special constables in front of City Hall, selecting citizens at random, sending them into the dark and noisy tent.

Eventually, the yard was cleared and nineteen circus hands (baggage and tent men) were escorted to the basement lockup at City Hall. Four others escaped and so did Lewis B. Lent, the well-known circus director. He would be found in Rockland, Maine, a few days later, where he was arrested on several charges.

Although the circus shootings were totally unjustifiable, three incidents had occurred to provoke the circus hands to take revenge upon innocent people: First of all, there had been confusion at the tent's main entrance earlier in the day. When the ticket agent was accused of giving incorrect change, he punched the patron in the face. A fight broke out between several citizens and circus people. Second, during the performance, a number of boys climbed the guy ropes for a better view. When they came down, the tent hands struck them viciously with mallets. Finally, one of the circus men had coaxed a young Fredericton woman to come away with him. When they were found together behind the tent, several of the local men intervened and took her home, much against the protests of the intended lovers.

Eighteen of the circus prisoners were released due to lack of evidence (and cell space). One American, George W. Harrison, was held over for an October court appearance. However, he was not brought to trial, the grand jury finding no bill of indictment. Leaving the York County Court House, Harrison praised the British justice system and thanked the city's policemen for their kindness manifested to him during his "compulsory residence" in the York County Gaol.

The circus troupes were always gone the next day, but Police Magistrate Marsh would soon face a challenge that would remain until the day he retired.

In 1878, the federal government announced the Canada Temperance Act, also known as the Scott Act. Two years later, it came into force in Fredericton due to a decision of the Dominion Supreme Court. By 1883, there had been ninety-five prosecutions in the city and $3,150 in fines.

Selling liquor was illegal and it was the job of the policemen to find those who were guilty of it. In one incident, Sergeant Dow VanDine approached a horse and wagon but the two guilty fellows plied the whip and drove off. The sergeant pursued them, caught up, and jumped from his horse into the back, serving the summons as they travelled at breakneck speed.

For wages of one dollar a day, it was difficult to recruit policemen. No one wanted to put on the uniform; in fact, there were no uniforms at that time. In the spring of 1882, the entire three-man force (VanDine and two others) resigned.

When the police magistrate went before city council, he informed them that he could not find "good and efficient" men. He suggested $1.25 per day and a suit of clothes per year. Council bargained for $400 per year and the uniform.

VanDine returned and joining him were two new officers whose devotion to the force became legendary over the next quarter century. Their names were Henry Paul Phillips (who went by Paul) and Zebedee (Buckwheat) Wright. During their first summer, they began their careers on a note of heroism.

It was July 27 of 1882 and two young brothers, George and Newton Lee, along with their friend Thomas Virtue, set out to get even against the prohibition of liquor sales. Their intention: murder. Their target: Sergeant Dow VanDine.

Armed with a shotgun, the boys arrived at the sergeant's Brunswick Street residence at midnight. They woke him up, and fired a shot, but missed. Four days later, a similar attempt was made on Colonel Marsh at his George Street residence.

A warrant was issued.

When VanDine, Phillips, and Wright went to the Westmorland Street home of the Lee brothers, they went straight for the barn where the three boys were hiding. Without hesitating, VanDine started up the ladder to the hayloft. He was immediately shot in the arm.

With all attention on the wounded officer, Newton Lee made a dash across the back yard. Phillips and Wright went after him, firing revolver shots all the way to Charlotte Street, where they cornered him in a small shed. When he was brought before the assembled crowd of 1,500, there were cries of "Hang him!"

George Lee was found hiding in the pig pen. Thomas Virtue fled across the river and disappeared. The Lee brothers wanted to join their friend, attempting to escape from the old Guard House in the Military Compound. Instead, they stood trial at the Officers' Quarters in October of that year and were found guilty, being sentenced to twenty years in Dorchester Penitentiary. The officer who accompanied them on the train was none other than Sergeant Dow VanDine!

In the late 1890s, Phillips and Wright were joined on the force by John O'Neill and George Rideout. The quartet made an impressive team as they risked their lives chasing rumrunners, a contrast to the impounding of dozens of cows that roamed the city neighbourhoods. They always carried their "billy" sticks, two walking the streets by day, two by night, now earning $1.25 for each shift.

One hundred years ago, catching bicycle thieves and horse thieves was a regular part of the daily routine for the four-man force. When the culprits were brought before the police magistrate, they were shown no leniency, often receiving a sentence of seven months in jail and their names in the local press.

On the lighter side, Fredericton had its share of revellers, especially when "the vulgar practice of *shivaree* reached the City." The blowing of horns, the beating of tin pans, the ringing of cowbells, and "other untuneful noises" associated with weddings prompted police to interfere in such unseemly demonstrations.

The male students at the University of New Brunswick and the Provincial Normal School caused no end of trouble. It became a graduation tradition for the PNS boys to serenade staff members at their homes—after midnight! When the teacher appeared at the bedroom window, the cheering and singing became louder, much to the consternation of the neighbours and the police.

The UNB boys also liked to sing and shout their college yell, but they wanted to impress the "lady students" at the Normal School. On one such occasion, twenty-five boys entered the school and disrupted the opening exercises in the morning. When they refused to leave, Sergeant Phillips arrived and charged the ringleaders.

When Paul Phillips became sergeant, he was assigned to day duty only. Owing to the fact that a telephone was installed in his home, subjecting him to the calls of citizens at any hour of the night, his salary was increased to $1.50 per day.

It was said that "oft in the still night" the services of a policeman were required, but there was no telephone in the basement police station at City Hall.

In 1910, Sergeant Phillips quit when he was instructed to return to night duty. After twenty-eight years, he handed in his equipment and declined to serve any further. He died eight years later and was buried in the Old Burying Ground.

His three close colleagues had already left the force. Zebedee Wright had been "summarily dismissed" after a quarter-century service; George Rideout went to Moncton to become chief of police; John O'Neill attended UNB and returned as city engineer before moving to the United States.

As the sesquicentennial of the Fredericton Police Department is celebrated this year, a composite photograph of the current ninety-four-member force, its auxiliary and associates, is on display in the foyer of the Queen Street headquarters. Nearby, among a collection of artifacts, is the original copy of the provincial legislative bill that authorized the formation of the police 150 years ago.

SECTION FIVE: NOTABLE LOCALS

YUKON GOLD RUSH CHANGED THEIR LIVES FOREVER

MARCH 4, 2000

Four Fredericton-area residents who left for the Yukon Gold Rush on March 1, 1898. From left to right are George Pinder, Robert Duncan Wilmot Hubbard, George Black, and George Amireaux.

IT WAS ROBERT SERVICE, the Poet Laureate of the Klondike, who said: "No spot on the map in so short a space has hustled more souls to hell." Perhaps he should have added: "Or was more difficult to reach."

But that did not stop New Brunswickers who, by the spring of 1898, had left in large numbers to travel across Canada by train, north by steamer, and then over the steep mountain trails by snowshoe.

Harry Waugh of Fredericton was among the earliest to leave and to stake several successful claims. He would return for brief visits and, on one of these occasions, he built a large home for his parents. It still stands, overlooking the St. John River at Douglas, currently occupied by a nephew. Harry died in 1910 in Chicago, but he continues to be remembered: a monument in Whitehorse lists his name with other gold-mining pioneers.

The first major exodus from Fredericton occurred on Tuesday afternoon, March l, 1898. It was front-page news, an event that brought one thousand citizens to the CPR train station on York Street to bid farewell to twenty-four young men who were leaving in a special coach attached to the Montreal Express, each paying a one-way fare of $37.50 to Vancouver.

Eight members of the group were organized as the Fredericton Mining & Development Company, backed by a syndicate of businessmen and politicians and thoroughly equipped in every way for excavating in the north. They even took with them a chest of *Mazawattee* tea, promoting this product for York Street grocer Enoch Hoben.

The leader was the popular George Black, a twenty-five-year-old lawyer who lived with his parents, but who had his own office at the corner of Queen and Carleton streets, in the same building as his uncle John Black, barrister and MLA. Being an eligible bachelor, George enjoyed the social life of Fredericton; however, he was ready to give up city comforts for the rugged land of gold exploration. He was also looking forward to seeing his older brother, John, who was already in the Yukon working on railroad construction.

The other members of the Fredericton company included William Boddy and George Graham of Prince William, George Pinder of Temperance Vale (whose father was an MLA), George Amiraux of Richibucto ("the life of the party"), Samuel Hoskins (an experienced cook from Lake George), and Humphrey Boone, who was to become a Fredericton hero in the Yukon.

Finally, they were joined by one of the city's brightest musical talents of the day—twenty-one-year-old Walter Chestnut, solo clarinetist in the 71st Battalion Band and Orchestra. He, too, lived with his parents and two older brothers (William and Harry), the latter having just founded the famous Chestnut Canoe Company in the back of their father's hardware store on King Street. Another brother (Robert) was already prospecting for gold in the Yukon. Unlike his fellow travellers, Walter was leaving his sweetheart behind.

Many of the other gold-seekers sharing the special coach on the westbound train were travelling on their own, but once they reached

Vancouver they would join various parties for the journey north. R.D.W. Hubbard, a twenty-two-year-old from Burton, was one of them, but he remained solo for the twelve years that he lived in the Yukon. Although he used his initials, it is interesting to note that his three given names belong to New Brunswick history, having come from his grandfather, Robert Duncan Wilmot, who was a Father of Confederation and a lieutenant governor of the province.

In Vancouver, the boys were met by a young man from Fredericton who would eventually become one of the foremost bankers in Canada. His name was Charles Neill and he would keep in contact with the mining company while they were in the Yukon, assisting with their correspondence, telegrams, and newspapers.

From the beginning, letter-writing became just as important as panning or sluicing for gold; news from east and west was as precious as the illusive nuggets that were being mined. Unfortunately, much of the voluminous correspondence from the Yukon to Fredericton has been lost; only rare individual letters having been saved by family descendants.

George Black appears to have had a plan that would save his letters for posterity and now, one hundred years later, researchers can go back in time and relive those harrowing experiences on the trails and in the camps, word for word, first-hand.

Not only did he write long and informative compositions in pleasant and conversational tone to his father and uncle, but George also wrote to the editor of *The Daily Gleaner*, encouraging all three recipients to publish his letters in the press for everyone to read. Today, these splendid accounts of the Yukon geography and the endless search for gold are preserved on library and archival microfilm.

George even took a little camera with him, sending photographs home, and requesting that *The Gleaner* publish them. As a result, these prints became some of the first and best black and white illustrations in the paper's early history. A group picture of the Fredericton Klondike party, taken in front of their tent, received so much attention that it was enlarged and exhibited in the window of John Adam's Framing Store on Queen Street.

But that was not all he sent home. There were pressed flowers ("to be mounted"), the dried skins of small animals ("we always carry pistols"), a mosquito specimen ("to show the large size"), the occasional gold nugget, and even the remains of an old flintlock musket, "probably a relic of the days when the Hudson Bay Company traded with the Indians along the Yukon River."

As the boys kept pitching their tent at Fort Wrangel, Skagway, the White Pass Summit, Lake Bennett, Tagish Post, and along the Stikine

Trail and the Hootalinqua River, conversation inevitably turned to Fredericton and what they missed most about home. "We have a steam launch, a row boat, and a scow. We named the steamer *City of Fredericton* and the scow after the good ship of the Fredericton Bicycling & Boating Club—*Zeezaboo*, prefixing the word *Nackawick* in honour of the designer [George Pinder]." They were proud to report that all three of their little boats, each floating astern the Union Jack, were successful in shooting the Whitehorse Rapids.

Once a month, two members of the party tramped back to the coast over the Chilcoot Pass to post a sack of letters and newspapers (*The Yukon Sun*, *The Klondike Nugget*, *The Whitehorse Star*) and to pick up mail. Three days, ninety-five miles! But it was rewarding to find forty or fifty letters waiting, along with back copies of *The Richibucto Review*, *The Saint John Sun*, and *The Daily Gleaner*.

Whereas thousands were unable to stand the strain of hardship and exposure, which could not be avoided, and whereas extortion, disease, and death claimed many, the crew from Fredericton was a hardy lot. "We are tenderfeet, but we keep our boots on and the soles of them are full of St. John River driving corks; we look tough and we are tough. You should see our whiskers grow. We use them to stick matches in."

They were the only party in the North "to keep Sunday"—no travelling and no mining. It was a day to socialize with other New Brunswickers whom they had met on the trail and whom they wrote home about. These included officers of the North West Mounted Police (NWMP), soldiers from the Royal Regiment Canadian Infantry (RRCI), and former acquaintances such as Harvey Lawrence (Burtt's Corner), James Humble (Stanley), Charles Pond (Boiestown), Perry Dibblee (Nortonville), George Bigger and Dan Lenihan (Fredericton).

By the Spring of 1900, the Anglo-Boer War was pushing the Gold Rush from the headlines. With their dreams of striking it rich never fulfilled, disillusioned people who came from all over North America were gradually giving up, looking for work elsewhere, or returning home, rich only in experience. The original eight of the Fredericton company were no exception; they too faced the grim reality of too many claims, not enough wealth. But only six came back.

Their one major loss and tragedy was the untimely death of Walter Chestnut. He became ill while climbing the White Pass and had to be returned to Skagway (Alaska), where he died in one of the makeshift hotels. His remains were taken to Victoria for interment, although the family stone in Fredericton bears his name and place of death.

George Black settled in Dawson City, opened a law practice, and handled the business affairs of a successful sawmill owner in the Klondike by the name of Martha Munger of Chicago. They were married in 1904 and the rest is history. With Martha's help, George was first elected to the Yukon Council, then appointed commissioner, and finally Member of Parliament. When George became ill, Martha took her husband's place in Ottawa, becoming the second woman to be elected to the House of Commons. She died in 1957 at age ninety-two; he died in 1965 at age ninety-four.

On one of his many visits to Fredericton during his political career, George Black gave his family a souvenir that he had carried with him throughout his gold-mining adventure. Today, his personal letter-opener is in the possession of his grand-nephew—Jack Fenety.

An Unusual Love Story with a Touch of Class

February 19, 2000

[LEFT] **Lord Ashburnham, circa 1920.**

[RIGHT] **Lady Ashburnham, circa 1920.**

ONE HUNDRED YEARS AGO a forty-five-year-old bachelor arrived in Canada from England. Captain Thomas Ashburnham was the fifth son of the fourth earl of an ancient and wealthy family, but there seemed to be little chance that he would inherit the earldom that consisted of three large estates and a London townhouse.

Tom had graduated from Cambridge, joined the Queen's Own Seventh Hussars and, as a result of his heroics in Africa and Egypt, was decorated by Victoria herself. When he retired, a large annuity from the family fortune supported his leisurely lifestyle, but he became the "black sheep" and was subsequently packed off to Canada, abandoned to a life of travel and solitude.

By 1903, he had settled in Fredericton, which was to his liking, probably because it had been a garrison town. He found lodging at Windsor Hall, a large hotel on the corner of Brunswick and Westmorland streets and became a familiar figure on the verandah each afternoon. His evenings were spent in various taverns, and he began to make regular telephone calls to Camp's Livery Stable on

King Street, as he summoned a horse and carriage to transport him to the Windsor.

The friendly voice at the telephone exchange belonged to Maria "Rye" Anderson, and it was a voice with which Captain Ashburnham became infatuated. Each time he called, they chatted and they laughed, and soon they fell in love, long before he requested their first meeting on Valentine's Day.

A courtship followed and in the spring of 1903 Tom made a hurried trip back to England to announce his intentions to his family and to purchase gifts for his future bride. On June 10, North American newspapers carried the headline:

CAPTAIN THE HONOURABLE THOMAS
ASHBURNHAM MARRIES A TELEPHONE GIRL
AT FREDERICTON.

However, the event was discreetly mentioned in the British press, although Tom was not the first of his line to have "married beneath him."

Maria Anderson was born in Fredericton in 1858. Her father, the chief engineer for the fire department, served on city council; her grandfather served as a soldier in the illustrious 104th Regiment. Both had been vestrymen at St. Anne's Parish Church, where "Rye" was baptized and also married, the bride and groom standing upon a beautiful robe which was made from the fur of silver jackals and which Queen Victoria had stood upon during several state occasions in London.

"Rye" Anderson was petite, attractive, and vivacious. A forerunner of the liberated woman, she wanted to seek employment outside her father's house, a rare desire for a young woman in the ultra-conservative Fredericton of the late nineteenth century.

When the New Brunswick Telephone Company came into being in 1888 and set up its central exchange on Carleton Street, Maria took a job as a night operator. There were 123 subscribers at the time and they all got to know the employee with the pleasant voice and the soft laughter.

Returning from their honeymoon, Maria no longer worked at the telephone exchange and Thomas gave up his tavern visits to remain at home with her. Home was a large residence on upper Brunswick Street, the Captain having purchased two large houses that touched the sidewalk at numbers 163 and 165.

One of these buildings had been a popular inn, the other had been the Anderson family homestead. Because they were so close, the Ashburnhams had them joined at the second floor by a glassed-in conservatory, a porte cochère being formed at the ground level, the driveway running through to a magnificent garden. Two full-time employees cared for the miniature estate, which is still known as Ashburnham House, although the stained-glass windows of the double front door have been replaced and the hitching posts along the sidewalk have disappeared.

The Ashburnhams liked the west end, as opposed to Waterloo Row; their home soon became the centre of an elite social life in the capital city. With money sent from England, the rooms were lavishly furnished. Maria's personal quarters were in the lower house at 165, where she began to host her famous luncheons and afternoon teas. Thomas occupied the upper house at 163, which contained a small library and a collection of military memorabilia and hunting trophies, making his study comfortable for writing letters to his family and solicitors.

A decade passed and the ties with England became more distant. Then, in the winter of 1913, the least of the captain's expectations came true when a telegram was received announcing the death of his brother, the fifth earl. The three brothers next in line had all died of an hereditary bronchial illness, so Thomas became the sixth earl and, because he and Maria had no children, the last in the Ashburnham line.

Thus, Maria Anderson of Fredericton became The Right Honourable The Countess of Ashburnham, her life never being quite the same again. In the spring of 1913, the new lord and lady sailed for England where Maria would become the mistress of her husband's vast landholdings. But they were to stay for only one year.

There is no doubt that "Aunt Rye" won the hearts of those who met her, especially the cousins, nieces, and nephews, but she was never really accepted by the British aristocracy, her name even being struck from the presentation list for the court of King George V and Queen Mary. And, because he knew little about administrative duties, Thomas played no part in the running of the estates.

As the World War One clouds gathered, Lord and Lady Ashburnham returned home to Fredericton, bringing with them three servants and a number of family heirlooms. For the next ten years they continued to be celebrated socialites and the press followed their every move, especially their volunteer involvement with local organizations.

By 1924, the earl longed for his ancestral home in England and so another visit was planned. It was to be his last. He died in London at age seventy on May 12, his body being taken to Ashburnham Church for a funeral that was synchronized with a memorial service in Christ Church Cathedral (Fredericton).

Under the provisions of the will, Maria was given a life annuity of $10,000 and Ashburnham House in Fredericton, where she returned to live with her younger sister, Lucy. An older sister, Jane, lived nearby, and five brothers travelled from their homes to make regular visits.

The Ashburnham estates in England were greatly reduced in size by the impact of death duties. It was necessary to sell half of the tenant farms and much of the contents of the grand houses. What was left was passed to the nearest male heir, the son of Tom's eldest sister, and then to a grandson, who donated Ashburnham Place for use as a Christian retreat.

For the Countess of Ashburnham, her social activities continued as she opened her home for church and civic groups, politicians, and visiting dignitaries. She was and still is best known for her philanthropic acts of kindness and generosity. She forgot no one, especially her late husband; in 1926, she donated a stained-glass window in his honour for UNB's Memorial Hall.

Throughout the 1930s, Maria maintained the lifestyle to which she was accustomed when the earl was living, but she exceeded her means and slowly went into debt. Her health began to deteriorate and on October 9, 1938 she died of a heart attack and was buried in the Rural Cemetery, her tombstone bearing the full title of her acquired peerage.

It was the end of an era, just before World War Two, but it concluded on a note of sadness. To settle Maria's debts and accounts, an auction was held to sell the contents of her home and her personal belongings. Fortunately, certain items were saved and preserved in Fredericton, among them Lord Ashburnham's antiquated roll-top desk and Lady Ashburnham's elegant wedding gown, the latter being a rare symbol of a Cinderella story that actually did come true.

Photography and Philanthropy: The Lasting Legacy of John and Martha Harvey

December 9, 2000

John Harvey as a young man, circa 1890.

Martha Harvey as a young woman, circa 1890.

CHRISTMAS WAS THE SEASON they loved best, although their Yuletide motives were noticeably different.

By 1900, John Harvey, a professional photographer, had become a household word. His successful business in downtown Fredericton was advertised throughout the province, and the studio that has carried his name for over a century still operates in the same building.

Martha Harvey had remained anonymous as she single-handedly uplifted the lives of those less fortunate, no matter what creed or colour. She founded community organizations that continue to enhance the city, but her name, after a lifetime of volunteering for others, has been relatively forgotten.

He was flamboyant and enjoyed the limelight; she was reserved and wanted no recognition. As they pursued their own interests, they tended to complement one another, their happy marriage destined for longevity.

Unfortunately, Christmas 1900 was to be their last together; John Harvey's untimely illness and premature death were soon to follow.

Left with two small children, a large home, and a thriving portrait studio, Martha Harvey stepped out of the shadows and became a woman ahead of her time. Alone, she carried the legacy into the twentieth century.

Her husband, John Harvey Jr., was the son of John and Sarah (Rutherford) Harvey, the parents having been born and raised in northern England. In the early 1850s, they sailed for America with their first son, Robert. After a few years in the United States, where their first daughter, Isabella, was born in 1853, they came to Canada and settled in Fredericton.

John Harvey Sr. became a carriage trimmer and harness maker, his home and business located at 80 Queen Street (the 200 block today). Here, three more children were born and raised: Margaret (Annie) in 1858, John Jr. in 1861, and Sarah (Janie) in 1864. The family was then complete.

By 1880, nineteen-year-old John Harvey Jr. realized that photography was becoming a booming business in Fredericton and he wanted to be a part of it. Elegant studios were opening; elaborate advertisements were appearing. Could a population of 6,200 support one more professional camera?

He opted not to apprentice with well-established local photographers such as Taylor, Schleyer, and Buckhardt, each of whom had progressed from daguerreotypes to tintypes, from wet plate to the dry plate process. Instead, John Harvey travelled to the United States and took two years of intensive artistic training in the best studios of New York.

Upon returning to Fredericton in 1883, John boarded with his parents and began doing portraits on a small scale, hoping to set up his own studio as soon as possible. The competition, which was definitely challenging at the time, was situated all along Queen Street and that is where he wanted to be.

On Thursday morning, May 22, 1884, John Harvey opened his new studio at 142 Queen Street (372 today). He rented one-half of a small brick building just below the People's Bank (the stone facade of which is still there) and directly opposite the Randolph Block (now Greenarm Corporation). *The Gleaner* described the new studio as one of the best in the city, "handsomely furnished, well-lighted and well-ventilated." *The Capital* promoted Harvey as "a first-class photographer who merits a liberal patronage."

The advertisement that Harvey placed in the newspapers was large and personal: "I have purchased a complete set of improved instruments, together with the latest scenery and furniture. I have also one of the finest north lights in the Province. Having worked in the leading firms in New York, I am now in a position to do the finest and best work ever done in the photograph business in this City."

And he did! By July, *The Farmer* carried the headline HARVEY'S STUDIO IS THE PLACE TO GET YOUR PICTURES TAKEN and, in a new advertisement, John encouraged people to drop by and look at his showcases. "We are now on a standing equal to any Gallery in America."

In November, there were two additions: a new room to his already extensive premises and a new employee, Mary Lugrin, a member of Fredericton's large and prominent Lugrin family of printers and publishers. Her experience in the "finishing" department was gained in the United States and, as a result, everyone was admiring the colouring on the photographs at Harvey's Studio.

For Christmas, John published in *The Reporter* "extra inducements" for the public who were interested in good photography. According to him, photographs were much better than Christmas cards or Christmas souvenirs. The result: an overwhelming rush for his first holiday season in business.

For the next six years, Harvey's Studio grew and prospered. According to the Fredericton Assessment Records for that time period, John was making seven hundred dollars annually. By 1890, there were two more additions: a full-time assistant and a wife.

John Walter Lister Jr., the new assistant, was five years younger than John Harvey, but their backgrounds were similar. Lister's father was also born in England, coming to Canada at age twenty-one, settling in Fredericton, and being appointed caretaker of the Legislative Building. To avoid confusion, the younger Lister went by "Walter" and, over the years, he became a very important part of the studio.

Martha Fleming, the new wife, was a year younger than her husband. At six o'clock, Tuesday morning, September 23, 1890, they were married at the new Kirk (St. Paul's Church) before taking the train to New York for their honeymoon. According to *The Daily Gleaner*, "both are very popular in this town, and the bride is well known as an energetic worker in the Kirk congregation."

Martha Johnston Fleming was born in Fredericton, August 12, 1862, daughter of John and Jane (Harper) Fleming. Her middle name came from her mother's side of the family; her first name was in honour of her paternal grandmother who, with her husband Joseph Fleming, came to Fredericton from Ireland in 1826.

Joseph was appointed keeper of the newly built Alms House, a large stone building on Maryland Hill. He had that position for many years and, when he retired, his son John, who had been master steward at UNB, succeeded him.

There is no doubt that the family's involvement with the Fredericton Alms House influenced Martha's compassion toward her fellow human beings later in her life, but, as a young girl, she had six brothers for whom she cared greatly—Charles, Joseph, James, Alexander, Robert, and John Jr., the last becoming the owner of Fleming's Haberdashery Shop at 480 Queen Street.

After their marriage, John and Martha lived with his parents on Queen Street. In 1892, a daughter was born and named Bertha Hastings Harvey. Two years later, a son was born and named John Fleming Harvey (nicknamed Don).

In 1894, it was time for their own home, which they built at 245 York Street. A year later, they purchased the Queen Street building where the business was located. The studio remained in the west half, the other side being rented to a confectionery merchant who made his candy on location.

On December 1, 1899, a Christmas feature appeared in *The Daily Gleaner*. A reporter wrote about his pleasant visit to the studio, which began at the door, where he was attracted by "new-style photos in the showcase." Inside, "the genial proprietor was busily engaged in retouching negatives, dozens of which were piled upon a table beside him, while his assistant, Mr. Lister, was attentively watching dozens of other negatives laid out in the sun, from which prints were being made."

In 1901, the studio was closed on two occasions: February 2 for the funeral of Queen Victoria; August 31 for the funeral of John Harvey. For months he had been confined to his home, critically ill with heart problems. He was just thirty-nine when he died on Thursday morning, August 29.

After her husband's death, Martha took over the ownership and operation of Harvey's Studio and looked forward to the twentieth century. It was a time when very few women were in business for themselves, a time when women were struggling to even get the right to vote.

She appointed Walter Lister as manager, hired another employee to the staff, updated and refilled all the showcases, installed a negative-printing machine (so that prints could be made with a strong electric light), and opened all the rooms for tours (which she often conducted herself).

She wanted to continue with the high standards established by her husband and, because she was strict, she succeeded. A month after his death, the local press said that a visit to Harvey's was well worth an inspection, "reflecting credit on those who have the business in charge."

In 1917, she sold the business to Frank Pridham, with one major condition: the name was to remain in perpetuity. And it did. Pridham's son-in-law, Ted Atkinson, joined the company, becoming president, followed by his son, Andy, who manages the business today at the same site, making Harvey's Studio possibly the oldest continuous picture-taking operation in Fredericton, in Canada, and in North America—almost 120 years!

With the business sold, Martha Harvey was quite independent and eager to carry on with her philanthropic work, her many organizations, and her fervent interest in all that went on in the capital city. A number of editorials were written, praising her as "one who lived an unselfish life, one who was everybody's friend" *(The Daily Mail)*.

In many cases, the extent of her charity was never made public beyond those she helped, and that is the way she wanted it to be. But it is known that wayfarers never left her home without warm food or the price of a meal and financial help to start them on their way.

She was deeply interested in the beauty of Fredericton, seeing that trees were looked after by experienced caretakers, tending to the Old Burial Ground where her grandparents and her parents were laid to rest, and crusading for the preservation of historic buildings such as Old Government House.

She was a life member of the Fredericton, the New Brunswick, and the National Women's Institutes, through which she was able to introduce many community reforms such as the wrapping of bread in bakeries, the use of bottles for milk deliveries, and free milk for children and seniors. The institute later honoured her by setting up a UNB scholarship in her name

She expanded the Fredericton Exhibition from a few craft entries to over one thousand exhibits by women! She was on the boards of the Children's Home, and the Social Service Council; she was active in the IODE, and the Order of the Eastern Star; and she was a charter member of Saint Andrew's Presbyterian Church.

After the franchise for women in 1918, Martha organized the Conservative women of York and Sunbury counties. She was a staunch party supporter who worked long hours during election time, and a fluent speaker who put forth many convincing arguments. Today, she would very likely be a successful candidate!

Her last major accomplishment was the founding of the York-Sunbury Historical Society, which she began with small meetings in her own home in 1927.

Through her persistent efforts and financial contributions, the society was finally established in 1932. Martha encouraged Mayor W. G. Clark to become the first president and she became one of the first directors.

Due to her unexpected death, January 16, 1934, she did not live to see the society incorporated on July 20 of that year or housed in permanent accommodations many years later in the Officers' Quarters.

In 1981, the society established the Martha J. Harvey Award in her honour. It is given annually "for outstanding contribution in the field of New Brunswick history." This year, the award went to the Heritage Department for its magnificent restoration of Old Government House, the current location for the society's annual Christmas party, hosted by the lieutenant-governor.

April 27, 2002

Remembering Fredericton's Forgotten Poet

Francis Joseph Sherman became a captain while serving in France in 1916. When he was discharged in 1918, he held the rank of major.

Come, for it is April, and her hands have loosed the tether
That has bound for long her children,— who her children more than we?

THESE LINES FROM THE POEM "In the North" were written in Fredericton more than one hundred years ago by Francis Joseph Sherman. During the last two decades of the nineteenth century, he joined Charles G. D. Roberts and Bliss Carman in leading a Canadian poetry movement that began in Fredericton. As a result, the three poet sons of the capital city gained for their common birthplace a well-known and popular title—the Poets' Corner of Canada.

In 1947, a National Historic Site monument, bearing the names of all three, was unveiled on the UNB campus. It stands today in front of the Harriet Irving Library, a fitting memorial and an appropriate location as all three attended the University of New Brunswick.

Throughout the twentieth century, the international reputations of Roberts and Carman often overshadowed the biography and work of their younger colleague. Thus, the splendid poems of Francis Sherman have been under-appreciated, his brief dramatic life almost forgotten.

His story began at the Barker House Hotel, which was located on Queen Street, across from Officers' Square. Following his birth on February 3, 1871, his parents continued to live at the hotel for one more year before moving into a home of their own at #71 St. John Street (approximately where the stage door of the Playhouse stands today).

The father was Louis Walsh Sherman, an American who came to Fredericton in 1866 at age thirty-three; the mother, who was ten years younger, had been born in Fredericton as Alice Maxwell Myshrall. They were married on November 25, 1868, in St. Anne's Parish Church on Westmorland Street.

Living near the river end of St. John Street placed the Sherman family in the busy east end of Fredericton and, for little Frankie, this section of town became his world for the next twenty-eight years. Nearby was Christ Church Cathedral, the York County Court House, and the elegant Queen Hotel. Across the street was Province Hall, which was replaced by the present Legislative Building after the fire of 1880.

L. W. Sherman built a massive wharf at the foot of Church Street and became a general commission merchant, paying particular attention to the shipping of lumber, even leasing a wharf in Saint John. His partner was Zebulon Rowe and their advertisement was supported by several impressive references.

According to Roberts, Sherman's Wharf also became the centre for schoolboy activities. "Around it, under the shelter of the high bank, we swam, we launched our birch canoes, we explored for spruce gum the great log-rafts sometimes tied up below it."

Although Frankie Sherman was only three years old when Roberts was fourteen, he too spent his boyhood summers playing and swimming around his father's wharf. Three of his playmates became life-long friends: Charlie Neill and the Winslow brothers, Wentworth and Jaspar. Later, a number of his poems alluded to the St. John River.

Another part of his early life was his maternal ancestry. Grandfather Joseph Myshrall was a widower whose house was around the corner between the Queen Hotel and Camperdown Lane. He had been a deputy sheriff, a city marshall, a railway commissioner, and finally a liquor merchant, operating a wine shop on the ground floor, living upstairs with his older daughter Louisa, who was the leading female singer in the cathedral choir.

Grandmother Achsah (Maxwell) Myshrall had died in 1856, long before Frank was born. She was from Charlotte County and the granddaughter of James Maxwell, a Loyalist from Connecticut and a major in the New Brunswick Militia. She and her husband, who died in 1884, were buried in the Old Burying Ground.

At the Collegiate School, located on lower George Street, Frank Sherman followed in the footsteps of Roberts and Carman. The plain wooden building with its little bell tower was the forerunner of Fredericton High School; it was where all three future poets came under the profound influence and guidance of headmaster George Parkin (who was later knighted).

Sherman continued to follow Roberts and Carman "up the hill" to UNB, entering in the fall of 1886 at the age of fifteen, one of his classmates being Mary Kingsley Tibbits, the first female enrolled at the university. Because he did not have full entrance requirements, he was listed as a "partial student." However, he took no examinations and left the following year, the only one of the poetic trio who did not proceed to a degree.

In the fall of 1887, Sherman accepted a junior position with the old Merchants' Bank of Halifax (later the Royal Bank of Canada), first in the Woodstock branch and a few months later in Fredericton. By the age of twenty-six, he became the youngest manager in Canada and was ready for a transfer and even greater responsibilities. His ability as a banker was evident from the very beginning as he continued to rise to the top in the financial field.

When not working long hours over his desk at the bank, Sherman was reading the classics and writing verse. ("No one can hold a higher opinion of Matthew Arnold than I do," he once said.) Bishop Kingdon, who lived next door, found him to be one of the best-read persons he had ever known and allowed Frank to use his personal library. There would be follow-up discussions on the front porch or during walks along the Green, an experience that transcended any other form of higher education.

During his banking years in Fredericton, it was necessary for Frank to live at home because, in 1890, a major upset had occurred in the Sherman family. According to the city's assessment rolls, the father's business appears to have deteriorated and, as a result, he left the city, probably returning to the United States. Apparently, he was never heard from again, his disappearance causing dire hardship for the family and speculation to this very day.

Thus, Frank's banking salary was needed to help support his mother and his five younger siblings—Lawrence, Ralph, Bessie, Myra, and Stella. This close-knit family remained together and continued to live in the little house on St. John Street (which had been willed by grandfather Myshrall to his daughter Alice).

All six of the Sherman children were successful, the oldest brother becoming a surrogate father, leading the way and setting a strong example with his own accomplishments. They were musical (Frank playing the violin the sisters singing in the cathedral choir); they were athletic (hiking in the summer, snowshoeing in the winter); they were sociable (receiving invitations to the city's fancy balls, private parties, and upper-class weddings).

Frank belonged to the fashionable Thirty-Two Club, an exclusive group of prominent bachelors, including J. J. F. Winslow, Loring Woart Bailey, Jr., W. O. Hartt, A. B. Wilmot, Theodore Goodridge Roberts, Charles FitzRandolph, and poet John Bodkin. Each year these gentlemen gave a grand ball at the Queen Hotel; among the female guests were the Misses Sherman and a beautiful and vivacious young lady by the name of May Whelpley.

Miss Whelpley was at the centre of Fredericton social life in the 1890s. She was extremely popular with the young gentlemen about town and her dance programmes were always filled. Unfortunately, she was unable to dance, but her many suitors were delighted just to "sit out" and talk with her. One of these suitors was the handsome young banker and aspiring poet—Frank Sherman.

May was the devoted daughter of George Thomas Whelpley, "one of Fredericton's most highly respected and generally liked merchant princes" and a descendant of the famous family who established the Long Reach skate factory in the lower St. John River valley. He had his grocery store business in the Barker House block but his family homestead was located at #28 Waterloo Row (no longer standing). It was here that May lived with her parents and her brother Charles.

And it was here, at a very early age, that May suffered from infantile paralysis, leaving one of her legs shorter than the other. For the rest of her life, she wore a leg brace and a heavy-soled shoe to help her get around. She also had her own horse and carriage, which took her about the city and "up the hill."

At the age of seventeen, in 1889, May Whelpley (along with ten other young ladies) entered UNB, registering as a "partial student," remaining for two years, studying mostly languages. When her mother passed away in 1891, she left to "keep house" for her father and to become the fiancée of Frank Sherman.

It was a familiar sight in Fredericton to see May and Frank in her carriage, riding into the countryside for picnics, or walking across the Green, carrying cushions and paddles to the river's edge, his birch-bark canoe waiting to take them over to the Nashwaak River.

They might have married, but family differences intervened and, although the Whelpleys and the Shermans did not approve, the engagement was never broken. May and Frank continued to see each other and she became the inspiration for his first book of verse, entitled *Matins*.

It was published in Boston in October of 1896 and, although every line was written for his beloved May, the collection of poems was dedicated to the father he lost. In a two-page review in *The Bookman*, Bliss Carman had only praise, saying it was "the most notable first volume of verse of the past year, notable for its beautiful lines and stanzas, and for the unwritten beauties between them." By the end of December that year, there was not a single copy left in Fredericton bookstores.

When Rudyard Kipling received a copy in England, he began to correspond with the young Fredericton poet, two of his letters to Sherman being preserved today in the UNB Archives. "It must be a gorgeous thing to be one of the band of new singers," Kipling wrote, "whose eyes are well opened on the country of their birth and love—new men in a land that is both old and new."

In appreciation, Sherman and several of his gentlemen friends, including the four members of his banking staff (Frank Shute, Mont Wiley, Morris Aitken, Fred Dever), started the Kipling Club of Fredericton. They met regularly to read and discuss the life and work of the British author, annual dinner meetings being held at the popular Hatt's Cafe.

If the members of this literary club looked forward to more poems from Frank Sherman, they were not disappointed. His Boston publisher subsequently released *In Memorabilia Mortis*, a collection of sonnets, a poetic form of which Sherman was a master. The same firm also assisted in the private printing of several small booklets, each inspired by May Whelpley: *A Prelude*, *Two Songs at Parting*, *The Deserted City*, *A Canadian Calendar*, and *An Acadian Easter*. (All were collected and published as *The Complete Poems* in 1935.)

When his poems began to appear in the leading periodicals of the day, alongside the work of Roberts and Carman, *The Daily Gleaner* in Fredericton took notice and introduced a new column in their expanded weekend section, starting in 1898. It was entitled "The Poets Fredericton—The Charms of the Celestial City in Verse." The first to appear was "A Road Song in May" by Francis Sherman.

He had achieved distinction in two very different fields—poetry and banking. It made his departure from Fredericton in February of 1899 a little easier. Before he left for Havana, Cuba, where he was to establish the Royal Bank of Canada, there was a grand farewell dinner at the Queen Hotel, businessmen from all over the city joining to give testimonials in his honour. He was visibly affected, concluding his remarks with these words: "I can never forget my native town and hosts of friends, and I anticipate with pleasure the coming to visit my old home."

And he did. Every year he returned to see the woman with whom he was still in love and who continued to inspire him. However, by 1906, May Whelpley was dying from tuberculosis and, although Sherman was with her near the end, he had to terminate his Fredericton visit because he could not bear to see her suffer. She died on November 11, four months after her father had passed away. On her bedside table were copies of Frank's books, each one inscribed "for Maisie."

With May Whelpley gone from his life, Frank Sherman never wrote another line of poetry again. Ironically, he now had the time, because he was at the height of his banking career. He returned to Montreal to be assistant general manager at head office, sharing the post with his boyhood friend, Charles Neill.

In 1915, Frank retired from the bank and joined the Canadian Forces, going overseas on military service, returning to Canada in poor health. Happiness came when he met Ruth Ann Sullivan of Philadelphia, whom he married in 1922, without her realizing that he had been a poet. They lived in Atlantic City, where two sons (Francis and Jerry) were born and where Frank Sherman died, June 15, 1926.

He was the first of the Fredericton poets to be returned home for a funeral at Christ Church Cathedral and burial at Forest Hill Cemetery. Carman followed in 1929, Roberts in 1943.

Frank was laid to rest in the Sherman family plot, between his mother, who had died in 1914, and a memorial stone for his brother Lawrence, who was killed during the war and who was buried overseas. (His brother Ralph was selected as a UNB Rhodes Scholar, entering the Anglican ministry, becoming an Archbishop in western Canada; his three sisters became schoolteachers.)

Today, visitors have only a short walk between the unpretentious tombstones that mark the graves of May Whelpley and Frank Sherman. They are on either side of the old section of the hillside cemetery, separated by a narrow roadway running through the middle.

He had written his last poem in 1901. Entitled "So, After All, When All Is Said and Done," it was a final note, a prophecy, and it ends with these lines:

But, after I am dead, my troubled ghost
Some April morn shall tremble and be glad,
Hearing your child call to a child of mine
Across the Northern wood it dreams of most.

November 23, 2002

York County Farm Boy Successful in City

Alexander Addison Sterling was born in St. Mary's parish, York County in 1838, the son of farmer George Henly Sterling and Susan Elizabeth McLean, the grandson of Loyalists on both sides—Captain Jonathan Sterling (Maryland Loyalists) and Captain Archibald McLean (New York Volunteers).

Alexander was the third of four brothers—John (1836), George Jr. (1837), Allen (1842). They were raised on their father's farm, beginning their education at the local one-room school. When they became old enough, the brothers walked two miles to the Nashwaak River each day, crossing by boat, continuing on to Fredericton by foot to attend the old Collegiate School on lower George Street. After the return journey in the evening, farm chores were waiting.

In time, the father's family donated land for the Baptist church in Penniac and established the Sterling Wharf at Taymouth; the mother's family named McLean's Brook at Durham Bridge, McLean's Flats, and the McLean Cemetery. Thus, roots were established along the Nashwaak Valley, but the young Alexander wanted more than pioneer life in rural New Brunswick.

He left home in 1852 to begin a career in commerce, his first job as a clerk in a Fredericton dry goods store for four years. In 1857, he travelled to Toronto, where he became an apprentice for one year with a large hardware establishment, learning the business from the warehouse to the front office. It was not an easy start in life, but it was an experience that prepared him well for the future.

Returning to New Brunswick, Alexander took up farming and lumbering with his brother George in Maugerville, continuing their partnership with a successful sawmill. George eventually became a member of the provincial parliament for Sunbury County, Alexander, a representative for the parish of Maugerville in the Sunbury County Municipal Council. It was the first step into public life and A. A. Sterling never looked back.

When he returned to Fredericton in 1867, he was twenty-nine years old, a quiet, unassuming young man with good looks, a sharp mind, and keen powers of observation. He opened his own general store on upper Queen Street, in the middle of the 300 block (south side), and he lived in a small apartment over the shop.

In 1867, New Brunswick was playing a major role in Confederation, Lemuel Allan Wilmot becoming the province's first native-born lieutenant-governor. The premier was Andrew

The Sterling family. From far left: Estelle, Alice (seated in front) Helen (standing in back), Alexander (father), Louise (standing in centre with white dress), Mabel (standing in back), Sarah (mother), Spencer (with arms crossed), Sadie, and Archie. Fredericton photographer George Burkhardt took the picture in the late 1890s.

Rainsford Wetmore, the mayor of Fredericton, William Needham. All roads led to the capital city, a thriving centre for politics, education, religion, and commerce. It was where A. A. Sterling wanted to be; it was where he would create a new life. However, he never forgot the adjoining parishes of St. Mary's and Maugerville, visiting often, saving his lumber permit for vacant land on the Tay Creek for the rest of his life.

In 1869, the local newspapers carried an obscure announcement for Thursday evening, August 12: "Christ Church, Maugerville, Reverend Canon Harrison married Alexander Sterling of Fredericton and Sarah Haws of Saint John."

The bride was twenty-two years old, elegant, beautiful, and "of a retiring disposition." She was the youngest of the eight children of John Haws and Calista Calvert, a prominent and wealthy Saint John family, the father being a shipbuilder and county magistrate. He was also "a tough old hard Scotsman," who employed a large number of workmen and who contributed greatly to the prosperity of the port city.

Before the end of the nineteenth century, eleven children would be born to Alexander and Sarah Sterling. Unfortunately, Herbert (1870) and Alex Jr. (1886) died in infancy. Florence died of dipthe-ria at age six in 1879; Estelle died of scarlet fever at age twenty in 1901. All four deceased children were buried in the Old Burying Ground in the centre of town.

According to the 1891 census, Helen was eighteen; Mabel, fif-teen; Sadie, thirteen; Spencer, twelve; Alice, seven; Archie, two. Louise would be born in 1892, all seven surviving children reach-ing adulthood, the five sisters remaining close friends for the rest of their lives.

When his children were growing up, A. A. Sterling wanted them to have the best public education possible. Thus, when the city council appointed him to the office of trustee for the Fredericton School Board in 1875, he gladly accepted. He remained in the posi-tion for fifteen years, never absent from meetings, an energetic work-er improving the system for all children.

In 1875, he also became an active member of the Order of the Sons of Temperance, holding the office of grand worthy patriarch for New Brunswick one year later. Little did he realize at the time that he would one day be part of the province's judicial system, dealing with hundreds of prohibition offences in relation to the con-troversial Scott Act, regarding the sale of alcohol.

In the early spring of 1883, it was rumoured in the local papers that A. A. Sterling was to receive a special appointment and, on April 4 of that year, the official document arrived from Lieutenant-Governor Robert Duncan Wilmot. It still survives and reads in part: "Reposing especial trust and confidence in your loyalty, ability, and integrity, I appoint, constitute, and declare you to be the High Sheriff of York County."

A. A. Sterling would become the second longest-serving sheriff in the history of York County, remaining in office until 1909, a total of twenty-six years! Edward Winslow Miller served from 1817 to 1852, Thomas Temple from 1864 to 1883. Colonel John Murray was the first York County sheriff, being appointed in 1785 but leav-ing no record of departure.

"Sheriff Sterling," as he was called for the rest of his life, even after he left office, became known all over New Brunswick and beyond. He held the respect of everyone with whom he came in contact, never losing interest in the humanitarian affairs of life. He became so popular as sheriff that petitions such as the following often appeared: "The undersigned electors of York County hereby express their appreciation of the honourable, straightforward, and efficient manner in which Alexander Sterling has discharged the duties of high sheriff, and his continuance in that position will be satisfactory to us."

In his courtroom in the York County Court House (still standing on lower Queen Street), Sheriff Sterling never compromised his ethics, especially in relation to political patronage. When he dismissed John Hawthorne from the office of York County Gaoler, ordering him to quit and to deliver up possession of the gaol, he received the following letter from a government lawyer: "Perhaps it has not occurred to you that Mr. Hawthorne owes his position very largely to services performed for the party, to which we are all supposed to belong, and that his dismissal has caused considerable unsatisfactory comment among our friends."

In his reply, Sterling was not prepared to change the situation: "I never thought of displacing him until the indefensible course he has taken rendered it necessary, in my judgment, in the proper discharge of the public duties for which I am responsible. I would like to meet with party members and fully explain the details, and I would ask that my attorney be present."

His correspondence was voluminous and much of it survives, even the draft copies of the letters that he sent, all being preserved in the provincial archives and various private collections. The most touching are those from inmates in the Boys' Industrial Home in Saint John. Sterling corresponded on a regular basis with those who had appeared in his courtroom, encouraging them to write and tell about their progress, promising that he would answer—and he did!

In Fredericton, Sheriff Sterling was so well known by every girl and boy that he was loudly cheered whenever he was invited to speak before large school gatherings. During the coronation celebrations for Edward VII in 1902, he was one of the main speakers on the platform at Parliament Square, his eloquent speech including many references to "the greatest Empire the world has ever seen."

Soon after he became sheriff, A. A. Sterling merged his grocery store into a wholesale business, specializing in choice flour (shipped by full boxcars from milling companies all over Canada) and exotic tea (imported from all over the world in thousand-pound orders). He now occupied several buildings on Queen Street and offered friendly competition to other wholesale firms in the city.

The Sterlings no longer lived above the store but had moved to a house on Charlotte Street in 1882, acquiring a full-time maid (Ella) and a part-time handyman (Sam). The next move came when the sheriff built one of the great mansions of Fredericton during the latter part of the 1880s. It was a major project and Sterling kept a detailed account of every payment in a small leather-bound book that he carried inside his vest pocket.

The location for the handsome new residence was on a vacant piece of land on the north side of lower Brunswick Street. The architect was Harry Mott of Saint John; the contractor was Joshua Limerick of Fredericton; the "unofficial" supervisor was Sheriff Sterling himself. Total cost: $4,500.

As the plans were being finalized, Sterling and Mott corresponded back and forth, making the following last-minute additions: two feet to the library (off the back hall, opposite the kitchen) on the first floor, making it twelve by fifteen; a verandah in front of the library, matching the one on the lower side of house; a larger water closet in the shed, making it five by six feet; all square turns on the front staircase—no round corners; a second pantry in the cellar; slate mantles for the fireplaces.

The installation of gas fixtures in every room and hallway, in order to provide abundant nighttime lighting, became a major expense—$245.55. On the first floor, the two parlours, the sitting room, and the dining room had four-globe chandeliers, each suspended from the centre of elaborate circular mouldings. The main hall, kitchen, pantry, and library had square lanterns. The four sleeping chambers on the second floor, and the two on the third, had three-globe chandeliers; the front and rear halls on these two floors had circular lanterns.

By the spring of 1890, the Sterling House, as it came to be known, was ready for the family to move in. According to the local papers, the final result, framed with magnificent landscaping, was "an ornament for the east end of Fredericton," at 767 Brunswick Street, in the shadow of Christ Church Cathedral. The sheriff's total real estate value, including his properties on upper and lower Queen Street, was now assessed at $12,000.

What could be left for the gentleman sheriff, who was also a successful businessman, a valued school board trustee, a staunch member of the Episcopal church (synod delegate, cathedral sidesman), a major shareholder in the People's Bank of New Brunswick, the president of the Fredericton Horticultural Society, and the favourite master of ceremonies at political banquets? The answer: horses!

Sheriff Sterling was an ardent horseman, one who loved, fitted, and trained fast-driving trotters and pacers, having a full stable of his own. As a stockholder and president of the Fredericton Trotting

Park Association, he drove his own horses around the one-mile track (south of Saunders Street) during the summer races, having ordered the best sulky wheels from Toronto. As his reputation spread through the Maritimes and New England, he received endless invitations to judge at various driving parks, such as Charter Oak in Connecticut and Moosepath in Saint John. He was paid handsomely, and Mrs. Sterling always accompanied him.

During the winters, he joined the Fredericton City Flyers and raced his beautiful mares up and down Queen Street on Sunday afternoons, wheels being replaced by the celebrated skeleton sleigh of the nineteenth century. Thousands cheered when A. A. Sterling appeared on the scene because he would set the swift pace and offer the greatest challenge. Although there would be a number of lively "brushes" with danger, the sheriff insisted that the sport remain "clean."

In 1910, A. A. Sterling was appointed chief assessor for the city of Fredericton, a position he held until the end of 1923, resigning because of a double tragedy in his family that year. His youngest son, Archibald Gibson, died following an appendectomy on August 9; his beloved wife, Sarah Anne, who had been in failing health, passed away on October 16. She was seventy-six, the last surviving member of her Saint John family.

The son was thirty-four, single, a successful city businessman who owned the Capital Bottling Company, and a prominent athlete, playing several seasons with FHS and UNB hockey teams. He and his mother were buried in the Rural Cemetery on the Woodstock Road where, four years later, Alexander Addison Sterling was also laid to rest, his death occurring on July 14, 1927. He was approaching his ninetieth year, the last surviving member of his St. Mary's family.

Of the six Sterling children who survived, Spencer married and moved to Montana, and Sadie married and moved to Washington. The four remaining sisters eventually lived together for the rest of their lives in the family home.

Mabel was the librarian at UNB and, in 1939, she was invited to give the alumni oration, the first time a woman had been so honoured at any Canadian university. She died in 1947 at age seventy-one.

Helen was the last surviving charter member of the first IODE chapter formed in Fredericton (and in Canada) in 1900. When she died in 1957 at age eighty-five, she was a member of the Sir Howard Douglas Chapter.

Alice was a math teacher in New Jersey, retiring after twenty-seven years, returning home to Fredericton, where she received an honorary Doctor of Laws degree from UNB (her Alma Mater) in 1949. She died in 1961 at age seventy-seven.

Louise was a businesswoman, inheriting her brother's bottling company, managing her father's property, and then returning to university later in her life. She died in 1971 at age eighty.

All four sisters were buried with their parents and siblings in the family plot, the remains and markers of Florence, Herbert, Estelle, and Alex Jr. having been moved from the Old Burying Ground.

The Sterling House still stands majestically at 767 Brunswick Street. Very few changes have occurred, but it is fitting that New Brunswick's ombudsman (another administrator of justice) now occupies this architectural treasure.

WHAT EVER HAPPENED TO RABBI MARTIN KRAUS?

AUGUST 19, 2000

The Mess Hut, which was divided into two kitchens and two eating areas. This sketch was done at the campsite by internee Gerd Walstein, who is now Gerry Wal, a retired president of his own creative design company in Toronto and Montreal.

FRIDAY AFTERNOON, AUGUST 16, 1940. It was warm and humid and, in the business section of the city, the front door at 394 Queen Street (a clothing and furniture store) was opened wide, welcoming customers and fresh air. The owner, Ben Medjuck, received a telephone call. A man's nervous voice was at the other end: "My name is Captain David Stark and my Commanding Officer, Colonel Adam McLean, asked me to give you a call."

Medjuck: "What can I do for you?"

Stark: "I would like to get in touch with someone who knows about kosher food. I've got over 500 Jews here and they're driving me crazy."

Medjuck: "Where are you?"

Stark: "We are in an internment camp near Ripples, 20 miles east of Fredericton on Route 10."

Medjuck: "I'll be there as soon as I can."

Throughout the brief conversation, Medjuck had hesitated, clearly realizing his precarious position of being a Jew at that particular time in history. He was a young clothier who had immigrated to Canada from Poland in 1921 at age ten, living in Cape Breton until his move to Fredericton in 1936.

Although Stark's call took him by surprise, Medjuck's first move was to leave the store in charge of his wife and then go and find the rabbi, who would probably be around because it was Friday and the Sabbath was fast approaching.

Rabbi Martin Kraus was in residence at 186 Westmorland Street, but he hesitated to leave because he was afraid of it getting dark before they returned. Twenty miles was a long way in 1940, especially over a desolate dirt road. If they became stranded, there would be no telephone handy and no one to put them up.

Kraus had also immigrated to Canada, leaving Hungary in 1929 at the age of twenty-three. He and his wife settled in Halifax, where they had two children (David, born in 1930, Alice the following year) and where Kraus ran a kosher meat market until 1936, at which time he accepted the position of rabbi in Owen Sound, Ontario.

In 1938, Rabbi Kraus and his family moved to Fredericton, where he became the fifth rabbi of the Fredericton Jewish Community, which was organized in 1930, the Sgoolai Israel Synagogue being built on Westmorland Street in 1934. By 1940, there were 146 members in his congregation. Ben Medjuck was one of them.

As it started to get late that Friday afternoon, Rabbi Kraus finally decided to go to Ripples. Medjuck had just purchased a $250 half-ton Hudson, so they drove as fast as they could because the Sabbath would be starting at sundown and they had to get back to Fredericton. Little did they realize what was ahead of them!

Approaching the Fredericton Internment Camp (as it was called officially and Camp B/70 unofficially), Kraus and Medjuck saw high gates, sentry towers, and guards with bayoneted rifles. After an identification check they were allowed inside the barbed-wire compound where they soon learned of the volatile situation.

There were about two hundred extremely orthodox Jews in the camp who had gone on a hunger strike because the food was not kosher, and there were about three hundred non-orthodox Jews who had also gone on a hunger strike because they thought kosher food was a lot of nonsense and they did not want a kosher camp.

Caught in the middle were two hundred Gentile internees and three hundred veteran guards who could not understand what all the fuss was about. Enter Rabbi Kraus to offer an explanation for the religious philosophy associated with the Jewish dietary laws. The guards never realized that the most obvious aspect of a kosher kitchen was the separation of meat and dairy products for washing, preparing, and eating.

Upon returning to Fredericton, Rabbi Kraus phoned the Canadian Jewish Congress in Montreal and on Monday morning the executive director arrived in the city. The rabbi accompanied him to the camp, driving once again over the pasture-like road. Consulting with military personnel, they were able to arrange for two kitchens (kosher and non-kosher) and two eating areas to be set up inside the large mess hut within the compound.

In time, kosher food arrived at the CNR Station on Brunswick Street, stored in the freight shed there, and then transported to the camp by army trucks. This was all done very secretively because the internment camp at Ripples was supposedly a hush-hush project.

Although local carpenters, electricians, and plumbers were hired to work at the site, and many of the guards were World War One veterans who lived in New Brunswick, others in Fredericton had begun to hear stories about the camp "away out in the woods," the only one in the Maritime Provinces during World War Two. There were rumours about a sealed CNR train going through North Devon on Tuesday afternoon, August 13, 1940. But who was on it and why?

The passenger list included a total of 711 enemy aliens or, as the Jews said: "Refugees from Nazi Oppression." They had been arrested or "picked up" in England because they were of either German or Austrian descent, all males from age sixteen to sixty. By October of 1940, the Gentiles were transferred and more Jews arrived, making the Fredericton camp entirely Jewish for its first year of operation.

Rabbi Kraus was officially appointed chaplain to the internees at the Fredericton Internment Camp and he accepted. He did not have a driver's licence and he did not own a car, so he had to get someone to drive him back and forth on a regular basis. His son David accompanied him on some of these trips. The rabbi became a valuable link with the outside world for the internees.

Today, his words of advice and encouragement are still remembered; diaries, journals, and letters from the camp years mentioning his name over and over, always in a positive light. He provided whatever they needed for the high holidays and Jewish festivals, including a regular supply of candles.

The interned pastry chefs from Europe showed their appreciation towards the rabbi by sending him back to Fredericton on one occasion with an elegant torte, eight layers high, each with a different filling, especially whipped cream, the outside covered entirely with chocolate icing, and the top decorated with orange sections.

Rabbi Martin Krauss

By the summer of 1941, the British and Canadian governments realized that Jewish refugees should not be behind barbed wire. The order of release was granted and many of the internees remained in North America, being sponsored for employment or university. All of them became successful citizens; several achieved the Order of Canada. When contacted years later, the former internees one unanswered question: "What ever happened to Rabbi Kraus?"

There are people in Fredericton who ask the same question as they recall the rabbi whose congregants would drive him to farms for chickens and cattle to be slaughtered ritually, or for fresh milk right into the pail. They remember when Louis B. Mayer (of Hollywood's MGM) would come from Saint John to visit Kraus and how the two would walk down Queen Street, followed by young David Kraus.

There are also memories of the rabbi's regular excursions to the corner convenience store for his daily "fix"—a Coca-Cola. His wife, with whom he conversed in Hungarian, always kidded him about his "Coke" habit and his chain-smoking. Unfortunately, the latter habit would eventually affect his health.

Before the war was over, Kraus became ill with pneumonia; the fact that he was transported to the hospital on the Sabbath gives an indication of the seriousness of his illness. The family doctor insisted that, for the sake of his health, he should move south to the United States. In January of 1944 Rabbi Kraus left Canada.

For the next half century, former internees of the Fredericton Internment Camp and older members of the Fredericton Jewish Community continued to ask the question, "Whatever happened to Rabbi Kraus?" There would not be a complete answer until the summer of 1994, when Rabbi David Kraus, the son, came back to Fredericton for a brief visit.

Apparently, the Kraus family settled first in Ohio and then made moves to Indiana, New Jersey, and finally North Carolina. Martin became the rabbi of orthodox congregations and the owner of kosher meat markets, and was always a teacher in nearby Hebrew schools. Son David attended theological college and returned to help his ailing father with services.

Four days before Passover in 1965, Rabbi Kraus died at age fifty-nine. He had been a perpetual scholar, happiest when studying a book of the Talmud or one of the books of the Bible. Work for him was only a means to have the time to study, and that approach influenced his son, who had learned more Judaica from his father during their early years in Fredericton than later at the seminary.

Before returning to his own congregation in South Carolina, David Kraus learned that the man who first drove his father to the internment camp had remained in Fredericton. Ben Medjuck became a successful businessman and a recipient of a Distinguished Citizen of the Year award. In 1995, he died at age eighty-four.

In August of 2000, David Kraus will be attending the Rabbinical Retreat in the mountains of North Carolina, an annual event which he never misses and where he became friends with Rabbi Max Selinger, who attends regularly from Florida. In one of their conversations, it was revealed that Dr. Selinger had been an internee at the Fredericton Internment Camp when Martin Kraus arrived at the site on that August afternoon sixty years ago.

FEBRUARY 5, 2000

REMARKABLE ENTERTAINER SET STAGE FOR CHILDREN'S FANTASY

This 1949 publicity photograph of Mary Grannan was done by John Steele of Toronto; it became the author's signature image.

BEFORE THERE WAS HARRY POTTER, the Simpsons, Pokémon, the Cabbage Patch Kids, Telletubbies, or Tickle-Me-Elmo (each promoted by a huge advertising conglomerate), we had Maggie Muggins, Mr. McGarrity, Kitty Kinsella, Georgie the Rat, Orville Bug, Fitzgerald Fieldmouse, Big-Bite Beaver, Greeny Grub, and Princely Pig—all created and developed by one person: "Just Mary."

Mary Grannan was a pioneer radio personality and a best-selling author. On February 11, 2000 she would have reached her one-hundredth birthday, having lived seventy-five years of the twentieth century, leaving an unmatched legacy in the history of Canadian media for children.

She was a born actress with a captivating voice, her career beginning at a young age when she and her two sisters staged theatrical productions on the steps and platform at the end of the clothesline in the backyard of the family home—a tiny wooden house nestled beneath arched elms at 325 Brunswick Street.

The Grannan sisters were born three years apart (Ann in 1897,

Mary in 1900, Helen in 1903) and they remained devoted to each other throughout their lives. Each attended St. Dunstan's School, graduated from the Provincial Normal School, and remained unmarried.

Mary taught for twenty years at the Devon Superior School and it was here she put her talent for storytelling into practise. Her grade one classes, with enrolment sometimes as high as seventy pupils, have never forgotten her. According to Mae (Savage) Nicholson, Eleanor (Monteith) Stillwell, and Marion (Brewer) Smith, "She was a wonderful teacher, sharing many of her original stories with us, changing her voice as she introduced each new character. Special concerts were big productions, with all the parts written by Grannan. She fired our imaginations and showed us the world through new eyes."

Mary Grannan's own Irish imagination soared when she took part in amateur theatricals at the City Hall Opera House (second floor of City Hall at the time), and she looked forward to the month of March when she produced and starred in the annual St. Patrick's Day play at St. Dunstan's Hall on Regent Street. Many senior citizens still remember *The Meddlesome Maid* of 1936!

J. Stewart Neill, the owner of CFNB Radio, became aware of her talent and gave her a chance to submit a program idea. The result was *Aggravatin' Agatha,* a comedy skit written and performed twice a week and sponsored by Valley Motors and Hudson automobiles. Mary played the incorrigible maid in the title; Gertrude Davis, a fellow teacher who still lives in Fredericton, played a wealthy dowager; Carl "Hap" Watson, now a retired NBC executive in New York, took the part of the chauffeur. It was a hit and each actor earned twenty-five cents per show!

Encouraged, Mary created "a series of fantasies that came right out of my head," playing all the parts and producing all the sound effects. Radio was made for fantasy and thus, *Just Mary* was born airing in a fifteen-minute spot on Sunday evenings between *Current Events* and *Jack Benny*. She said: "I have a captive audience."

And she did! When CBC offered her a job in Toronto in 1938, she accepted and soon *Just Mary* went nationwide every Sunday afternoon, forty-four weeks a year until 1962. She was appointed supervisor of children's programs and she never looked back. In the early days, a federal government committee on radio reported in *Hansard*: "She is one of the few *naturals* in broadcasting, both in script writing and in microphone technique."

Her listeners expanded to the United States and, before long, she was writing six different live shows a week and performing three of them herself. In the end, there would be a total of four thousand scripts, each fresh and sparkling, each having been composed in the early morning at a portable typewriter on the kitchen table in Mary's Toronto apartment, 89 Breadalbane Street. In the afternoon, she was off to the studios. Although there was continuous deadline pressure, she never missed a show.

In 1941, the first of her thirty books appeared and the five thousand copies of *Just Mary* sold within a month. Five years later, a new *Maggie Muggins* book would sell twenty-five thousand copies, a record for juvenile literature. Simultaneous publications in the States and Britain, along with multiple printings and subsequent editions, brought her total sales to four hundred thousand copies and earned the Canadian publisher $300,000!

She had readers from coast to coast, age six to sixty. She received mail from both sides of the Atlantic, including servicemen who carried copies of her books in their kitbags. How pleased she was when RCAF planes and anti-tank guns were named after characters in her stories.

Her tenth anniversary with CBC coincided with the centennial celebration of her native city. At the invitation of Mayor Ray T. Forbes, she returned home to Fredericton to sign the Golden Book and to be presented with the key to the city, the impressive ceremony being broadcast over stations of the Trans-Canada Network. However, only the locals were able to see the sophisticated lady with the couturier wardrobe, the enormous hats, and the elaborate jewellery, all part of the image that became Mary Grannan.

With fame came special projects: requests for school curriculums, new stories for popular magazines, speaking engagements, publicity parties in Chicago and New York, book tours and the signing of countless autographs. Lorne Green invited her to be a guest instructor at his School of Radio Art, Leslie Nielson being among the students. When the changeover was made to television in 1954, she auditioned the little girls who were to play the freckle-faced Maggie Muggins during the eight-year run, and she chose the actors who became the kindly old gardener, Mr. McGarrity.

The accolades and the awards were voluminous, including an honorary membership in the Mark Twain Society, a distinction she shared with Eugene O'Neill, John Masefield, Lionel Barrymore, and Albert Einstein. The *CBC Times* did a cover story and *Liberty* magazine named her Woman of the Week. *Time* and *Maclean's* did feature articles, as did *The Atlantic Advocate* and *Reader's Digest.* Her proudest recognition was the Beaver Award, the honour of distinction in Canadian radio accomplishment.

In 1963, Mary Grannan came home to Fredericton to retire and to spend her twilight years with her sisters (Ann died in 1971; Helen is still living at age ninety-seven). She entertained, gave lectures, and never refused an interview. It was also time to enjoy her large collection of books on the Wild West, the big top, and show business. As a little girl, she had wanted to run away and join the circus; instead, she ran away and joined the CBC.

"Just Mary" died on January 3, 1975, and was buried in the family plot in the Hermitage Cemetery. Her manuscripts have since been placed in the provincial archives; her complete published works can be found in the Legislative Library and the UNB Children's Literature Collection at the Harriet Irving Library. Some of her correspondence has surfaced but hopefully there will be more, as she was a prodigious letter-writer to her family, friends, and business associates. (A recently discovered letter, written while she was taking summer courses at Columbia University in New York in 1937, ends with this revealing statement: "Had I a BA, I would proceed to apply for the Normal [School] job—couldn't I do it just?")

This anniversary year provides an opportunity for the CBC to re-broadcast some of Mary Grannan's programs, along with the J. Frank Willis documentary of her life; for libraries and archives to display her books and memorabilia; for educators to encourage their students to read a Maggie Muggins story. Although the Grannan home is privately owned and is now an official historic site, the city, the province, and the nation should think seriously about assisting with its perpetual preservation.

April 26, 2003

Alden Nowlan: Required Reading Then And Now

Alden Nowlan reading at the podium in 1968.

APRIL 2003 WAS THE FIFTH ANNUAL National Poetry Month, a time to honour poets from the past and to hear from those who are writing in the present.

Had he lived, Alden Nowlan would have been seventy this year (he was born January 25, 1933). Unfortunately, he passed away almost two decades ago (June 27, 1983). Since then, the man and his legacy have been continuously remembered.

His fifty years were all too short, but it was a half century that was filled with a unique and a remarkable life. In the meantime, there are many who will never forget their acquaintance, however brief, with this literary genius.

When I was a high-school English teacher, I received a number of memorable assignments over the years and, looking back, I now wish that I had saved more of my students' delightful first-effort poems, heart-warming short stories, and overly idealistic essays.

However, among those that were carefully selected to remain in my files for nostalgic perusal, there is an exceptional one that was handed in during the fall of 1968. Pencilled on the reverse side of a direction sheet that I had given to each student, were four little poems by the Canadian poet, author, and humanist Alden Nowlan, winner of the Governor General's Award for Poetry in 1967.

It is interesting to note that this prolific Maritime writer did not attend high school. He once wrote, "I probably hold the Canadian record for truancy." In fact, Alden Nowlan's formal education terminated after thirty-seven days in grade five at a one-room schoolhouse in Hants County, Nova Scotia, which means, he continued, "I'm the only professional writer who would be classified as functionally illiterate by Statistics Canada."

But how did he happen to hand in a grade ten poetry assignment at Fredericton High School in 1968 at the age of thirty-five? Again, one must go back to Nova Scotia and the beginning.

He had taught himself to read when he was five and at ten he was reading Xenophon and Herodotus. He later said, "I was also reading Captain Marvel and Buck Rogers and, because nobody had ever told me, hadn't the faintest idea that comic books were generally considered inferior to classic Greek histories."

Throughout his teen years he had a variety of jobs—cutting and peeling pulpwood, clearing bushes for the Department of Highways, being a night watchman in a sawmill. And the self-education continued: "I was Jack London reborn, achingly aware of my enormous ignorance, gluttonously devouring any scrap of knowledge, reading great stacks of books on almost every imaginable subject....For years, too, my writing and reading vocabulary was much greater than my speaking vocabulary because, never having heard them spoken, I had no idea how to pronounce many of the words I'd read."

At nineteen he answered an advertisement by *The Hartland Observer*, a weekly newspaper in northern New Brunswick, and got the job of reporter and then editor. But the pay was so small that he had to have several spare-time jobs as well, putting on storm windows, selling magazine subscriptions, even managing a hillbilly band. However, there was still time to meet and marry Claudine Orser and to write and have published five books of poetry.

In 1963, the move to southern New Brunswick was made, Alden Nowlan becoming a reporter and then an editor for *The Telegraph-Journal* in Saint John. He remained in the port city until his appointment as writer-in-residence at the University of New Brunswick in 1968.

As he began to encourage aspiring young poets on the autumn-clad hillside campus, his son John was enrolled in one of my English classes farther down the hill, all the FHS grade ten students being housed at the time in the old Provincial Normal School (now the Justice Building). Thus, I received my first acquaintance with the Nowlan family, learning later that it was Claudine and Johnnie to whom Alden Nowlan dedicated the majority of his works.

John Nowlan was an attentive but very shy student, finding his lessons to be a difficult challenge at times. Although he had no desire to try to emulate his father, a trait that his fellow students rather expected, one could sense his pride and admiration when the works of Alden Nowlan were presented in class, especially "The Bull Moose" poem and the "True Confession" short story, both widely anthologized selections with which high school students could easily identify.

When John remained at the end of the day for extra help, our conversation would eventually turn to his celebrated father, who was rapidly becoming one of Canada's foremost contemporary writers. On the local scene, devoted fans began to look forward to Alden Nowlan's monthly page in *The Atlantic Advocate* and his weekly column in *The Telegraph-Journal*. These provocative and philosophical articles were always welcome in my classroom.

Early that fall, my English classes had to warm up their creativity by attempting to write several examples of a little poetic exercise known as the "cinquain," whereby a topic is named, described, and commented upon, and then concluded with a synonym.

On the due date, I received two sheets of poetry from the Nowlan family, one from the son and one from the father, the latter placing his on the back of the direction sheet, the first poem expressing Alden Nowlan's feelings in relation to the assignment:

Cinquain
old, foreign
chore for students
words without heart, breath
trickery

He then proceeded to do three more, all relating to a topical item of the day—the United States presidential election:

Nixon
eyebrows, jowls
switchblade eyes
the hunger for power
president

Wallace
hoodless klansman
cracking invisible whips
smiling like a tiger
demagogue

Humphrey
laughing teddybear
who didn't understand
he was the joke
loser

Everyone in the classroom enjoyed this surprise assignment, especially the teacher. Composed just for us, these little poems were filled with the imagery which we had grown to expect from Alden Nowlan. They even encouraged us to try a freer type of verse.

It was in the early part of 1969 that John suggested we have his father come to the classroom for a poetry reading, something Alden Nowlan had not done before. Public readings by professional writers were rare at the time, especially in high schools, and, if anyone were to be given credit for starting them, Alden Nowlan would have to be the person.

My students accepted the idea unanimously and word of the visit soon travelled throughout the school, the result being that the entire staff and student body wanted to see and hear the poet. To contribute further to our program, Alden Nowlan said that he would bring along two university students whose poetry he wanted to share with us along with his own.

When the day of the reading arrived, John brought the three poets to the staff lounge and introduced them to me: UNB student Al Pittman from Newfoundland, St. Thomas student Louis Cormier from Saint John, and Alden Nowlan. It was evident that they were nervous, lighting up cigarettes, sorting through manuscripts, wondering just what to expect from eight hundred sixteen-year-olds. Alden Nowlan had composed a biographical sketch of each poet for use in my introduction, it being agreed that the two younger poets would read first. After they autographed my copies of their books, we started down a long corridor towards the stage entrance.

For the next hour the cavernous auditorium in the old Normal School was hushed from the front to the very last row in the balcony. All eyes were on the three poets who sat in the middle of the wide stage, a stark wooden podium standing in front of them.

Pittman was introduced first and read from his two publications, *The Elusive Resurrection* and *Seaweed and Rosaries*. Cormier followed and read from his published collection *The Silent Cowboys of the East*. They were young and their verse was light, appealing to the youthful audience before them. There was spontaneous laughter at some of the lines; everyone was finally relaxed.

Then came the big man with the beard and the black suit.

Towering above us, his physical appearance commanded attention, but when he spoke with his deep sonorous voice, the students never took their eyes from this gifted man who projected an exceptional warmth and kindness.

He was serious, his poems were serious, his audience was serious. It was a moving moment as he talked about his writing experiences and then read from his award-winning collection *Bread, Wine and Salt*. When he finished, there was great applause and several encores, as though the voice were like a magnet from which there was no release. It was an assembly I shall never forget.

Following the program, students who wished to talk personally with the poets were invited to come to my classroom. They came in large numbers and lined the walls and stood in the doorway, crowding closer and closer to Alden Nowlan, who was sitting at the front desk. He talked with them honestly and sincerely about writing, some of his answers being similar to those he gave in an interview for *The Fiddlehead* magazine later that year: "I enjoy writing poems more. With poems it's a direct emotional release, whereas with the stories there's a lot of hard-bone labour involved....I always get a charge out of it when people I've never met write to me. I don't write to please a particular audience, but it pleases me when people respond to what I've written—especially when their background is different from mine; this reassures me."

When it was almost noon, Alden Nowlan tactfully brought the discussion to a close by inviting any of the students to submit their poems to him through me and then he would return them with constructive criticism from a poet's point of view. The first packet was ready a few weeks later and delivered by John to his father.

As busy as he was with his writing career, Alden Nowlan took time until the end of that school year to comment on each student poem that was submitted to him, typing individual responses for the particular students involved. And there was always a covering letter for me to read before I distributed the student letters. Here is part of the one for March 22, 1969: "I feel guilty about the slapdash typing (mine, not theirs) but I don't like to hold the manuscripts too long. I notice that some of these young poets don't want to write free verse and yet don't seem to realize that if a poem is to rhyme it must also scan. I have nothing against rhyme; in fact, it's probably best to learn to write rhyming verse before going on to freer forms."

Contrary to what he said about his typing, we were amazed to find all of his letters to be impeccably neat and carefully crafted, Alden Nowlan having acquired his typing skills while he was still a teenager: "The first typewriter I bought (by mail, of course) was also the first I'd seen. I bought it after reading that editors wouldn't even consider handwritten manuscripts. I remember that it took me several days to figure out what you had to do to make a space between the words."

The students who received a letter about their poems have had a part of the poet to treasure all these years. Now that he has gone, this correspondence will have an even greater significance, especially since several of these former students have been published. The mini-lessons that he conducted in these letters certainly had an impact, such as this one: "It isn't enough just to put down two words that happen to rhyme and then twist the sense of the lines to fit. The rhymes have to sound inevitable. The rhyming word has to sound as if you'd have put it there even if it hadn't rhymed. Look at Browning's rhymes to see what I mean. And at Yeats. Two great masters of English rhyme."

Throughout the 1970s, Alden Nowlan received numerous accolades as his work continued to be published. There were six more books of poetry, three of prose, and four plays co-authored with TNB artistic director Walter Learning. On July 13, 1971, I met him at a Tom Forrestall exhibition at the Beaverbrook Art Gallery and he told me about his forthcoming collaboration with Forrestall, a major volume entitled *Shaped by This Land.*

In turn, I was able to tell him to expect a complimentary copy of the FHS-published booklet of student poetry entitled *Writer's Cramp*. He was overjoyed at this news—his interest in young writers had never ceased and never would. He went on to become a member of the "Writers in New Brunswick Schools" project, and he frequently granted student interviews at his Windsor Street home, a major one appearing in the FHS newspaper *The Dome*.

On January 29, 1983, I saw Alden Nowlan for the last time at a Maritime book fair in Saint John. His wife was with him and, as we talked, our conversation tended to delve into the past—that first high-school poetry reading, student writers, and Johnnie: "You may be interested to know that Johnnie has made his peace with the educational system and has been doing very well at Ryerson in Toronto, where he has finished his second year, working towards a degree in Social Work."

Five months later Alden Nowlan was dead. He left wonderful memories for me and my students and a rich legacy of published work. Because he can be interpreted on many different levels, from scholar to layman, there is no doubt that Alden Nowlan will always be "required reading."

Former Fredericton Family Inspired Popular Novel

March 15, 2003

Mrs. Maria Louisa Partridge, seated, with five of her eleven children in 1906. From left: Harold, Charlotte, Ernest, Basil, and Muriel.

A HALF-CENTURY AGO, during the winter of 1953, the people of Fredericton were ignoring the political and diplomatic news on the front pages of *The Daily Gleaner*; instead, they were turning to page three to read the paper's new serial story from a novel entitled *The Penningtons*—eighty consecutive instalments beginning the last week in January and continuing throughout February, March, and April.

This was not the first *Gleaner* serialization and it would not be the last, but the Pennington story was different. The advertising began days in advance on the front page; there was even a three-month special subscription deal for just $2.25, encouraging readers not to miss a word.

Why would this particular story be so captivating? When it was first published in 1951 by the Westminster Press of Philadelphia, *The Penningtons* became a popular best-seller in North America and abroad; however, for the people of Fredericton, there were additional features.

The setting for the story was their city (under the fictional name of Kingsford); the Penningtons were none other than the Partridges, a large prominent family who lived in Fredericton from 1895 to 1906;

the author was Basil Partridge, the eleventh and last child of the first dean of Christ Church Cathedral.

Like some families of the cloth, the members of the Pennington/Partridge clan were far less conventional than one would ever suspect. Thus, the reader is kept in suspense wondering what is going to happen next, and if it really happened in Fredericton. The result: a very thin line between fact and fiction, although the author's foreword to the book states that "it is purely fictitious."

But not according to the clues! From the first page, the setting is unmistakably Fredericton, the sound of the cathedral bell pealing "above the winding, slow river and bridges; above the serene streets shaded by leafy archways; above the university and the Parliament Buildings, the mills, the railroad, and the infantry barracks; above the business section, the jail, and Government House."

In the fall of 1894, Bishop H. T. Kingdon of the Fredericton diocese named the Reverend Francis Partridge as the first dean, the newly created office being second only to that of the bishop, the main responsibility being the administration of the cathedral. Partridge took up his duties in the spring of 1895, arriving in the capital city of New Brunswick with his wife and nine children.

In the novel, the dean is called Richard Pennington and his wife is Victoria Louisa. Their long and dramatic journey to Kingsford is identical to that of Francis Partridge and his wife Maria Louisa, the latter couple following a stormy and difficult road to Fredericton.

According to Basil Partridge, his father was born in Gloucestershire, England, and received his early education at Lady Berkeley's Grammar School (founded in 1300). He then attended St. Augustine's College in Canterbury, excelling in medicine, music, and religion, taking all first-place prizes, later becoming one of only four honorary fellows in the history of the college!

As a student, Partridge had the opportunity to visit the magnificent cathedral in Bristol, where he had the privilege to hear nineteen-year-old Maria Louisa Gillett give an organ recital. He was immediately fascinated by her talent and her beauty. They met, they fell in love, and the rest of their lives became a remarkable story that would one day be turned into a novel, written by their youngest child.

After they were married, Maria wanted to stay in England and enjoy the comforts offered by her wealthy family. Francis was ready for adventure and dedication, looking towards the colonies for missionary work. He answered an advertisement in an obscure New Brunswick newspaper and eventually received the headmaster appointment at the Charlotte County Grammar School in the little seaside town of St. Andrews.

In 1868, Francis and Maria "married in haste" and sailed for Canada, leaving behind their families and a comfortable life in England. He had wanted her to wait until he was established, but she refused. Unfortunately, the young couple would "repent at leisure."

The four years in St. Andrews were not easy ones, suitable accommodation being the major problem. The Anglican rectory, where they had a small apartment, is still standing on Parr Street and it was here that their first child (Charles) was born in 1869. He was nicknamed "Charlie" and they loved him dearly. Tragically, in June of the following year, he died of whooping cough.

His father was in Fredericton at the time, being ordained a priest at Christ Church Cathedral by Bishop John Medley; his mother experienced the death alone and, as a result, was resentful towards the church for the rest of her life, a bitterness that becomes even more evident when she is portrayed in the novel as the temperamental Victoria Pennington.

Charlie Partridge was buried in the shadow of St. John's Chapel, outside of St. Andrews in Chamcook, a quaint little stone church where his father began his parish ministry while also teaching school. The church is still standing and the infant marker can be found in the nearby graveyard.

In 1870, a daughter was born and, although she was christened Katherine Helen, her parents called her "Nell." She grew up to be an attractive redhead, more than a little high-strung, and devoted to her father. As in the novel, she became a minister's wife, the marriage eventually turning out happily in the long run, producing three children and a move to California.

In 1872, Francis Partridge was unanimously elected rector of Rothesay, (Rothsage in the novel), subsequently moving his family to King's County where he was no longer a schoolteacher but a full-time clergyman. He became a familiar sight travelling the back roads with his horse and buggy, always carrying two little black bags, one medical, the other religious, ministering to both the physical and spiritual needs of his parishioners.

In Rothesay, two sons and two daughters were born: Francis Ernest (Ern) in 1872, Mary (Molly) in 1874, Arthur (Art) in 1877, and Charlotte Greville Partridge (Tot) in 1879.

Ern grew up tall, energetic, and handsome, but he and his father "struck sparks off each other." Apparently, they crossed swords many times and, on a final angry occasion, Ern announced that he was bored with "the strait-jacket of clerical life" and that he was getting out! His father handed him five dollars, saying "You'll be back in a week." He left for the United States and never returned, having little contact with "the family" thereafter.

Like her father, the attractive Molly had considerable presence. Following her education at the prestigious Edgehill School for Girls in Nova Scotia, she met and married a Montreal businessman, their wedding at Christ Church Cathedral being a social highlight. Besides raising two sons (one named Francis after his grandfather), Mary was active in church affairs all her life.

Art was like his father in physical appearance and sense of duty. After he graduated from King's College in Nova Scotia, he worked for various newspapers in the States before returning to Canada at the beginning of the Great War and enlisting in the Black Watch. Arriving in England, he accepted a commission in the Royal Navy, subsequently making headlines regarding a false suspicion of espionage. He remained a bachelor all his life

Tot was named for Lady Charlotte Greville, a patron of her father while he was a student at Canterbury. After she graduated from Fredericton Business College, she moved to the States and became a first-rate secretary. Marriage and the birth of a little girl soon followed.

Although these children were important to their father, his career continued to come first, much to the annoyance of his wife. As he was elected secretary of the Diocesan Synod of Fredericton in 1876 and appointed canon of Christ Church Cathedral in 1879, Maria openly criticized the bishop on several occasions, and she refused to become involved with the church. "I was never cut out for this life," exclaims Victoria in the novel.

With great reluctance, the Partridge family left New Brunswick in 1882 to spend the next thirteen years in the diocese of Nova Scotia, the father becoming the rector of the historic round church of St. George in Halifax. The move gave him the opportunity to study at King's College where, in 1884, he received his Doctor of Divinity. For the mother, it was a return to the urban life that she had missed.

Five more children would be born in Halifax, bringing the total to eleven: Muriel (Moolly) in 1882, Aubrey St. George (Aub) in 1884, Harold deVere (Hal) in 1886, Cyril Attenbury (1888), Basil Gilpin (1894). Cyril, named after an obscure English bishop, to the disgust of his siblings, died as an infant, leaving five sons and four daughters to arrive in Fredericton with their parents in 1895.

Moolly was engaged to be married but her father's custom of waiting a year caused the relationship to suffer and finally cease. Thus, she remained single, staying with "the family" when they moved to Rochester, New York, always keeping house for her mother. She was the only member of the Partridge family who returned home to the

Maritimes, spending the last part of her life in a little cottage above Fredericton in the parish of Kingsclear (Kingslea in the novel).

Aub was incompatible with the city of Fredericton. He also remained with "the family," moving to the States, obtaining a job with the Rochester Gas and Electric Company, where he spent his entire working life, content and successful. He married and had one son, whom he named Francis in honour of "the Dean."

Hal, on the other hand, loved Fredericton, especially the canoeing and camping, which were popular around 1900. His good friends were poets Charles G. D. Roberts and Bliss Carman. Besides working in a local bank for seventeen dollars a month, Hal also wrote poetry and had it published in various newspapers and magazines. He and his wife settled in Toronto, where he worked for Southam Press and where they raised their only child—Harold deVere Partridge Jr. (Pat).

Basil took the family completely by surprise because his mother was forty-six at the time of his birth and his father was forty-eight. Like his older sister Nell, he was also a redhead and, like his older brothers, he grew up to work in the newspaper world. After returning from the war in 1921, he spent the next forty-two years writing advertising copy before he ventured into fiction. Several of his short stories (all based on the Partridge family) appeared in *Maclean's* and *The Atlantic Advocate*.

Following the success of *The Penningtons*, Basil continued with the family saga and wrote two more biographical novels: *Chaplet of Grace* (his parents' early years) and *Larry Pennington* (his own personal story). Fredericton is a recurring theme in all three books.

In Fredericton, the Partridge family lived in the first Anglican deanery at 729 Charlotte Street, an historic house built by William Franklin Odell, dating back to the 1830s. Across the street was a stately red-brick elementary school, which Basil would attend; across the backyard gardens was the elegant red-brick Anglican rectory, where the famous Roberts family resided. (All three buildings are still standing and are in wonderful condition.)

However, the deanery in 1895 left much to be desired until Francis and Maria repaired and renovated it at their own expense, preserving the little attic over the kitchen for the dean's study. In *The Penningtons*, it is described as the favourite room for the children, reached only by the winding back stairs, bare and worn, their father going up there "to smoke his pipe in peace and enjoy forty winks on a horsehair couch in front of a potbellied stove."

The daughters in *The Penningtons* came to enjoy Fredericton, especially in the autumn: "The maples below the university in Kingsford would be stripped of all their glory and, in another month, the river would freeze up. The round of indoor parties would be beginning and university activities would be in full swing."

The sons in *The Penningtons* felt trapped in Fredericton: "Damn this nosy, gossiping little town! A man couldn't turn over in his bed at night without eight thousand and forty people knowing which side he'd turned on!"

Every Sunday morning the family walked to and from the cathedral in a column of twos, the dean in the lead, wearing the same accessories as the deans in England—black cloth gators and a black apron. The children remained home in the evening but Maria was always in the family pew to hear her husband deliver one of his powerful sermons, giving his opinions on controversial topics such as temperance and Sunday travel. She had convinced herself long ago that he should have been a bishop, her discontentment with the church never diminishing.

When the dean passed away in 1906 at the age of sixty, the family followed his last wish and buried him in the shadow of St. Peter's Church in the parish of Kingsclear. According to *The Penningtons*, "there were services twice a month at this small country church for farm people who came for miles to attend, the dean taking every other one of these services for years."

Maria was now free to leave Fredericton for good and, in the novel, Victoria gives one parting shot to the new Bishop Richmond (Richardson in real life): "I reminded him that the Dean had worked himself to death, and I felt that the diocese owed us something more than the pittance paid me." When she died in Toronto in 1928 at age eighty, she was buried in "the family" plot at Mount Pleasant Cemetery. Muriel was the only one to be buried beside her father.

Because the dean was an accomplished choir conductor, composer, singer, and cellist, the cathedral choir installed a large stained-glass window in the south nave in his memory. Some of his neatly penned musical arrangements still exist one hundred years later; several of his hymns and sermons were published individually.

To honour the dean's memory as a wise and kindly parent, his youngest son, who was the last of the children to die (in 1981), has left behind three superb novels, of which the plots and exploits are very true to life, showing the emotions and the challenges experienced by both the Penningtons and the Partridges.

SECTION SIX: SOCIAL LIFE

YESTERYEAR'S COLOURFUL CLUBS AND SINCERE SOCIETIES

FEBRUARY 1, 2003

THROUGHOUT THE 1800S and early 1900s, just about everyone in Fredericton belonged to a particular organization of people, either a club, a society, an order, an association, a lodge, or a religious group.

During the long winter evenings, various meetings were scheduled for every night of the week (except Sunday), a list of notices appearing daily in the local newspapers, February being one of the busiest months. It was a common practice to adjourn to a nearby restaurant for refreshments.

Many of these early clubs and societies were for men only, but it was not an easy procedure to join. Although there were detailed application forms and subsequent elections, prominent gentlemen were always accepted, the same names appearing with several different memberships.

An organized women's group was rare in early Fredericton and a mixed group of both sexes was even rarer. Small clubs had to face the challenge of finding suitable meeting places and attracting enough members to keep the venture alive.

Along the way, each group made a distinct contribution to the city's culture at the time, but many were short-lived and are now a part of the city's heritage. Other than a rare photo, a musty ledger, a brief news clipping, or a faded document, there is very little left to remember.

It was most appropriate that one of the first organized groups was the Fredericton Emigrants' Society, established in the late fall of 1819, "for the purpose of affording employment, information, and assistance to destitute settlers in Fredericton and the neighbouring country." From the very beginning, the popular nineteenth-century spelling of the word "emigrant" was used.

Monthly meetings were held at the old Market House on lower Queen Street (where the York County Court House now stands), the first being on November 26, 1819, with Judge John Saunders in the chair. It was unanimously resolved, "that His Excellency, Lieutenant-Governor George Stracey Smyth be solicited to accept of the office of Patron of this Society."

The treasurer's book of the Emigrants' Society survives and is now preserved in the Provincial Archives, providing researchers with a complete list of the charter members and the numerous donations that were made. Ten pounds, paid in advance, constituted a

The LaFontaine Club in the 1890s was established in honour of Jean de LaFontaine, one of the world's greatest writers of fables, who died in Paris in 1695, leaving twelve published collections of fables. Front row, from left: Robert Smith Barker (who became official secretary to eight lieutenant-governors); unidentified gentleman; Albert Patrick McCloskey; Nelson Campbell. Back row, from left George Dibblee; Gilmour Brown; Fred B. Coleman (the young businessman from Saint John who purchased and improved the Barker House Hotel); Edmund Head Allen (fifth son of Sir John Campell Allen, who became provincial secretary in the cabinet of Premier C. W. Robinson). The symbolic items being displayed relate to one of LaFontaine's fables.

permanent membership; however, many of the prominent gentlemen only subscribed to the one-pound annual dues.

The society opened the first Emigrants' Office in the provincial government's little stone building on the west side of Province Hall (the first Legislative Assembly Building). Every day (except Sunday) newcomers to the province could register their names and their circumstances. The first to be helped were the Welsh settlers who had arrived from Cardigan, Wales, after a forty-five-day crossing on the now-famous brig, the *Albion*.

The Fredericton Bible Society, formed in 1822, was an ecumenical group with one common purpose—promoting and distributing the Bible. At the sixty-second anniversary meeting in City Hall in

1884, Mayor George E. Fenety occupied the chair, and seated upon his right was Lieutenant-Governor Robert D. Wilmot, patron to the society. At the seventy-fourth anniversary, held in the York Street Temperance Hall in 1896, Fenety was still president, but the patron was now Lieutenant-Governor John J. Fraser. All members of the ladies' branch attended as well.

In December of 1825, Lieutenant-Governor Sir Howard Douglas became the patron of the newly formed Fredericton Society of Saint Andrew, an organization that continues to thrive today. The original goal was for the relief of indigent Scots but, as time went on, the Society became involved with other matters of Scottish interest, particularly along religious, cultural, and fraternal lines. Among the Society's well-preserved papers, there is the list of the twenty-six charter members, many of them later laid to rest in the Old Burying Ground on Brunswick Street.

On February 20, 1826, "The Fredericton Society for the Encouragement of Good & Honest Female Servants" was formed, with Lady Anne Douglas, wife of the lieutenant-governor, as patroness. This was an all-female group consisting of prominent ladies, especially the three directors: Arianna Saunders, wife of Chief Justice John Saunders; Elizabeth Odell, wife of Provincial-Secretary Franklin Odell; Isabella Hailes, wife of Lieutenant-Colonel Harris W. Hailes.

One of the Odell daughters was treasurer of the Servants' Society, one of the Douglas daughters, the secretary, each of these young women having her own servant-in-waiting. Along with their mothers and the other ladies, they paid half a guinea (ten shillings) to join and another half a guinea annually. Eventually, a list of the forty-five subscribers was published in *The Royal Gazette*, and it was impressive.

The object of the Servants' Society was to encourage and reward female servants who could provide testimonials of their good conduct for a two-year period. If the women behaved themselves, financial rewards would be distributed in pounds, shillings, and pence. However, one of the rules stated that "all acts of dishonesty, insolence, and disobedience shall be punished by publick disgrace."

In the 1830s, the wealthy women of Fredericton organized again when they established the Benevolent Society, an early forerunner of today's Food and Clothing Bank. During the fall of each year, contributions were solicited "to enable the necessary supply for the winter to be laid in." A register was then kept daily at the place of issue, "exhibiting the name of the applicant relieved, the number in the applicant's family, the party recommending, and the amount of relief afforded."

The Benevolent Society received contributions of potatoes, meat, and clothing at various schools each weekday. Financial subscriptions were also received and, by the 1840s, affluent men and women from all over the city were volunteering their time to provide for the needy citizens of Fredericton.

In 1859, the Young Men's Literary Society had its first meeting on January 11, the initiatory lecture being given by the Reverend Dr. Charles Spurden, principal of the Baptist Seminary, and later second master at the Collegiate School. His topic: "British India." The result: an overwhelming response with increased membership.

This early literary society laid the groundwork for several debating clubs that were organized towards the end of the nineteenth century, followed by the Rudyard Kipling Club of the early 1900s, the English Literature Association of the 1920s, and the Bliss Carman Society of the 1940s.

Two other long-running and successful organizations also reflected the intellectual and cultural side of the capital city: The Fredericton Historical Society, formed in the city hall auditorium in 1881, with Mayor G. Fred Fisher in the chair; the Natural History Society, formed in the York Street School assembly hall in 1893, with Dr. Loring W. Bailey of UNB in the chair. Only professional gentlemen were allowed to become members of these two learned societies, applications being made in writing to the president.

The object of the historical society was to gather "any and all documents, papers, and manuscripts which bear or throw light on the history of the province, with a view to their preservation and chronological arrangement." The object of the Natural History Society was to present informative and interesting papers relating to scientific topics. Both of these societies were the predecessors of two important organizations of the twentieth century: the Fredericton Science Club and the York/Sunbury Historical Society.

Fraternal societies began in Fredericton in the late 1700s with the various Masonic lodges leading the way. Many of the secret societies that followed had their own halls or private meeting places: the Foresters, the Black Knights, the Good Templars, the Oddfellows, the Orangemen, the Knights of Pythias (and the subsequent Damon Club), the Knights of Columbus, and the Royal Arcanum ("a profound secret or mystery known only to initiates"). There was even a Fredericton nest of the Order of the Owls, organized in 1911 with seventy-five members!

Sister organizations in connection with the fraternal orders soon emerged, but the women of Fredericton tended to become more involved with benevolent societies along religious and patriotic lines—the King's Daughters, IODE, the Daughters of England (associated with the Sons of England), Women's Institutes.

One of the most successful fraternal organizations for youth in Fredericton was started on the evening of February 9, 1893, by Alderman William Rosborough and thirteen charter members. It was called the Protestant Association of Prentice Boys (York Lodge #21) and, a year later, the capital city membership was over fifty. Candidates for admission had to be at least sixteen years of age and definitely Protestant.

The foundation of the Prentice Boys originated in Ireland in 1688, when thirteen apprentice boys closed the gates of the city of Londonderry against the armies of King James, shouting "No Surrender." In honour of this heroic action that supported religious and civil liberty, a lodge was formed in Ireland; the idea later crossed the Atlantic. In 1951, the national convention was held in Fredericton, hosted by the Gibson Lodge #37, the Prentice Hall on Union Street being the headquarters, proudly displaying the emblem (crossed keys and crossed swords).

Many of the upper-class social clubs in early Fredericton originated with a local idea, but several of these groups of young professionals were short-lived: the Horse and Buggy Club, the Union Social Club (responsible for dances and masquerade balls), the Horse Shoe Social Club (which had its own orchestra), the Birches Camping Club, the Macawber Club (an operatic entertainment group), the Fredericton Musical Club (which met at various residences for drawing-room concerts and elegant suppers), and the Auld Lang Syne Whist Club.

The Hochelaga Club caused a local controversy because of its name. This social and "self-admiring amusement group," composed of twelve single gentlemen (with the same number of ladies as honorary members) even christened their new sleigh "Hochelaga." As a result, *The Capital* newspaper and its readers questioned a name that was connected with the early history of Montreal and not Fredericton.

Club members responded, agreeing that an inappropriate name had been chosen and that this would likely be amended. Unfortunately, the "Hochelagas," as they were known around the city, became defunct before a change could be made, their brief existence only encompassing the month of February 1884.

On the other hand, the Star Social Club was a leader from 1887 until 1894, disbanding because its twenty-five members were young businessmen who wanted to devote more time to their careers. They left behind one of the finest club rooms in the city, located over

James S. Neill's store on lower Queen Street. They also left their "Constitition and Bye-Laws," a beautifully penned document that is now preserved in the Provincial Archives. Undertaker George W. Adams was the first president.

During the time the Star Club was in operation, it formed its own successful baseball team, and organized elaborate excursions for friends and the general public. Annual moonlight cruises along the St. John River would be accompanied by a military band for dancing; annual drives to Springhill would conclude with a sumptuous picnic and musical entertainment.

The Assembly Social Club was re-organized every December throughout the 1890s and into the early 1900s in order to provide the winter's entertainment for the senior elite of Fredericton. Several quadrilles and fancy-dress balls were planned, the location being either Windsor Hall or the Queen Hotel, those in attendance being among the first families of Fredericton: the Allens, the Chestnuts, the Edgecombes, the Winslows, the Wetmores, the Gregorys, the Wilmots, the Sterlings, the Babbitts, the Limericks, the Neills, and the Roberts and Tibbits families.

There was also a Junior Assembly Club, sometimes called the "32 Club" or the Young Bachelors' Club—thirty-two young gentlemen in the process of making a place in business, politics, or education. Thirty-two young ladies would always be invited, along with several parents as chaperons. At all their grand affairs, a catered luncheon would be served at midnight, and then the dancing would continue until the early morning hours. It was Fredericton at its best...socially!

After World War One, the popular social clubs (including the Mandolin Club with its own orchestra) began to disappear, new and serious societies having already emerged, each of them filling a need in the community. Two shared the old Officers' Quarters (where the York/Sunbury Museum in now located): the Fredericton City Club in the stone section, the Great War Veterans' Association in the wooden wing (which used to face Queen Street). Two others complemented each other, aiming to improve life mentally and physically: the Fredericton Boys' Lending Library Association and the Association for the Prevention of Tuberculosis.

Several organizations founded before and during World War Two are still going strong today: the Rotary Club, the Fredericton Art Club, the Elks, the Y's Men's Club, the Kinsmen, and the Kiwanis.

However, by 1940, two important groups were formed as a result of the war: the Soldier Comforts Association met monthly in the city council chamber, its dedicated members (men and women) operating a hostel for officers and soldiers; the Girls They Left Behind Them Club met weekly at various homes, where letters, snapshots, and souvenirs from England were shared among wives, mothers, daughters, and sisters as they sat with their knitting.

When the Federation of Canadian Clubs opened its fourth annual conference at Fredericton's City Hall in 1912, there were hundreds of delegates from across Canada, including those from the women's Canadian Clubs. Lieutenant-Governor Josiah Wood formally welcomed the guests; Dr. W. S. Carter, Fredericton's chief superintendent of education, presided over the event.

An important subject on the agenda was "The Duty of Canadian Clubs to the Immigrant," the following resolution being moved, seconded, and carried: "That this Fredericton conference recommend to all Canadian Clubs the object of helping immigrants to understand and appreciate Canadian citizenship."

The capital city of New Brunswick had come a long way from its little "emigrant" society of 1819.

TORCHLIGHTS AND TOURNAMENTS
THE SPIRIT OF EARLY FIREMEN

DECEMBER 7, 2002

An 1858 torchlight procession arriving at Government House to honour Queen Victoria's birthday. The firemen are in the foreground with their smoking torches and a decorated hose cart; they also released the fire balloon hovering over the mansion (to the right of the flag). The mayor is standing at the base of the flagstaff; the lieutenant-governor is one of the four men in front of the porch.

THE FIRE DEPARTMENT'S HEROISM and gallantry displayed while fighting the city's major fires for almost two centuries have already been well documented and illustrated for posterity. However, the spirited involvement in the community is another side that should not be forgotten.

It was in the mid-nineteenth century that the firemen's famous torchlight procession made its spectacular debut in Fredericton and continued until the early 1900s, enhancing one special event after another.

In 1858, the big occasion was Queen Victoria's thirty-ninth birthday celebration on May 24. At 3:00 P.M., Fredericton's five fire companies assembled on the cathedral grounds for the first of two parades on that day. Their destination: Government House on the Woodstock Road.

The two hundred enrolled firemen, regulars and volunteers in full uniform, came from their respective hose stations (makeshift wooden buildings with crude bell towers), strategically located from one end of the city to the other: corner of Queen and

Northumberland streets (No. 1 company), middle King Street (No. 2 and No. 3 companies), corner of Queen and St. John streets (No. 4 company), Sunbury Street (No. 5 company), the last location now called University Avenue.

For the afternoon parade, each company pulled a hose cart and a hand-operated pump engine. Marshalled under the direction of Charles Brannen of No. 1 company, the firemen marched up Brunswick Street, preceded by Mayor William Needham on horseback. A few of the Swizzletown Celestials (the forerunner of the Calithumpians) acted as outriders, creating amusement for the huge crowds along the route.

At 9:00 P.M., the five companies met at the King Street "central" engine house for the flaming of the torches and the subsequent quick-step march up King Street to the Woodstock Road. Once again, the destination was Government House, but this time the parade was led by the Freemason's band (in full uniform) and His Worship the mayor (in a fireman's uniform). The "fire laddies," as they were affectionately called, followed with their torches and were joined by hundreds of local citizens.

Passing through the gate at Government House Lane, the bandsmen and firemen came to a halt on the spacious lawn, where Lieutenant-Governor John Manners-Sutton stood at the foot of the steps leading to the entrance of the mansion. He was flanked by his private secretary, an aide-de-camp, and one of his five sons. Lady Manners-Sutton did not appear, having lost a baby daughter the month before; the child had been born at Government House and was interred in the Old Burial Ground.

The mayor paid his respects first and then the five companies of firefighters were deployed in succession, saluting His Excellency, forming a flaming semi-circle, the entire brigade facing the lieutenant-governor, "while the moon, just rising above the spruce trees, beamed calmly o'er all."

The magnificent scene was witnessed by the people of Fredericton, who filled the remainder of the lawns and the Woodstock Road. Fortunately, in their midst, there was a young Saint John artist by the name of Edward John Russell, who was making a sketch of the ceremony, capturing the moment for all time, sending his result to *The Illustrated London News* in England, where the drawing was made into a rare engraving and published in the July 17 issue of that year.

The sounds of the evening can only be imagined today, especially the rousing cheer proposed by the mayor, and then the hushed silence as Manners-Sutton addressed the crowd: "Fredericton ought to be proud of her fire companies, for any city on this great continent might be proud of such a brigade... I need not tell you that I reciprocate your feelings on the occasion of Her Majesty's natal day."

The mayor responded by eulogizing the spirit and the efficiency of the different fire companies, "who are so often called upon to combat a foe more insidious than a foreign enemy." He then remarked that, after honouring the brave, they must remember the fair, and called for three cheers for Lady Manners-Sutton, which were given heartily as she watched and listened from an upstairs window.

The companies then fell into order and marched back through the streets of Fredericton, where their brilliant appearance captured the imagination of young and old. Before they retired to their stations, the firemen concluded the evening at eleven o'clock by giving a massive display of fireworks on the Green. The tradition of the torchlight procession had begun, and succeeding lieutenant-govenors looked forward to the illuminated visits in the dark of night. They were not disappointed.

When three of Queen Victoria's sons arrived in Fredericton for individual visits in the 1860s, the firemen's torchlight procession was a major part of the proceedings, making a memorable impression on each—Prince Edward (a future King of England) in 1860, Prince Alfred (a member of the Royal Navy) in 1861, and Prince Arthur (a future Governor General of Canada) in 1869.

For all three visits, the route was the same: down King Street to Church Street, through Church to Queen, and up Queen to the Woodstock Road, five hundred torches flaming like a long meteor of fire, lighting up the night sky. At Government House, a semi-circle was formed around the front entrance, the royal visitor and his host (the lieutenant-governor) coming forward to acknowledge the firefighters. The events were witnessed by thousands who had joined the parade.

For nineteen-year-old Prince Arthur, there was a special ceremony. The fire department had just acquired its first steam engine and named it *Alexandra* in honour of the Princess of Wales (Arthur's sister-in-law and the future queen of England). On a balmy September evening in 1869, the parade marshall addressed His Royal Highness and invited him to inspect the new steamer.

The prince descended the steps and made a close examination of the steamer, asking questions about its power and capacity, being impressed when informed that it could send a jet of water to the height of the wooden hand on top of the Methodist church steeple! Upon returning to the steps, the prince requested that the torchlight procession circle the lawn three times. When No. 4 engine approached, a young lad descended and presented His Royal Highness with a bouquet. Everyone applauded, gave three cheers, and sang the national anthem.

In August of 1873, Canada's third governor general and his wife, Lord and Lady Dufferin, were in Fredericton for a state visit. On the evening of their arrival, the firemen's famous torchlight procession took place, escorting Their Excellencies and Lieutenant-Governor Lemuel Allan Wilmot and his wife from Government House to the Exhibition Palace (in the vicinity of Saunders and York Streets). The elegant carriages of the vice-regal party were added to the rear, behind the torch bearers, hose carts, hand-pump engines, and the *Alexandra*.

Following the palace reception, and after winding through the streets of Fredericton, the procession returned to Government House. The firemen, holding their torches high, formed a line in front of the main entrance and cheered loudly as the Dufferins and Wilmots approached to inspect, both couples showing great interest in the operation of the firefighting equipment. The ceremony concluded when two young firemen stepped forward and presented bouquets to the ladies.

In 1874, Mayor Edward Wetmore and his five councillors presented No. 3 hose company with a new steamer, the firemen christening it *City of Fredericton*. Thus, when future vice-regal visits occurred, there were two steamers in the procession. The old hand-pump engines were gradually coming to an end, although they were not discarded immediately, and for good reason.

In 1883, Fredericton hosted the first provincial firemen's tournament, every item of firefighting equipment being brought back into service for parades, exhibits, and demonstrations (including the old leather buckets from the early bucket brigades). The big event took place on Monday, July 2, also the 16th Dominion Day celebration. Over five thousand excursionists arrived by special riverboats and trains, three thousand coming from Saint John alone!

The Fredericton firemen made all the preparations, polishing and decorating late into the evenings, building a large platform for the fireworks on the riverbank (between the Normal School and City Hall), organizing every sport event in all age categories. Young boys were recruited to haul the old hand engines, each child to be dressed in a newly made fireman's uniform.

The mile-long firemen's parade in the early morning was the finest ever held in the city, every fire department in the province being represented, along with several visiting marching bands. In the lead was the grand marshall (Alderman D. J. Stockford), followed by several VIP barouches, the visiting brigades, and the Fredericton firemen. The steamers and the hook and ladder wagons came last, each drawn by four plumed white horses.

In the afternoon, there was a baseball match at Officers' Square (the Saint John "Nationals" defeating the Fredericton "Originals"), and races on Queen Street. The entire area was a solid mass of spectators. One of the races, open to all firemen, had ten men on a team running 220 yards with a hose-cart and 200 feet of hose, connecting with a hydrant, unreeling, and attaching to a branch pipe. In the ladder race, five men on each team had to run one hundred yards with a ladder, raise it to a building, and then have one of the five reach the top.

The fireworks began at nine o'clock and continued until eleven o'clock, Queen Street being packed again from Regent to Westmorland. According to *The Capital* newspaper, "it was a magnificent display of all sorts, sizes, and kinds, ending with a beautiful piece on which the words GOOD NIGHT came into view." At different intervals, the firemen had special red flares illuminate the surrounding blocks of downtown buildings, revealing the upstairs windows crowded with faces, "an immense moving sea of people filling up the entire Phoenix Square below."

Five years later, the Fredericton Fire Department hosted the tournament again, this time bigger and better: visitors numbered six thousand! Brigades came from Saint John, Woodstock, St. Mary's, Halifax, and Houlton, Maine. Trains ran to and from Marysville every hour of the day-long event. For the first time, the Boys' Company of twenty-two youths marched in the big parade as Fredericton's future firemen, receiving special attention from Mayor John Douglas Hazen.

The afternoon of competitive sports was highlighted by the tug-of-war between Fredericton and Houlton, the latter winning the $30 prize. In the evening, all visiting firemen joined the local companies for a brilliant torchlight procession through the city, marching to the music of several bands, ending at Parliament Square for the fireworks display.

There were Fredericton tournaments again in 1906 and 1912, but the big one came in 1933 when the headline in *The Daily Gleaner* read FIRE-FIGHTERS OF MARITIMES WILL BE WELCOMED. It was a four-day event from July 24 to 27 and, on the opening day, the headline read MARITIME FIREMEN OWN FREDERICTON TODAY. The key of the city was given by Mayor W. G. Clark.

The professionally published souvenir booklet (including the official program) was then distributed. A copy is preserved in the provincial archives.

The grand morning parade of one thousand firemen and nine bands had never been surpassed by any other Maritime gathering to that date. For the thousands of spectators who lined the route of evergreen arches, it was an impressive spectacle. For the multiple sports events that followed, spirited recreation, rather than service, was given first place. As one visiting fireman put it, "I wish they would hold the tournament in Fredericton every year."

Fredericton Fire Chief Karl A. Walker led the popular torchlight procession through the streets of the city. Senior citizens recalled smaller torch parades of yesteryear but never had they witnessed anything like 1933. The long lines of firemen, holding their flaming torches high, paraded for hours, finally terminating at Parliament Square for the proverbial lavish fireworks.

Over the years, visiting firemen saw many changes in the Fredericton department. The salaries had increased dramatically from City Hall's $3.50 donation in the 1880s for each fireman annually! The new $8 uniform in 1899 consisted of a blue frock coat, trimmed with buttons and braid, and a black cap, the fire laddies holding tournaments and festivals at Scully's Grove to pay for the cost.

In 1902, two horses were purchased to haul a modern hose carriage (capable of carrying 1,200 feet of hose), two drivers being permanently employed. In 1914, a handsome and commodious brick structure replaced the wooden station on King Street, the old district station no longer in use.

The new central station had stables for the horses, apartments for the drivers, an office for Chief Harry Rutter, space for all the firefighting equipment, and a $1,200 alarm system. Eventually, every home in Fredericton would have a list of the thirty-six alarm boxes located around the city. (One of the lists is now in the archives.)

The new fire hall (still standing as Bell Boy Cleaners at 441 King Street) had its grand opening with a firemen's ball, hosted by Lady Ashburnham and Mayor Moses Mitchell. All that was missing was a torchlight procession through the streets of Fredericton.

Cricket and Curling— Firsts in Sporting Heritage

February 15, 2003

Two Fredericton cricket teams (eleven players each) in the early 1900s, a member of one team taking the picture. The two gentlemen in the bowler hats were the umpires. Some of the players are holding their blade-like bats made of willow wood.

THE THEME OF THIS YEAR'S New Brunswick Heritage Week (February 10 to 17) is "Our Sports"—an area in which Fredericton led the way with the early games of cricket and curling.

Cricket in summer and curling in winter were essentially gentlemen's games (in the beginning), each arriving from the Old Country, flourishing in the capital city, becoming immensely popular with the local citizens and leaving a unique legacy.

Cricket came first. This national game of England (starting in the thirteenth century) was played in Fredericton as early as 1835, the proof being found in a dated watercolour, showing students playing a match on the lawn between the first Collegiate School and the old parish church (site of the cathedral).

Before that time, the various British regiments garrisoned in the city had introduced the game and, by 1850, the Military Elevens (the number of players on a team) were challenging the Local Elevens. By 1870, the regiments had left, but the sport was firmly established with the Fredericton Cricket Club, the Union Cricket Club, the UNB Cricket Club, the St. George's Cricket Club, the

Eureka Club (with its pie-bald breeches), the Celestials, the All-Comers, the Incognitas, the Mutuals, the Made-Up Club (with its blue trousers), the old Fredericton Eleven (veterans), and the new Fredericton Eleven (youngsters).

The 1879 minute book for the Fredericton Cricket Club survives, a rare and valuable document that is preserved today in the provincial archives. The penmanship is clear and legible; the correspondence is in order, including the draft invitation for the Governor General (the Marquis of Lorne) to participate in a match during his visit that summer; the newspaper clippings are organized, revealing detailed descriptions and score tallies of all the matches that year.

The membership list at the front is composed of forty-five prominent gentlemen, each recommended by the club's Managing Committee, each paying one dollar for the honour of joining. They elected the following officers for the 1879 season: Lieutenant-Colonel John Saunders (patron), former mayor John A. Beckwith (honorary president), future mayor Thomas Carleton Allen (president), George B. Seely (vice-president), A. F. Street (captain), L. C. MacNutt (secretary-treasurer). The managing committee consisted of Harry C. Rutter, Edmund Head Allen, John Robinson, and A. G. Beckwith.

In order to appreciate the 1879 minute book, a little knowledge of the game is helpful. Even though the basic concept is similar to that of baseball, the rules for cricket are definitely more complex!

A match is played between two rival teams of eleven players each as they bat a ball in successive innings, attempting to score runs. The opposing side plays the field, bowling the ball, trying to knock over a small three-post wicket at each end of the field, each being defended by a batsman.

When the ball is hit into the field, the batsmen (carrying their bats) change places and a run is scored. Batting continues until a wicket is "taken out" or a batsman is retired, another taking his place and so on until ten of the eleven are out, the last unable to bat alone.

Before the 1879 season began, the Fredericton cricketers received word from Ottawa that they could use Officers' Square for their practice and matches. This was made possible through the influence of Sir Leonard Tilley (Federal Minister of Finance at the time). Ten years later, they were granted permission to use the military square in front of the Soldiers' Barracks, "but it was under the provision and guarantee to make good any damages."

With Anderson's Field, Kenny's Grove, the pasture, and the

Green, there were now six playing areas for the uptown and downtown teams. Thus, handwritten invitations were sent back and forth and, when a challenge was accepted, wickets would be pitched at 2:00 P.M. on the appointed day. If the game started in the morning, there would be a short intermission for lunch, but it was not unusual for a match to continue for nine or ten hours, or even a few days!

A memorable match occurred on Saturday afternoon, May 19, 1894, at Officers' Square. The verandah in front of the Officers' Quarters was crowded with "distinguished personages and a number of the fair sex," witnessing a thrilling match between the All-English born and the All-Canadian born of No. 4 Company of the Royal Regiment. The English won with a score of 114 to 67 but not before one of the leather balls landed across Queen Street in the doorway of Shute's Jewellery Store. Bouncing, it struck the globe of the electric light ("breaking it into a thousand pieces") and then dropped through the glass of one of the showcases.

Several of the local players also had memorable games, becoming legends in their time: John Beckwith handled the bat so skillfully that he would have felt disgraced if the bowler took his wicket; Dan Tobin, as wicket-keeper, was never known to allow a ball to pass him; John O'Brien, with his left, round-hand bowling, was a terror to all opponents, especially the military; William Maxwell frequently sent the ball from Barracks Square to Wilmot's Alley or into the river; E. H. Allen made his mark by terrorizing the batter with his under-hand bowling.

The game was open to all classes with regard to enjoyment and participation, but it became exceedingly fashionable for professionals, because they had the means and the time. There is no evidence that women played the game in Fredericton, although they were always a large part of the spectators. In England, ladies' cricket was not uncommon, two popular clubs being the Bramley Maids and the Hambledon Maids.

By the end of the nineteenth century, every gentleman in Fredericton had turned into a cricketer and, with the establishment of the Infantry School and the Royal Regiment, there were even more teams for competition. However, following World War One, only small clubs at UNB and FHS were functioning at College Field and these soon disappeared. The game has never been revived successfully.

Although cricket did not last in Fredericton, the Scottish game of curling did, and today the "roaring game" is just as popular as it was when it made its debut in the city almost 150 years ago.

The man responsible was John Neill, who arrived in the city from Scotland in 1842, bringing with him the skill to start a successful hardware business and the determination to introduce Scotland's national sport to North America.

In December of 1854, Neill went all over Fredericton trying to recruit subscribers for a curling club. The following gentlemen paid one shilling in dues and, along with founder and first president John Neill, became the charter members of the Fredericton Curling Club—Robert Fulton, John Taylor, Robert Thorburn, William McLean, Alexander McKilligan, Barry Phair, and James Moore—two teams!

A year later, two dozen stones, each made of polished granite and each weighing forty-four pounds, were imported from Scotland. However, when they landed in Saint John, custom officials did not know what to make of them, thinking they were lap stones for shoemakers or models for cheese moulds.

Finding ice was the next challenge. They tried the south shore of the St. John River, the mouth of the Nashwaak, and Heron's Lake (now Killarney Lake), all three locations unprotected from the winds and the bitter cold of New Brunswick winters. Thus, the brooms were used not only for the art of the sport but to keep the curlers warm as they swept away the drifting snow on the ice.

In 1860, travelling by horse and sled to curl on Heron's Lake came to an end, the Fredericton Curling Club formally petitioning the officers of the 63rd Regiment (in garrison at the time) for the use of the square in front of the Officers' Quarters (now the York/Sunbury Museum). The request was granted, but there were two conditions: the individual curling rinks (then 138 feet by 10 feet) were to be made on the gravelled pathways and not the lawn; the officers wanted to assist with the preparation and subsequently play the game.

When the hard work of flooding began, the dedicated curlers and officers hauled numerous casks of water from the river to the square. Unfortunately, when they tried to sink a well outside the Military Compound fence, intending to pump water to the rinks, all they struck was clay.

By 1869, there were thirty members in the club, but it was a year of mixed emotions including both the invitation to join the Royal Caledonia Curling Club of Scotland and the departure of the last British Regiment. The square in front of the old Soldiers' Barracks was now free and the curlers were allowed to use it for more ice space. This rink became so popular that lights were provided for night-time games.

However, maintaining two outdoor rink areas was laborious and, by the early 1880s, a covered rink with a comfortable club room became a priority. The winter of 1883 was the turning point. On February 1, the club hosted its first Annual Curlers' Ball at the York County Court House; on February 6, John Neill presented the club with a silver rink medal in honour of the eight charter members, their names being engraved on the back; on March 27, property was leased on Brunswick Street as the site for the first covered curling rink in Fredericton.

The formal opening of the new rink took place on New Year's Day, 1884, John Neill throwing the first stone, resulting in a "capital shot." Many young people were in attendance because the club consented to allow skaters to use the rink on certain days. When shares in the building were sold, the shareholders were incorporated as "The Fredericton Skating and Curling Club."

Because it was small, the new rink was unable to accommodate Fredericton's first two-day bonspiel on January 13 and 14, 1885. Instead, the snow on the St. John River in front of the city was cleared and several sets of concentric circles were marked on the ice, along with hog lines, back lines, and hack lines. An elegant new trophy, presented by Fred B. Coleman (owner of the Barker House Hotel), would become the property of the winning club.

Fredericton's two oldest rivals were invited from Saint John—the St. Andrew's Club and the Thistle Club—each being allowed to send four rinks. From the skirling of the bagpipes to the fading echo of "Soop, Mon, Soop," competition was fierce as "the brithers o' the broom" tried to lay their stones nearest to the "tee" (centre of the circles).

The host club was more successful and so the famous Coleman Trophy remained in the capital city, only to meet a tragic fate years later. However, one of the professionally printed programs is preserved in the archives today, a picture of the trophy on the cover.

In the summer of 1898, the Fredericton club decided to tear down the city's first covered curling rink, the little building with its two sheets of ice being in drastic need of repairs. A larger and more modern rink was planned for the same site that year. William Minue was the architect; Albert Saunderson, the contractor. Completion date: November 1. Total cost: $1,480.

On November 2, 1898, the annual meeting was held in the new rink, many of the curlers seeing the impressive results for the first time. The wooden building was 165 feet by 64 feet, with a roof that was supported by a system of trusses and braces. The ice surface was extensive enough for three rinks. A platform extended all around. A large spectator gallery inside the main entrance ran the entire width above the reception area.

During the year of its Golden Jubilee (1904), the club's ninety members honoured the occasion by personally contributing $275 for the addition of a special room for visiting teams. *The Daily Gleaner* remembered the fiftieth anniversary by publishing a detailed record of all matches, scores, players, and medals since 1870, there being no surviving statistics before that year.

The centennial year for the Fredericton Curling Club was 1954 and, by then, there was *The Hog Line* newsletter (begun in 1941) and artificial ice (installed in 1946). There were also three hundred members! Dr. George M. Young of Wilmot United Church was one of ten honorary members. He was the club's chaplain and historian, having prepared a professionally published centenary booklet.

The year 1954 also marked the organization of the first Ladies' Curling Club in Fredericton. Once again, the rink was too small to handle the large and diverse numbers of men and women who wanted to join the sport. Thus, in 1961, the Capital Winter Club was formed and another rink was built on Rookwood Avenue. The founders were Alden Clark, Paul Lynch, Bill Allwood, Doug Rouse, Ivan Forbes, Dave Ballantyne, Ron Burgess, Bob Velensky, Doug Etter, Jack Morrison, Chet Campbell, and Bob Chalmers.

Ironically, the new rink would be shared by both clubs after the one on Brunswick Street burned to the ground on July 8, 1978.

Everything was lost in the fire, including treasured trophies, rare photographs, and the twenty-five sets of new stones purchased on the club's one-hundredth anniversary. According to the police department, "arson was definitely the cause."

It was decided that a third rink would not be constructed on the site; instead, the Fredericton Curling Club joined forces with the Fredericton Golf Club and built a combined facility on the Golf Club Road. The grand opening: October 4, 1980.

In 2004, the Fredericton Curling Club will be celebrating 150 years of sporting heritage, with curling as one of the oldest organized games in New Brunswick. The club's code might be the reason for its longevity—"playing the game with a spirit of good sportsmanship and conducting oneself in an honourable manner."

JANUARY 4, 2003

CFNB RADIO WAS BORN EIGHTY YEARS AGO

The old CFNB studio on the second floor at 69 York Street. The year is 1934; Cleve Stilwell is the announcer and Cedric Cooper is the pianist.

JANUARY 12, 1923, was one of the coldest days in Fredericton's history—thirty-two degrees below zero Celsius!

Despite the weather, there was a warm feeling of accomplishment inside the home of J. Stewart Neill, Jr. at 212 Waterloo Row. From the family living room, the first sounds of Atlantic Canada's first radio transmitter were sent over the airwaves with ten watts of power.

Only five householders in the city owned radio receivers, but all they could hear on that memorable day eighty years ago was continual static interspersed with occasional strains of music. However, it marked the beginning of a long and successful career in broadcasting for radio pioneer Stewart Neill.

He was thirty-eight years old at the time, the son of James S. Neill, Sr. (a prominent hardware merchant) and Mary Todd Hill of Nashwaaksis. Following high school, he went into banking, but in 1904, he and his brother John joined their father in the business on lower Queen Street (across from Court House Square). From that year forward, James S. Neill & Sons Limited became synonymous with Fredericton commerce.

Stewart Neill was fascinated with the infant broadcasting medium of radio long before 1923, especially the retail possibilities of "receiving sets" and radio parts for "building your own." Subsequently, a radio department was established at the Neill store and, during the summer of 1922, Fredericton's first public receiving station was installed at the store, ready for operation.

The person in charge of the new radio department at Neill's was George F. MacRae, a UNB student who never regretted taking a year off from his engineering course "to put the operation on its feet." He not only installed aerials and radio receivers in many homes in Fredericton and the surrounding communities, but, with his experience in wireless work, MacRae was able to conduct workshops at the Neill store for amateurs (especially young boys with crystal sets).

It was expected that the first musical concert would be heard on July 19, but "atmospheric conditions were decidedly adverse as a result of the electrical storm which raged during the evening." A few days later, on July 25, a radio broadcast from Schenectady, New York, was a definite success. A large number of Fredericton people gathered at the Neill store to hear for the first time ("with remarkable distinction") a radio concert of instrumental selections.

But there was competition. Another hardware business, operated by Robert Chestnut & Sons and located above the southwest corner of York and Queen streets (opposite Phoenix Square), set up a radio department under the direction of one of the grandsons (Kenneth R. Chestnut) and a staff of technical assistants. As with the Neill family, interested people were invited to gather at the Chestnut store for musical concerts from the large broadcasting stations in the United States.

On August 20, 1922, the Neills received the first concert heard in Fredericton from New Jersey. The complete program, broadcast from station WJZ in Newark, was as follows: "Piano solo; several scenes from Verdi's opera Rigoletto, each being carefully described, then the parts sung with orchestral accompaniment; miscellaneous reports; baseball scores; songs by Miss Brookbender, who had sung for the troops during the War and who also sang for Edison phonograph records."

Two days later, the Chestnuts were successful in getting in touch with station WVP, Army Signal Corps, Governor's Island, New York, and receiving "an excellent musical program." They were also successful in getting the correct time announcement at eleven o'clock, as sent out by the government station at Arlington, Virginia.

And the competition continued. Outside speakers in front of the

Neill store brought the World Series "live" to Fredericton. In November, the details of the Mickey Walker-Jack Britton welterweight championship bout were heard "live" at the Chestnut store from Madison Square Garden in New York. It was a furious fifteen-round contest with Walker emerging as the new champ.

In December, James S. Neill & Sons introduced a popular new feature when hundreds of children gathered at their store to hear from Santa Claus by radio. The crowds became so large that policemen were required to control the traffic. A few days before Christmas, Santa Claus made the Neill store his headquarters.

For Christmas 1922, both the Neills and the Chestnuts had runaway sales with the hot new commodity on the market—radios. One Fredericton customer received programs from as many as twenty-nine stations; a Marysville customer had success from as far west as Kansas City and as far south as Havana, Cuba.

Shortly after New Year's, 1923, Stewart Neill travelled to Saint John and purchased a transmitter, which was made in New Brunswick and which he set up in his home, having applied to the Department of Transport in Ottawa for a broadcasting license. By putting his station on the air, he gave the family hardware store the added boost to sell even more radios than their competitor.

Life in the Neill home on Waterloo Row changed dramatically and, subsequently, radio changed the entertainment ideals of people living in Fredericton and beyond. For a radius of fifty miles, daily concerts could be picked up from the Neill station between four and five-thirty. The music consisted mainly of recordings spun on a phonograph situated in front of a live microphone in the centre of the living room. Family members learned to be very quiet around the house.

During that first year on the air, programming improved. Evening concerts from seven to eight o'clock on Monday, Wednesday, Friday, and Saturday were offered; vocal and instrumental music by local and imported talent became a part of the agenda; readings, speeches, and conversation were designed to interest young people.

For Christmas 1923, Fredericton's two daily newspapers, *The Gleaner* and *The Mail*, carried large radio advertisements for "The Hardware People Up Town" (Chestnuts) and "The Hardware People Down Town" (Neills). Both stores offered a complete line of radio sets from $60 to $350, including the Maritime three-tube set with aerial, battery, and headphones for $100 and the Northern Electric peanut tube set for $105—"gifts the whole family can enjoy by listening in on the many fine concerts every night."

With a radio station at home and a radio department at the store,

Stewart Neill wanted to make 1923 a radio Christmas, realizing that every boy between the ages of twelve and seventeen was interested in radio, and thus promoting anything and everything in radio. "Why not start him with some of the necessary parts to complete a radio set or, if he already has a set, there are many useful accessories."

In 1924, the people of Fredericton were totally surprised when James S. Neill & Sons purchased the stock and store of Robert Chestnut & Sons. On March 8 of that year, the Neills closed their downtown store and moved all their stock uptown to the Chestnut store (still standing near the southwest corner of York and Queen). They were now New Brunswick's chief distribution centre for radio sales.

The Chestnut family had occupied their upper Queen Street location for ninety years; however, financial pressures and the added responsibility of a new canoe factory on upper York Street led them to sell their hardware business, bringing the commercial competition between two old Fredericton families to an end. Ironically, they purchased the downtown Neill store for a future apartment complex and it still stands as the DiGiacinto Building.

The Neills then had the entire radio market (station and sales) to themselves. But there were big changes ahead. In 1927, James S. Neill (the father) passed away at age seventy-eight; in 1928, Mary Ann Logan Neill, wife of Stewart had had enough of her home being used as the entertainment capital of New Brunswick. As a result, the station was moved to the second floor of 69 York Street, a brick building that housed Neill's sporting goods at the time.

The power for the radio station increased to twenty-five watts and the new call letters became CFNB—Canada/Fredericton/New Brunswick. All programming was live and included a full schedule of evening entertainment and noon hour shows, the latter gradually filling the entire afternoon. Although phonograph records were loaned by music stores, local talent clamoured to gain exposure.

Throughout the 1930s, power increased to one thousand watts during the day and five hundred watts at night, with a full schedule of live and local programming from seven in the morning until sign off at midnight. There was still heavy static during the long summer evenings but, with the cool autumn weather, reception improved, and people settled in for good winter listening.

They heard the familiar voice of CFNB's first announcer and first "disc jockey," George MacRae, who never identified himself, as was the custom in the early days. The news was read by the well-modulated voice of Cleve Stilwell who, at the end of each day, was greeted by his next-door neighbour with a list of words that had been mispronounced over the airwaves. The sound of live background music was provided by local pianist F. Cedric Cooper, who was also a Fredericton insurance agent with an office on York Street.

On the top floor of Neill's warehouse, located behind the Queen Street store, there was a small quiet office where the daily news was received by Morse code and immediately transcribed by a staff of several young women. These transcribers (who made $8 per week) worked eight-hour shifts, sitting for hours, listening to the tapping of the dots and dashes, removing the tape from the cylinder, checking the transcription, and then delivering the copy to the newsroom nearby.

In 1935, the Department of Education invited Devon Superior School teacher Mary Grannan to write a radio script about her unusual but very successful methods of teaching primary classes. Broadcast over CFNB, it became her first radio success and, with the encouragement of Stewart Neill, she turned to radio in earnest, giving talks on art, travel, literature, and fashion.

At age thirty-five, Grannan was a commanding woman with a wonderful voice, and a penchant for big hats and chunky jewellery. When she wrote her comedy series "Aggravatin' Agatha" for CFNB and starred in the title role of the incorrigible maid, her radio career was on its way.

The "Agatha" series also made two other Fredericton actors into household names—Carl (Hap) Watson, who took the part of the chauffeur, and Gertrude Davis, who played a wealthy dowager. The program was scheduled for Sunday evenings at 7:45, just before Jack Benny, and all Fredericton listened to the weekly comedy skit, for which the three performers each received twenty-five cents a show!

Grannan also wrote children's stories, presenting them locally over CFNB before moving to Toronto and the CBC, where she had two successful decades as "Just Mary" and the creator of Maggie Muggins. Carl Watson moved to New York and became an executive with NBC; he passed away in 2000, at age ninety. Gertrude Davis remained in Fredericton, simultaneously working in radio and teaching elementary school; she passed away in 2001, at age ninety-four.

In 1948, Mary Grannan returned to her native city for two anniversaries—Fredericton's centennial and CFNB's twenty-five years as a community radio station. In a ceremony that was broadcast from coast to coast, she was presented with the key to the city by Mayor Ray Forbes. Standing beside her was Stewart Neill, whom she never forgot and to whom she never failed to give credit for starting her radio career (dedicating her seventh book to him). She returned home to retirement in 1962, passing away thirteen years later at age seventy-five.

By that time, CFNB had had its fiftieth anniversary in 1973. Its power had been increased to fifty thousand watts full time (the maximum allowed North American stations). The corporate name had changed to Radio Atlantic and the station had moved from its post-war location over Neill's expanded store (corner of Queen and York streets) to a new building on Hanwell Road. But it was still a privately owned family concern, son Malcolm becoming president when Stewart Neill died in 1963.

For forty-two years after World War Two, the one constant at CFNB was a tall energetic man with a voice that was made for radio. His name was Jack Fenety and he became a Maritime legend as he progressed from announcer to company vice-president, and finally to consultant when Bathurst Broadcasting bought CFNB in 1982. He continues to live in Fredericton during his retirement.

When Jack Fenety signed off for the last time in 1988, it was the sixty-fifth anniversary year of CFNB. There would not be a seventy-fifth. On June 24, 1996, Mayor Brad Woodside, a former announcer and disc jockey at the station, had the "honour" of pulling the switch that finally silenced the twin-tower transmitter located near Harvey Station. Because of economic and cultural changes, one of Canada's oldest radio stations left the airwaves, taking with it those familiar words, "This is 550 on the dial in Fredericton, New Brunswick."

Gone, too, were the familiar voices of George Mountain (*Saturday Night Polka*), John Richards Jr., Bill (Wee Willie) Scott, Larry Dickinson, Russell "Doc" Daiken, Gordon Catt, Harold "Hymie" McFee (*My Concert Album* for 30 years) Dave Bennett (*Reaction Phone-in*), George Brown, Trafford "Pop" Donovan, Don Jamieson, Rick Green, Bob Stilwell (son of Cleve), David Morell ("the voice of the Express"), and Eva Searle (who died in 1998 at age 101).

And gone were the family favourites such as *Western Swing, The Listening Post, Medjuck's Hit Parade, Ma Perkins, The Marconi Band Music Show, The World Tomorrow, Fact and Fancy, The Gospelaires, Charlie McCarthy and Edgar Bergen, The Diamond Trio,* the Sunday morning church broadcast, *Burgess Bedtime Stories, The Shadow,* and the *New York Metropolitan Opera.*

It has never been the same for the loyal listeners of CFNB. On cold winter days and evenings, they long for Fredericton's golden age of radio.

IRISH ORGANIZATIONS ONCE PART OF LOCAL SCENE

MARCH 17, 2001

A group of Hibernians from the St. Mary's division. Back row, left to right: Harry Crowley, Ed Morton, Alex Brogan, Matthew Murphy. Front row, unidentified.

YEARS AGO there was the Irish Literary Society, the Irish Friendly Society, the Irish Benevolent Society, the St. Patrick's Society, and the Ancient Order of Hibernians (the Latin name for Ireland being Hibernia). These organizations were non-political and non-profit. Each played a significant role in the social, religious, and cultural fabric of the city, and there was no lack of citizens who wanted to participate.

According to the 1871 census, the total population of Fredericton was approximately 6,000. Those who were of Irish descent numbered 2,800; those who had been born in Ireland, 770.

Like many immigrants, the early Irish community in Fredericton had its own unique ancestry, its own national identity, its own enduring faith. And, on March 17 each year, there was a celebration in honour of Saint Patrick. In time, Ireland's greatest holiday and holy day was adopted by the capital city.

As early as March 17, 1845, *The Fredericton Advertiser* reported that "a numerous and highly respectable assemblage of Gentlemen, natives of Ireland, or claiming Irish extraction, celebrated the anniversary of their Patron Saint by dining together at the house of Mrs. Perks, in this town."

The chair was taken at 6:30 in the evening by the Honourable Thomas Baillie, the president of the St. Patrick's Society. He had connections in Ireland and, when he came to New Brunswick to be surveyor-general and commissioner of crown lands, he brought his own staff of smocked Irish servants.

The vice-president of the society was the Honourable Lemuel Allan Wilmot, a member of the executive council of New Brunswick and a future lieutenant-governor. He was a Methodist, his maternal ancestry being Irish. When he settled into Old Government House, he, too, employed servants from Ireland.

Also in attendance, at that St. Patrick's Day tribute so very long ago, were Samuel Fleming (treasurer), Timothy O'Connor (secretary), several provincial legislators, and local citizens of various ranks and denominations. They drank the usual toasts; they expressed feelings of loyalty to the Emerald Isle.

During the next four decades, the St. Patrick's Society took on a permanent role in the city, a major event becoming the annual concert on March 17. The location was the old opera house at City Hhall until 1876, at which time the new St. Dunstan's Hall on lower Regent Street was built.

In 1881, *The Fredericton Capital* reported that it did not remember seeing the hall so crowded since opening night. The entertainment was for the sons and daughters of Erin, and in honour of the memory of the "old sod." However, there was regret "that the vocal portion of the program did not contain more selections from the national airs of old Ireland."

On March 4, 1887, the Fredericton branch of the Ancient Order of Hibernians (AOH) was established—the second in the Dominion of Canada. The first was founded a few months earlier (December 6, 1886) in Woodstock, New Brunswick.

Fredericton had a charter membership of thirty-seven, and the following officers were elected: J. H. Barry (president), Walter Broderick (vice-president), Harry MacKay (recording secretary), J. Broderick (financial secretary), T. C. Bohan (treasurer).

On October 12, 1887, Milltown, in Charlotte County, became the third Canadian branch. Before long, branches were springing up all over the province and the rest of Canada. The AOH had finally arrived!

The order, which was dedicated to Saint Patrick, originated in Ireland in 1565 and developed gradually among the Roman Catholics. Because of hardships and persecution (the dark days of Ireland's history), it was time to defy the tyranny of England and defend the religious and civil liberties of the Irish people.

In 1836, a branch of the AOH was established in New York, from where it spread all over North America, becoming the largest and most prominent organization of the Irish nationalist movement. As it grew, so did the size and significance of St. Patrick's Day celebrations.

The south-side Fredericton branch of the AOH became Division No. 1 when a No. 2 Division was organized on the north side in the parish of St. Mary's. Both divisions received an elaborate charter from the head office in Chicago, plus the monthly journal—*The National Hibernian*.

Soon there was a York County board of directors and a provincial executive. In 1893, M. McDade of Fredericton was provincial president; in 1895, John Toomey filled the position.

James D. Hanlon, an orchestra leader in Fredericton, became county president in 1898 and again in 1899. In 1900, he was secretary at the provincial level, and Reverend John J. Ryan of St. Mary's was provincial chaplain.

In 1904, Dennis J. Shea was president of Division No. 1. His officers were James P. Fairell, Jeremiah McAnnety, Edward C. Barry, and H. C. Mackey. The president of Division No. 2 was Alexander Brogan of Marysville and his officers were John Duffy, Frank Shortell, Alfred Hanlon, and James Hayes.

By 1905, there were 1,339 members province-wide, each county having several divisions. Northumberland had the most with eight. By 1907, Thomas L. Kane of Fredericton was county president and had the honour of installing officers.

The standard initiation fee for each member was one dollar; the monthly dues, thirty-five cents. Each member had to be Irish or of Irish descent, a practising Catholic, not less than sixteen or over forty-five years of age, and in good physical condition. Every division employed a doctor to examine the health of all candidates.

Fredericton Division No. 1 was affiliated with St. Dunstan's Church (on Brunswick Street at the time), holding their semi-monthly meetings in the hall on Regent Street. St. Mary's Division No. 2 began to have their services in the new St. Anthony's Church on Union Street (Devon) in 1906, their meetings taking place nearby in the old church, which became a hall.

Because of their proximity and their fraternal bond, these York

County divisions worked together to promote the goals of the AOH motto: Friendship, Unity, and Christian Charity. Committees were formed to visit and care for sick members, to assist and secure jobs for unemployed members, to establish libraries and provide literary material where needed. Beyond the order, a number of large scholarships were introduced for the youth of the parish.

In 1914, in the shadow of war, two major AOH events took place in the city of Fredericton. In July, a ladies' auxiliary of the AOH was formed with 107 members. Among the first to join were Katharine Grannan and her three schoolteacher daughters—Ann, Mary, and Helen.

In August, hundreds of male and female delegates from Nova Scotia and New Brunswick divisions and auxiliaries gathered in Fredericton for the fourteenth Biennial Convention. It was the largest to that date and the most successful, previous Maritime conventions having been held in Halifax, Woodstock, Sydney, Chatham, Saint John, Milltown, and Fredericton (1890 and 1896). Moncton was the fifteenth site.

The Fredericton event opened with a moonlight sail along the St. John River on the Steamer *Victoria*, with the 71st Regimental Band in attendance. The next day there was a grand parade about the city, accompanied by the Fredericton Brass Band and led by William Grannan (carrying the Union Jack) and Charles Sproule (carrying the Irish flag). They were followed by a barouche with Mayor Moses Mitchell and provincial AOH President E. C. Barry of Fredericton.

At the conclusion of the afternoon business meeting, several resolutions were passed: a declaration of loyalty to King George V and AOH readiness to defend the flag; a congratulation for the Honourable John E. Redmond and his success with home rule; a provision for monuments to the fever-stricken victims buried on Partridge Island, Middle Island (Miramichi River), and Grosse Isle (St. Lawrence River).

During its forty-year existence in Fredericton and St. Mary's, the AOH proved that in contrast to the organization's more serious accomplishmentsthere was a lighter side to it. This occurred once a year on St. Patrick's Day—the national holiday of the AOH.

Under the auspices of the AOH, and sometimes in co-operation with the St. Patrick's Society, musical concerts and drama presentations provided lasting memories for all denominations as the seats were filled year after year. The AOH Drama Club gave outstanding amateur performances, bringing Irish plays to Fredericton audiences and paving the way for local thespians of the future. Some of the programs were under the patronage of the lieutenant-governor and, on several occasions, all proceeds were in aid of the Irish Home Rule Fund. When membership decreased in the late 1920s, the AOH came to an end.

Since then, very little memorabilia relating to Hibernianism has surfaced for research purposes. The Provincial Archives does have the Fredericton auxiliary account books, placed there by the niece of Elizabeth McGinnis, one of the last members to join. There are also several documents and a few photographs.

A rare artifact that has survived from St. Mary's Division No. 2 is a gold AOH pin, bearing a crest that displays four symbols: the rising sun, clasped hands, a harp, and several shamrocks. It was once worn by James Hayes of Devon and is now in the possession of his grandniece Mary Hayes.

A Newspaper Tradition from the Nineteenth Century

January 8, 2000

Most courteous patrons, on this joyful day,
All News-Boys wish their best respects to pay,
To those whose generous favour, freely given,
Sustained their Press through pinching forty-seven.
With friends like you our Press shall never yield
A venial aid, nor shall it e'er a shield
Supply, to screen corruption, or the knaves
Who wish both Printers and their Patrons slaves.

SUCH ARE THE WORDS of the first verse of fifteen that are neatly printed on creamy-coloured satin beneath the title, "The News-Boy's Annual Address / To the Patrons of *The Head Quarters* / Fredericton, New Brunswick, 1st January 1848." The other fourteen verses tell of the famine in Ireland in the previous years, and extol the power of the press.

The delivery of the News-Boy's Annual Address on New Year's Day was a well-established custom in Fredericton during the early and mid-1800s. It was an ambitious undertaking with ulterior motives—a way of thanking the customer and also for requesting a generous tip at the beginning of the year.

The New Brunswick Reporter & Fredericton Advertiser printed these introductory lines in 1844:

I come kind friends with my tell-tale sheet,
Though long at your doors I must not stay;
O smile on your boy with favour sweet,
And gladly he'll speed on his devious way;
Tho' cold the day—tho' deep the snow,
Greet me with kindness, and pleas'd I go.

Notice the lack of subtlety in these opening lines from *The Head Quarters* for 1857:

Hail Patrons all! Another New Year's Day
I've lived to greet you with my annual lay
To gather news and leave it at your door.
Weekly through Fifty-six, I've travelled o'er
The City, wind and weather still defying,
And "News! The News!" each Wednesday ev'ning crying.
But since the toil is o'er I will not fret!

(Provided always you will not forget.)
So now, while hearts are warm with Christmas cheer,
I call to wish you all Happy New Year!
Hoping from each, whatever should his rank be,
Some more substantial present than "I thank ye!"

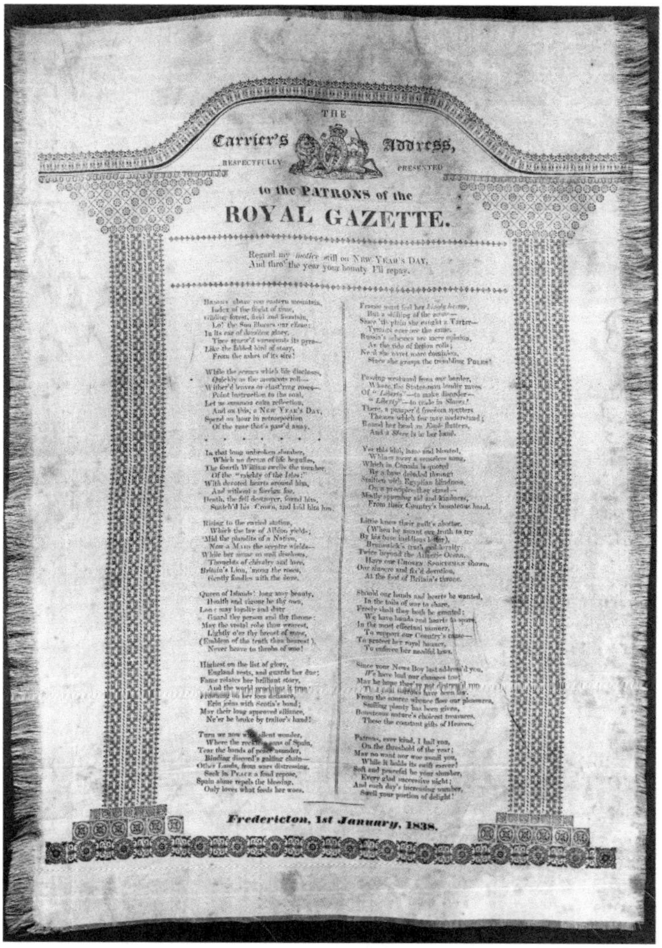

THE
Carrier's Address,
RESPECTFULLY PRESENTED
to the PATRONS of the
ROYAL GAZETTE.

Regard my *notice* still on NEW YEAR'S DAY,
And thro' the year your bounty I'll repay.

Fredericton, 1st January, 1838.

Remarkable as this doggerel poetry is, far more wonderful is the elaborate printing design that forms an ornamental framework for the verses, the border being grouped with fine and delicate tracery. Printers of today should marvel at the perfection with which the tiny pieces of type have been put together. Everything was hand set in the printing press establishments of the 1800s, and printing on satin was especially difficult, a task to admire in this current era of computer graphics.

If the address (or letter, as it was sometimes called) did not appear in a separate form, such as a rectangular piece of fringed satin or a hand-out sheet, it filled the entire front or back page of the newspaper. Seldom was it located on an inside page. Whatever the case, all patrons received a copy with the New Year's Day edition.

Early Fredericton newspapers, such as *The Head Quarters*, *The Reporter*, and *The Royal Gazette*, were consistent: a News-Boy's Address appeared every New Year's Day. There almost seemed to be competition among these three major publications as to which would have the best rhyme scheme or include the most current events. *The Head Quarters*, which was subtitled "Literary, Political, and Commercial Journal," certainly came out ahead in 1846 with a collection of witty couplets such as,

The Famine in England in the year FortyFive,
Has turned out a joke on the Corn Law Hive.

Fortunately, there was little competition from the smaller newspapers of the day—*The Capital*, *The Globe*, *The Herald*, *The Star*, *The Sentinel*, and *The Telegraph*, the last being Fredericton's first paper. It was founded by twenty-two-year-old Michael Ryan of Saint John, and only lasted from August 6, 1806, to February 7, 1807. In fact, all these little papers were short-lived projects, individually owned, most of them appearing on a weekly basis.

It is doubtful the newsboys or carriers of the nineteenth century wrote the verses they delivered, although the titles suggested that they did. It was probably the editor, the publisher, or the proprietor (generally all the same person) who created the poetic effusions, but no by-lines ever appeared to give the credit.

Perhaps it is just as well that the reader did not know who penned this final stanza for *The Head Quarters*, January 1, 1854:

No more from the News-Boy but wishes for weal,
He must now continue his range.
Hand out the first piece you just happen to feel,
And never mind waiting for change.

Or these concluding lines (after thirty-five stanzas), which are just as blatant, in *The Reporter*, January 5, 1882:

My annual tour has been made,
My story has come to an end;
My good will to each one conveyed,

For each one I hail as a friend;
Forget not, forget not the Newsboy,
To your purses and hearts take him in
And help him the New Year to enjoy,
By providing the much needed TIN.

The early years of the 1800s were a training time for the future leaders of the New Brunswick press. Three Saint John youths who were apprentices as well as delivery boys in those years were Harry Chubb (founder of *The New Brunswick Courier*), William Durant (founder of *The Times or True Briton* and *The City Gazette*), and George Lugrin, who worked for *The Royal Gazette* and who, at age sixteen, did not hide the fact that he was the poet for January 1, 1808, writing in first person and even including his name:

Once more kind Patrons the Season's return'd,
So famous for bringing good cheer,
And George as is usual with vendors of News,
Again wishes a Happy New Year.
The comforts last Season your bounty procured,
Are uppermost still in my mind,
And I trust (if too sanguine I hope you'll find excuse)
This year the same bounty I'll find.

The Royal Gazette served as the provincial government's official medium and also carried world news and local items. In 1815, George Kilman Lugrin moved *The Royal Gazette* from Saint John to Fredericton and became the first King's Printer in the capital city, holding the position for the next fifteen years. He raised a large and prominent family in Fredericton and even established his own newspaper—*The Watchman*.

Lugrin's two sons, George Jr. and Charles S., became printers with *The Royal Gazette* but in 1863 Charles S. Lugrin founded his own weekly, *The Colonial Farmer*, which lasted until 1879. Here is the introductory stanza that Charles probably wrote for the News-Boy's Address, New Year's Day, 1865:

Money is TRASH, said Shakespeare in his play,
But he'd think otherwise, if living in our day;
Your News-Boy knows, for he has read the papers,
That money now almost makes Suns of Tapers.

This is a rare address in that the style keeps changing and midway through the poem Charles Lugrin writes:

Once more we change our theme and rhyme,
And sing in other measure;
For subjects vast demand our time
And occupy our leisure.

He concludes with a timely topic for that year:

So hip, hip, hip. Hip, hip, hurrah. Hurrah for Federation.
New Brunswick, Scotia, and the Isles will make one mighty nation.
With hip, hip, hip, and hip hurrah. Hurrah for Le Canadien.
Canadian men and boys brave, will be our brethen all then.

A son of Charles S. Lugrin, who was named Charles Henry Lugrin, also became a newspaperman, attending UNB and then combining law with journalism. Before going to Saint John to become editor of *The Morning Telegraph* and then west to *The Victoria Colonist*, he established *The Fredericton Evening Herald* in 1881, a weekly which eventually continued as *The Daily Herald.*

All three generations of the talented Lugrin family would use the major portion of the New Year's Day address to recap the news events of the preceding year, similar to the year-end reviews presented by the media today. But nineteenth-century Frederictonians would have paid two cents for *The Reporter* on Saturday, January 3, 1885 and received a forty-seven-stanza history lesson, something like this:

During the Year,
Sir John was honoured by the Queen anew;
The first of Colonists the badge to wear,
Brave, patriotic, wise, Canadian through and through.

The Year saw Blair
Arouse the Teachers' righteous indignation,
By cutting down their mean and paltry fare,
And crippling thus the cause of Education.

The Year with dread
Saw Cholera with rapid step advance,
And hurry to the regions of the dead,
Thousands on thousands in Italy and France.

The longest address discovered so far totals 312 lines, moulded into thirty-nine stanzas, held together with various types of rhyme. It appeared in *The Head Quarters* for January 1, 1885 and probably caught the reader's interest with this opening:

Ere Christmas Holidays have passed away
Comes freezing, sneezing, pleasing New Year's day,
When all who "take the paper" and who pay
(I mean no evil)
Expect as regularly the news
The Quaint effusions of an embryo muse,
And few their quarters on that day refuse
To th' Printer's devil.

This particular address is also unique in that it contains a poem within the poem; "The Battle of Alma" is an individual history lesson in verse that describes a major event for 1854—The Crimean War.

The York-Sunbury HIstorical Society collection has two different newsboy's addresses, both printed on satin: the one reproduced on page 273 is to the patrons of *The Royal Gazette*, Fredericton, January 1, 1838; the other one, which consists of twenty-four stanzas and which is in a more fragile condition, is to the patrons of *The New Brunswick Reporter*, Fredericton, January 1, 1848. Unfortunately, the donors are unknown.

The News-boy's Address quoted at the beginning of this column was a gift to the New Brunswick Museum in 1932 from Mrs. F. H. White of New York City, the artifact having belonged to her father, Mr. M. H. Hart of Fredericton.

Are there more of these individual addresses waiting to be discovered and subsequently preserved for future generations? Hopefully, yes; if not, old and young alike can still enjoy reams of rhyming verse by perusing the old Fredericton newspapers on microfilm, either in libraries or in archives. Who knows, readers might find a rhyming couplet that is a gem amongst all the others, such as this one from *The Head Quarters*, January 1, 1845:

I sip my nectar—nib my pen anew—
Snuff my dim tallow, and my Muse pursue.

GOING TO THE MOVIES—MANY YEARS AGO

MARCH 30, 2002

MARCH is an important movie month around the world as it leads up to the annual Academy Awards. The first Oscars were handed out for 1928, the year the "talkies" hit the big screen. The sound was provided on long-playing records, synchronized with the film.

But motion pictures came to Fredericton long before. It was a time when large audiences were mesmerized by the flickering images of legendary silent screen stars such as Charlie Chaplin, Tom Mix, the Gish sisters, and the Barrymores.

The first show house in Fredericton was called Wonderland and the grand opening was on Monday evening, August 19, 1907. However, the entire operation was as mysterious as some of the films that were shown.

A former optical businessman named Charles Hallett representing a motion picture chain in Boston had arrived in town with his financial backer, a professional singer, and a picture-machine operator. They hired a local woman to play the piano and then they leased the old YMCA hall on lower York Street for two months. There was one condition: all pictures had to meet with the approval of the YMCA directors.

There was no need to worry; the initial advertisement encouraged the whole family to attend because there would be "nothing but clean, up-to-date moving pictures and illustrated songs." Featured on opening night were a number of short reels, including *Anarchist Mother-in-Law* and *Pioneer Life & the Indians.*

Wonderland offered a continuous three-hour performance every evening, except Sunday, with "special attention to ladies and children." Admission was ten cents for adults, five for children, and, according to the sign out front, everyone was encouraged to "come when you like, stay as long as you like, sit where you like."

During the first week, crowds had to be turned away each night, but on Saturday, the Wonderland closed abruptly, when two mysterious gentlemen arrived in Fredericton looking for Hallett.

Without any explanation, Hallett and his little company fled for points unknown, never to be heard from again. Fortunately, they had settled all their bills and left nothing behind, except the Wonderland sign in front of the YMCA. On Monday (August 26), the crowds gathered as usual, only to find the place closed.

There was a definite demand for motion picture entertainment and the void was filled when the Fredericton Nickel was set to open the very next night (August 27) in the Anglican Church Hall at the corner of Brunswick and Carleton (later the IOOF Hall and now a community centre).

The principal owner of the Nickel was J. Everett Watters, a former Saint John resident and a former UNB student. The operation was similar to the Wonderland—continuous evening entertainment from seven until ten-thirty at night, but with a five-cent admission for everyone, "the best five cents worth the public ever got."

Crowds streamed in for the opening, every chair taken, to see *A Sailor's Love Story* and *A Boar Hunt*. The greatest attendance came on Saturday nights, when Hanlon's Orchestra accompanied the moving pictures and the illustrated songs (the audience singing along), and when there was a $5 ticket draw.

The Nickel ran all fall that year, but Watters and his partners decided to close in mid-December for the Christmas holidays. They also wanted to consult with leading film houses in Toronto and Montreal. But they never re-opened in 1908.

By then, there was competition from the New Wonderland, which had opened on August 31 (1907) under local management and which was subsequently taken over by Keith Motion Pictures for a grand opening at the City Hall Opera House, the initial program including *Aladdin and the Wonderful Lamp* and *The Vengeance of the Algerine*.

Although Keith's was a large circuit enterprise from outside the province, local singers and musicians were hired. The company advertised that their films were longer (four thousand feet each night) and "strictly high class," with special sound effects. When the new year began, they capitalized on the fact they were the only picture house in town. But not for long.

In 1908, William T. H. Fenety, the son of former Fredericton mayor George E. Fenety, opened the Unique motion picture theatre in the Masonic Hall on Carleton Street, two doors from the Church Hall. It was the start of a long history for the Fenety family and the movies, William having already been involved for a number of years with bringing travelling drama companies to the city.

The changeover to film was a new challenge, but William and his son (Witter W. O. Fenety) met it with ingenuity. They were going to offer the latest motion pictures, the best-illustrated songs, and "a singer who can sing."

As the name indicated, the Unique was "refined and up-to-date," with an inclined floor, which gave everyone the opportunity to see the screen, and big electric fans, which gave proper ventilation during three evening shows.

Opening on September 18 with "five great motion picture reels during each one-hour showing," the Unique ran until June 26, 1909, at which time it closed for the hot summer months. It was also the intention of the management to make extensive improvements. The closing feature was entitled *The Bad Lands*, "a picture abounding in Indian & Cowboy life to the limit."

When the Unique re-opened on August 23, 1909, a new and improved machine which would finally present a motion picture that was "absolutely flickerless" had been installed. Fredericton had its first permanent movie house. It would stay in operation until mid-September of 1917.

In the meantime, the Fenetys had opened their first Gaiety theatre in the nearby Church Hall, the ground floor of which had been completely remodelled with modern opera chairs and a modern lighting system. The ventilation was improved and the very latest type of projection machinery was installed. The manager was son Witter and the grand opening was May 9, 1913.

The Fenetys had cornered the market but there were local attempts to compete with the Unique and the Gaiety. Some were short-lived, such as the Crystal Palace and the Carleton; others persevered.

On September 1, 1909, the Bijou opened in a newly constructed community hall (with four exits in case of fire) on upper Queen Street and remained in operation until the end of January of 1912. The opening feature was *La Tosca* with Sarah Bernhardt, and all patrons received a souvenir program.

In the spring of 1910, David Melchor Richards of Devon leased the lower flat of the Anglican Church Hall for a term of three years (four hundred dollars annually) for his new motion picture theatre—the Palace. One month later, the Palace closed when Richards purchased a large tenement building just down the street at the corner of Carleton and King. Here the famous and long-running Gem theatre was born.

The Gem opened its Carleton Street door for the first time on Saturday evening, May 28, 1910. The main feature was *Othello* (the silent screen version); the accompanying music was provided by a local orchestra; the cool and breezy atmosphere was created by oscillating fans.

For the next seven years, there would be three hourly showings every night (except Sunday) at the Gem. Up the street, the Unique and the Gaiety were doing the same thing. Theatre Row on Carleton Street was now established and the competition assured Fredericton of first-rate motion pictures.

Before he retired on July 5, 1917, David Richards leased the Gem to Fred G. Spencer, a theatre-chain operator from Saint John. As a result, the place was closed during that summer "to undergo alterations and improvements" valued at $10,000. When it re-opened on September 20, it was advertised as a modern theatre in a brand-new setting, with a seating capacity of 451. Balcony seats were now ten cents; lower floor, fifteen cents.

Because it was wartime, Spencer allowed the Daughters of the Empire to take charge of the grand opening, the entire receipts (at twenty-five cents admission) being donated for patriotic purposes. The special program included Norma Talmadge in *The Law of Compensation* and Molly King in *The Seven Pearls*, the latter the serial of a novel to be shown over the next fifteen weeks.

The year 1917 also saw big changes for the Fenety father and son movie team. Both of their Carleton Street venues, the Unique (Masonic Hall) and the Gaiety (Church Hall), closed and then amalgamated. The Fenetys moved into a new building on Queen Street (opposite the post office). The New Gaiety Theatre (as it was called) had its grand opening on November 23 with Mary Pickford starring in *The Little American*. Souvenir programs were provided.

The New Gaiety was Fredericton's first theatre to be built especially for the purpose of showing movies. No expense was spared in making it one of the finest in New Brunswick—seven hundred seats, attractive lobby, proper exits, perfect ventilation, indirect lighting, steam heating, totally concrete and steel, and "thoroughly fireproof."

The year 1918 saw even more changes for Fredericton's only movie theatres, the Gem and the Gaiety, when the pioneers of the business passed away—David Richards in May, William Fenety in August.

The Gem building was left to Mrs. Richards, although the theatre would still be managed by the Spencer chain; the Gaiety theatre was left to the five Fenety children, but Witter, who was the manager, became the sole owner after purchasing all shares from his siblings.

When the war was over, the Fredericton public demanded bigger and better motion pictures with more and more famous stars. Thus, the Gem and the Gaiety competed with costly major attractions. As a result, the adult price at both theatres had to be increased to twenty cents, the children's price remaining the same.

In December of 1919, the Gem purchased a quarter page in the daily newspapers to advertise its big Christmas feature—*A Midnight Romance*. Another quarter page was purchased to publish a letter stating that the chairman of the Board of Censors permitted the theatre to state publicly his special recommendation for this picture.

Unfortunately, the film was not shown. At four o'clock on Sunday morning, December 21, the Gem was completely destroyed by fire, apparently caused by a heating apparatus under the main entrance. The estimated loss was $25,000. This figure included 15,000 feet of film valued at $2,000 and box-office receipts totalling $500.

Although Mrs. Richards only carried $8,000 insurance on the building, and Mr. Spencer carried $4,000 on the movie equipment, they both wanted to rebuild and reopen. In the meantime, Spencer became the only entrepreneur to obtain a long-term lease of the City Hall Opera House—three years at $90 per week!

He spent $2,000 on renovations, including a new film-projection booth and additional fire escapes, and, by March 8, 1920, he launched the grand opening of the opera house movie theatre with Mary Pickford in *The Heart of the Hills*.

Before his City Hall lease expired, Spencer wanted to have his own building in Fredericton. When Mrs. Richards decided to sell her property at the corner of King and Carleton, Spencer was given first chance and accepted. His new Capitol Theatre would be born from the ashes of the ill-fated Gem, although the new $25,000 building would be twice as large, with accommodation for six hundred.

The new theatre opened its King Street door to the public on October 23, 1922, giving patrons their first look at the simplicity of the interior design, especially the parabolic curve of the auditorium walls. The picture screen was located in an insert at the apex of the curve, with the orchestra pit and a small announcement stage in front. The first-night audience saw Harold Lloyd in *Grandma's Boy*, plus *It Is the Law* ("a powerful western drama"), and the *Pathe News Review*.

In 1930, Witter Fenety purchased the Capitol and kept it operating as his second theatre until the end of 1973. The last movie to play was entitled *Rage*, starring George C. Scott. In August of 1979, the building was demolished to make way for the Carleton Place office complex.

For over two decades, the New Gaiety on Queen Street was Fredericton's leading movie theatre, but an unexpected disaster was waiting in the wings.

In the early morning of May 26, 1939, fire broke out in the old Barker House stables between King and Queen (across from the post office) and spread rapidly to all adjoining buildings, causing damage estimated at $200,000. Within two hours, the Gaiety Theatre became a raging inferno and subsequently a total loss, including a $20,000 sound projection system.

Because he was well covered with insurance, Witter Fenety planned to rebuild immediately, and he began by purchasing the former site of the Barker House Stables. His third Gaiety Theatre would be much larger—over nine hundred seats!

On opening night, September 18, 1939, the feature film was *Andy Hardy* with Mickey Rooney. When the Gaiety closed on March 31, 1981, the feature was appropriately entitled *The Last Picture Show*. By then, Witter Fenety and his son Billy had brought to Fredericton the best that Hollywood had to offer. But they were unable to compete with the multiple mini-theatre chains on the outskirts of town, and they refused to move from Queen Street.

In October of 1981, the auditorium was demolished for a parking lot. The front entrance and the long lobby were left and have been used for various business ventures since then. The specially made seats were also saved; some of these can be found today in the choir loft of Wilmot United Church on Carleton Street.

Although the downtown motion picture houses have all disappeared, local residents and even visitors still talk about their fond memories of the Gaiety, the Capitol, the Gem, the Unique, the Bijou, the Palace, the Wonderland, the Nickel—and the movie magic of many years ago.

Capital City Tourism Had Successful Beginning

June 21, 2003

A group of young ladies and gentlemen (chaperones included) pose in front of Camp Comfort during one of the many excursions to Camp Comfort Island.

In the late 1800s, Fredericton formed a small tourist association and began to promote "the Celestial City and its environs on the St. John River."

By the end of the nineteenth century, it was time to publish a major tourism booklet—the first professional tourism advertisement that would be attractive to the locals as well as visitors.

The idea for the publication began in the spring of 1897, when a special tourist committee decided to sponsor an adult essay contest devoted to a description of Fredericton and the St. John River. Maximum number of words: twelve thousand.

The members of the committee were Dr. James R. Inch, superintendent of education for New Brunswick; Mayor Wesley VanWart, a prominent Fredericton businessman; and C. Fred Chestnut, an apothecary who had a shop on Queen Street and who eventually became mayor of the capital city.

They wanted forty per cent of each essay to describe Fredericton, thirty-five per cent the St. John River, and the remaining twenty-five per cent to be a description of the Fredericton area as a sporting centre (camping, hunting, fishing). They also wanted a nom de plume for each entry to avoid identification of the author by the judges.

The first- , second- , and third-place winners were to be announced in May of 1897 and, in June, the first-place winner would travel to Boston (all expenses paid) to supervise the publication of the essay in booklet format. Two Boston printing firms had already placed bids for the project and were waiting for a decision from Fredericton City Council.

The four newspapers in Fredericton at the time (*The Reporter, The Herald, The Mail,* and *The Gleaner*) were also waiting anxiously. They wanted to promote the tourism idea by publishing the names of the winners on the front page.

In the meantime, City Council made a grant of $250 towards the publication, and substantial contributions were also made by individual citizens who strongly believed in advertising "our city." All names and amounts appeared in the local press. The man in charge of the fund was tourism treasurer Fred B. Edgecombe, a well-known businessman in downtown Fredericton.

Finally, the successful competitors were announced. First prize of eighty dollars and the trip to Boston: city alderman Frank H. Risteen. Second prize of twenty-five dollars: science professor Loring Woart Bailey of the University of New Brunswick. Third prize of fifteen dollars: principal Eldon Mullin of the Provincial Normal School.

Risteen (age thirty-five) fulfilled all the rules of the tourism contest; he even went one step further and prepared his essay during a camping expedition along the Tobique River in Victoria County. His nom de plume, "Pabineau," derived from Acadian through Mi'kmaq. It meant "low bush cranberry," and was the name for a river, a waterfall, a lake, and the Pabineau Indian Reserve—all in the northern part of the province. Frank Risteen visited them all.

Unknown to the judges, Risteen was a successful travel and nature writer, his articles, stories, and poems about New Brunswick having already appeared in American newspapers, and popular magazines such as *Outing, Forest & Stream, Rod & Gun, Shooting & Fishing*, and *Recreation*. As a result of the contest, Frank Risteen's gift for transferring the enchantment of the province's wilderness and the beauty of Fredericton into the printed word would reach an even larger audience.

From an early age, Risteen was an outdoors enthusiast and an accomplished marksman, hunting, fishing, and camping all over New Brunswick, especially along the St. John River, with his two younger brothers, Fred and Harry. He always had the high score in provincial and dominion rifle matches, bringing the purse and the trophy home to the local rifle association, of which he was the star member.

He loved Fredericton and its history. It was the city of his birth. His father (Joseph Campbell Risteen) had established a successful woodworking factory at the corner of Queen and Smythe streets (still standing with the date 1872). The family home was also on lower Smythe Street and, when Frank married Minnie Staples of St. Mary's Ferry (now Devon), he built his own majestic residence nearby.

By profession, Frank Risteen was a Supreme Court stenographer and an official reporter (by appointment) for the provincial legislature. He taught himself stenography, then gained newspaper experience by reporting for *The Fredericton Morning Star* and *The Saint John Daily News*. However, the purpose of his freelance writing was to make Fredericton and New Brunswick well known, and his prize-winning essay did just that. Describing the view from the summit of Brick Hill (top of Smythe Street today), he wrote the following:

"The entire city with its checkerboard streets, its spreading elms and many churches, enclosed as in a sylvan amphitheatre, lies spread beneath our feet. The horizon is formed by the sombre gray of the Nashwaak hills on the right and the lofty slopes of Cardigan and Keswick on the left. The white steeple of the Marysville church—the uncompromising brick walls of the cotton mill—the Nashwaak seen at intervals, then lost in a tangle of riotous vegetation—the massive front of Currie's Mountain standing guard at the head of the tide, and the noble St. John itself stretching far to the east and west in a sheet of burnished bronze, are conspicuous features in a scene whose equal one might seek in vain to find."

Thus, Frank Risteen and the Fredericton Tourism Committee must have been proud in July of 1897, when ten thousand copies of the tour guide rolled off the presses and were distributed throughout Boston, Philadelphia, New York, and other American cities. The price was twenty-five cents and the response was phenomenal. As a result, subsequent printings and revised editions were to follow.

Entitled "The Celestial City" and subtitled "Fredericton, New Brunswick, and the St. John River, for the Tourist and Sportsman," the fifty-six-page booklet was also circulated in Upper Canada, although the attraction of a trip "down to the Provinces" had already been appreciated by many. Because of Risteen's eloquent and enticing prose, larger numbers of visitors were now expected. And Fredericton was ready.

Hotel accommodations were plentiful and first class, the Queen, the Barker House, and Windsor Hall setting the style. The plank sidewalks were in good repair, especially the one along York Street leading to the railway station. The trees were "trimmed up," the cows confined within proper limits, and the public squares along Queen Street "scraped up" continuously. All fences and outbuildings were whitewashed and the wharves along the river bank repaired and looked after.

The thirty-two illustrations for the booklet included the Parliament Buildings (as they were called then), Old Government House (which the author emphatically pointed out was empty in 1897), the Officers' Quarters, Christ Church Cathedral, and Wilmot Park. Beyond Fredericton, there were scenes of Marysville, Oromocto, and Sheffield. Images included one of Arthur Pringle, a popular guide from Stanley, with one of his American clients and a dead moose.

There were also rare photographs of the summer "camps" along the St. John River in the vicinity of Springhill. Some of these mini-resorts were quite elaborate, all of them built of logs and each having a large open fireplace at one end. Although the bill of fare was the inevitable pork and beans served at picnic tables, the scenic surroundings were spectacular and, after spending a day at one of these rustic retreats, American and Canadian tourists had a memory for life.

Even the names were romantic, Risteen advertising all of them in his booklet: Pine Bluff, Beech Knoll, Scoodewapscooksis, Kaskiseboo, Ravine Lodge, Old Orchard, The Birches, Porcupine, Bohemia, Sunny Crest, and Cherry Bank. However, the most popular and the most photographed seems to have been Camp Comfort. Professional photographer George Taylor left behind several splendid glass slides of it in his collection, preserved today at the provincial archives.

Also preserved in the archives is the partial account book and minute log belonging to the Camp Comfort Club of Fredericton. The members of this elite club were the eventual owners of the camp and the hosts for many tourists and locals who wanted to enjoy a short summer excursion a few miles above the city.

Apparently, Camp Comfort was the first sporting camp in the Fredericton area. It was built by a group of Fredericton sportsmen (including the Chestnut brothers) on a small island named Camp Comfort Island, located near the present Hartt's Island with Springhill in the background. Folklore suggests that it was built in the autumn of 1886, but that it was carried away the following spring by the ice in the river. It was rebuilt and once more demolished by the ice. The third try was successful and the camp remained on solid ground for a number of years.

When the little minute book began in July of 1895, fourteen gentlemen from Fredericton (barristers, doctors, military personnel, educators, and businessmen) each paid twenty-five dollars a share to join the Camp Comfort Club. The officers were Albert James Gregory (president), Albert Foxcroft Street (vice president), and Colonel Thomas George Loggie (secretary-treasurer). The other members were Colonel W. D. Gordon, W. F. Mitchell, D. C. Chalmers, Jeremy Taylor, Lieutenant-Colonel Surgeon R. McLearn, John Black, Frederick St. John Bliss, Dr. W. E. Smith, Thomas Bradshaw Winslow, Hedley Vicar Burpee Bridges, and Allan H. FitzRandolph.

The account tally for the summer of 1895 indicated that the existing log cabin was purchased for $250 and that Joe Paul was hired for $5 to do repairs and renovations and to remain as the regular cook (with an assistant). Another $5 was paid to James E. Camber for one year's rent of the little island, Mr. Camber owning much of the real estate in the Springhill area. Two other expenditures: a framed picture of Queen Victoria for one of the walls and a Union Jack for the flag pole.

On August 16, 1895, the club was ready for its first major social event at the camp. According to *The Herald*, "nearly a hundred ladies and gentlemen enjoyed the hospitality of the members of the Camp Comfort Club and their estimable wives during the afternoon and evening at the Club's beautiful premises on the island opposite the Springhill Hotel." The guests of honour: Lieutenant-Governor and Mrs. John James Fraser!

The party travelled up on the steamers *Randolph* and *Bismarck*, in canoes and boats, and by horse and carriage. At six o'clock, an elaborate supper was served, the coffee being made on a real old-fashioned campfire, which Joe Paul and his helper kept piled high with fuel. At dusk, strings of Chinese lanterns were hung among the trees, and a military orchestra struck up the music for the lancers. "Inside the camp, the merry dance began." It was eleven o'clock before the picnic ended with the singing of the national anthem.

During the next several years, there would be a number of successful picnics at Camp Comfort, including those for the officers of the Royal Berkshire Regiment, the York County councillors, and tourist groups from all over North America. However, every Saturday was set aside for members' only day, and the last two weeks of every August were exclusively for the members' wives and lady friends.

The club held its monthly meetings in Fredericton at either the Barker House or in the anteroom of the Officers' Quarters. New members were proposed, elected, and sold shares. When Queen Hotel owner John Edwards joined, he donated one of the hotel's large ice chests. Someone else gave a cooking stove and, when assessments were calculated, everyone shared the expenses. The club's annual picnic always brought the summer season to a close.

Camp Comfort continued to be featured in succeeding editions of the popular tourism booklet "The Celestial City." From *The Toronto Globe* to *The Truro Daily News*, editorials encouraged readers to obtain a copy and become informed about the Springhill camps, the St. John River, the city of Fredericton, and the nearby communities. Members of the local tourist committee were overwhelmed by the positive letters of inquiry from those who had studied the booklet.

Unfortunately, Frank Risteen never experienced the future success of his wonderful essay, and he never had the opportunity to become a member of the Camp Comfort Club. He passed away (of tuberculosis) at the age of thirty-eight.

When his robust health began to deteriorate in 1899, he and wife moved to California, hoping and looking for a cure. It was never found. He died on February 9, 1900, his remains being returned to New Brunswick and interred in the Rural Cemetery on the Woodstock Road, beside his beloved St. John River.

One known copy of "The Celestial City" survives today, and it can be found in the provincial archives. It is in excellent condition, the navy blue cover only slightly faded and displaying the white embossed letters of the title and the crest and motto of the capital city.

Frank W. Risteen was a city alderman for Wellington Ward in the late 1890s. His writing skills and his appreciation for Fredericton and the St. John River helped to promote early tourism.

Image Sources

Cover: details from photographs courtesy Pearle Ross Estate, PANB #P120/3/119, and PANB #P120/4/3, and engraving, *The Illustrated London News*/UNB Library Archives

Remembering War
p.2, (PANB #P5/317); p.5, (PANB #P120/20/122); p.8,(courtesy William Crocket); p.14, (PANB #P120/1/77); p.20, (*The Daily Gleaner*); p.21, (*The Daily Gleaner*); p.26, (courtesy Michigan State Archives); p.31, (PANB #P37/385); p.35, (courtesy York-Sunbury Museum)

Famous Visitors
p.42, (courtesy UNB Library Archives); p.48 left, (PANB #P61/351); right, (PANB #P5/561); p.53, (*The Daily Gleaner*); (p.58, (courtesy York-Sunbury Museum); p.64, (courtesy Chalmers Hospital Foundation); p.70, (courtesy Pearle Ross Estate); p.76, (PANB #P14/64); p.82, (author's collection); p.88, (courtesy UNB Library Archives); p.89, (courtesy UNB Library Archives);

Historic Landmarks
p.94, (PANB #MC 375); p.99, (author's collection); p.100, (author's collection); p.106, (PANB #P120/3/19); p.112, (courtesy The Daily Gleaner); p.118 left, (Public Archives of Canada #C-85125); right, (Library of Congress #62-2883); p.120, (UNB Archives); p.124, (courtesy York-Sunbury Museum); p.130, (Courtesy York-Sunbury Museum); p.136, (courtesy Federal Department of Agriculture); p.142, (courtesy Federal Department of Agriculture);

Natural Disasters and Human Folly
p.144, (author's collection); p.150, (PANB #P11/149); p.154, (UNB Library Archives); p.155, (courtesy Annie Cairns); p.159, (courtesy Mona MacMillan); p.165 left, (PANB #P37/460); p.165 right, (courtesy York-Sunbury Museum); p.171, (PANB #P120/4/3); p.176 (courtesy Fred Ross) p.180 (author's collection); p.185, (PANB #P350/184);

Notable Locals
p.191, (courtesy Partridge family descendants); p.192, (courtesy Fred Lucy Hubbard); p.197 left, (courtesy York-Sunbury Museum); right, (courtesy York-Sunbury Museum); p.201 left, (Harvey Studio Fonds, PANB #P14/87); right, (courtesy Patricia Humphrey); p.207, (author's collection); p.214, (courtesy York-Sunbury Museum); p.220, (courtesy Gerry Wal); p.223, (courtesy Rabbi David Kraus); p.225, (author's collection); p.229, (Stanya Studio); p.235, (courtesy Partridge family descendants);

Social Life
p.243, (courtesy York-Sunbury Museum); p.249, (*The Illustrated London News* / UNB Library Archives); p.255, (PANB #P47/27); p.261, (PANB #P14/54); p.267, (courtesy Mary Hayes); p. 273 (York-Sunbury Museum); p.278, (courtesy Phyllis Batt); p.284, (PANB #P5/174); p.289, (PANB #P37/244)